TOM S

THE LIFE AND DEATH
OF ST KILDA

HarperCollins*Publishers*

HarperCollins*Publishers*
77–85 Fulham Palace Road,
Hammersmith, London W6 8JB

This paperback edition 1994
16

This revised edition previously published
in paperback by Fontana 1975
Reprinted three times

First published in Great Britain by
Fontana 1975
Reprinted nine times

ISBN 0 00 637340 2

Set in Pilgrim

Printed and bound in Great Britain by
Clays Ltd, St Ives plc

The Life and Death of St Kilda

Tom Steel was born in 1943 in Edinburgh, Scotland, and was educated at Daniel Stewart's College. He graduated from Emmanuel College, Cambridge, where he read History, in 1965 and joined the staff of Rediffusion Television as a programme researcher. From 1968 he worked for Thames Television as producer and director on such programmes as *Today, This Week, People and Politics* and several network documentaries, including the series *Destination America* and documentaries like *A Far Better Place*, which told the story of St Kilda.

Since 1977 he has worked as a freelance producer and director on numerous programmes for Channel Four, ITV and the BBC.

His book *Scotland's Story*, written to accompany his twenty-four part Scottish Television series, is also available from HarperCollins Paperbacks.

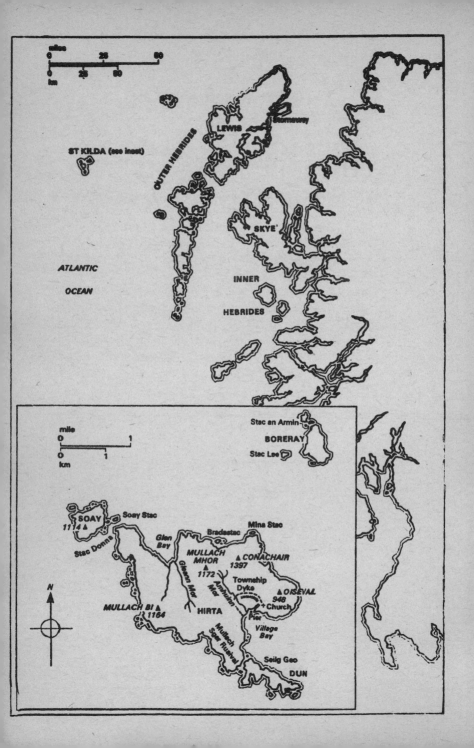

Contents

Acknowledgements

The author must first thank the National Trust for Scotland, who published the first and much shorter version of this book in 1965. The Trust has kindly allowed me to publish this new and more extensive history. I am particularly grateful to the Trust for allowing me to use the same title, and for granting me access to the collection of books, articles, and documents presented to them by the late Fifth Marquis of Bute when he generously bequeathed the island group to the nation in 1956. As regards the material contained in the Bute Collection, the author is grateful to the late Mr James Fisher who discovered the whereabouts of Mrs Ann MacLachlan's daughter. From her Mr Fisher obtained her mother's diary and kindly passed on a copy of it to the fifth Marquis of Bute. Mr Fisher likewise discovered the diary of Mr George Murray, the schoolmaster, and Mr George Atkinson's *A Few Weeks' Ramble Among the Hebrides in the Summer of 1831*.

Acknowledgement must equally be made to Thames Television Limited of London for allowing the author to quote freely from the transcripts of interviews carried out by him for the documentary film *A Far Better Place* which was first transmitted on the Independent Television network in April 1972. The interviews are a valuable record of the reminiscences of many of those associated with St Kilda, some of whom have since died.

The many writers of the St Kilda story have been liberally quoted in this volume. The author is grateful for their enthusiasm to put on record their impressions of life on the island, and above all must acknowledge his debt to their respective publishers. In particular, I must thank the late Mr Alasdair Alpin MacGregor for permission to quote from *A Last Voyage to St Kilda*, and Mr James Mackay whose book, *St Kilda, Its Posts and Communications*, is the definitive work on that aspect of the island's story. Thanks must also be extended to Miss Mary Cameron, who put on record her memories of childhood life on St Kilda when her father was missionary to the islanders after the First World War.

I must also thank my father, who was not only responsible for stimulating my interest in St Kilda and its people at an early age, but who also gave valuable help and advice regarding the present book.

I would like to thank, in terms of the 1988 edition, all those who have written to me since 1975 with additional information, the essence of which I have attempted to include. I am grateful to the Rev. John Barry and others for their painstaking work on the wrecked Second World War aircraft on St Kilda, Brigadier Spackman, whose book *Soldiers on St Kilda* is a detailed record of the military presence on St Kilda since 1957, and to the St Kilda Club's newsletters and *St Kilda Mail* which have enabled me to relate the activities of the National Trust for Scotland since it acquired the archipelago in 1957.

THE ILLUSTRATIONS

The photographic record of life on St Kilda is rich. I am aware of some 400 photographs that were taken on the island before and during the evacuation, and I have included a representative selection in this book. Many of them have never been reproduced before. Where possible a photograph's date has been indicated. Frequently, however, it proved impossible to trace ownership or to fix a precise date.

The Director of the School of Scottish Studies of the University of Edinburgh must be thanked for allowing several photographs in the School's care to be reproduced. A relation of the island's owner, R. C. MacLeod of MacLeod, was responsible for taking plates 5, 11 and 29, which were presented to the School by Miss Susan Martin. Plate 38, also part of the School's large collection, is from a print presented by Dr W. Kissling.

Gratitude must similarly be recorded for Mrs Cockburn's kind donation of her husband's lantern slides to The National Trust for Scotland, a large number of which are contained in this book. Dr A. M. Cockburn, who visited St Kilda in 1927, took plates 15, 20, 25, 26, 30, 31 and 40. Mr Frank Lowe, who visited St Kilda a few years before the evacuation, has to be thanked for allowing the reproduction of plates 6, 24, 34, 41 and 42. Professor W. Fisher Cassie took plates 10 and 28 when he was on Hirta in 1952. The author and publishers are also indebted to Mr Robert Atkinson who has allowed plates 18, 37 and 46 to be included. They were first reproduced in his book, *Island Going*, which was published in 1949 by Messrs Collins. Messrs Cassell and Company, London, have to be thanked for allowing the reproduction of Cherry Kearton's pictures, plates 17 and 33, which were taken in 1896 and the negatives of which have been lost.

Plates 9, 35 and 43 were taken at the time of the evacuation of St Kilda in August 1930. The author gratefully thanks the properietors of the *Glasgow Herald*, who took the pictures for publication in *The Bulletin*, for permission to reproduce them here. Plate 45, taken in Morvern, Argyll, after the resettlement of the St Kildans, is reproduced by kind permission of the *People's Journal*.

The remainder of the illustrations are from the collection that has been made over the last twelve years by the author and his father. Plates 1, 2, 3, 4, 16, 39 and 47 are from photographs taken by the author. Plates 7, 21 and 36 are from the studio of G. W. Wilson. Many of those associated with St Kilda before the evacuation have over the years given the author some of the photographs reproduced: Mr Lachlan Macdonald, himself an islander, gave the author plate 8; the late Miss Anna Mackenzie of Dunvegan, the daughter of the island's last Factor, provided plate 22, and plate 44 was taken by Mr W. H. Whellens whose daughter has given permission for it to be reproduced. Miss Mary Cameron, the daughter of one of the island's last missionaries, has kindly agreed to plates 12, 13 and 14 being included, and the author must thank his father, Tom Steel, for allowing him to reproduce plates 19, 23, 27 and 32, which were taken by the late Mr Alasdair Alpin MacGregor and subsequently given to him by his widow.

Introduction

St Kilda is the most spectacular of all Britain's offshore islands. The main island of the group, Hirta, boasts the highest cliffs and the largest colony of fulmars in Britain. The neighbouring island of Boreray and her two rocks of Stac Lee and Stac an Armin are the breeding grounds of the world's largest colony of gannets. The little archipelago, in fact, is a land of superlatives and as such has always fascinated the minds of men.

But the greatest fascination is that for over two thousand years man lived upon St Kilda. On the island of Hirta people once led a unique and unchanging way of life. They were crofters, like most of their neighbours in the Hebrides, but crofters with a difference. Cut off from the mainland for most of their history, the islanders of Hirta had a distinct way of living their lives. Isolated from the majority of the Scottish people the St Kildans were forced to feed upon the flesh of the tens of thousands of seabirds that returned year after year to breed on the rocky islands. Moreover, their very self-sufficiency meant that throughout their history they possessed a sense of community that was to show itself increasingly out of place.

It is not easy to imagine the lonely life led by the St Kildans. It is difficult for us to accept that they had more in common with the people of Tristan da Cuñha than they ever had with the city dwellers of Edinburgh or Glasgow. Any similarity between the St Kildan way of life and that led upon the mainland was superficial. Isolation had a determined effect upon their attitudes and ideas. The St Kildans can only be described as St Kildans and their island home little else than a republic. The people, like those of most isolated communities, sacrificed themselves year in and year out securing, often precariously, a livelihood for themselves and their children. In the practical business of living, St Kilda bore little relation to the mainland where people were becoming more concerned with evading secondary rather than primary poverty. When the island was finally evacuated in 1930, not only had

Nature defeated man but, in a real sense, man had defeated his fellow men.

Now, over fifty years after the evacuation, the whole story can be told, and in particular what happened to the St Kildans after they decided to abandon Hirta and settle on the mainland of Scotland. It was not until 1968 that the records of the Scottish Office pertaining to the 1930s were made available to public examination. In the Public Records Office in Edinburgh lie more than two dozen files that once were the property of the Department of Agriculture. From the collection of letters, minutes, and memoranda can be gleaned the true tragedy of the evacuation – not only the human distress involved, but the parsimony and bureaucratic behaviour of the civil servants concerned in the event – behaviour which makes one question whether they can ever be capable of true compassion.

The evacuation of St Kilda was to illustrate the basic insecurity of the society that had developed on the mainland of Scotland. It was an insecurity that showed itself when faced with a seemingly small and insignificant community such as was found on Hirta. It was thought that if the St Kildans could not adapt and accept the values of the dominant society, the only solution was to bring about a state of affairs which would result in evacuation. In this sense, the British government's obsession with the costs involved in providing the St Kildans with a nurse and a postal service mirrored the feelings of a society that not only demanded money should not be wasted in such a way but, more importantly, would not accept that anomalies may, let alone should, exist.

Throughout most of the last century, St Kilda was subject to pressures. Education, organized religion and tourism all attempted to throw into doubt the St Kildans' way of life. For centuries the world outside stood aloof from the people of Hirta. They were content on the mainland to allow such a remote community to go its own way. As long as the people of St Kilda were so isolated, they were insulated from the forces that wished them to conform. The strength of the community, however, became weakened as contact with the mainland increased. When disease decimated their number and wind and sea made the acquisition of adequate supplies of food difficult, the St Kildans were forced to turn eastward for help.

The majority of books written about St Kilda appeared during the nineteenth and early twentieth centuries. The authors for the

most part were products of the buoyant and vital society of
Victorian and later Edwardian Britain – a society in which it was
generally thought that man could do little without doing good.
The writers felt it was their duty to help others less advanced (and
therefore less fortunate) to attain the civilized level of their own
society. Help, as interpreted by the articulate spokesmen of a richer
and more advanced society, was best given by persuading the
islanders to give up the struggle.

In 1930 the people of Hirta unwittingly threw themselves into
the twentieth century. As adults, they had to accept those values
that most of us on the mainland are taught to believe in from
birth. For instance, the islanders found it difficult to base their
existence upon money. They had never lived in a world in which
they bought goods and services of each other. They had of course
accepted gladly the opportunity of making a little money for themselves at the expense of tourists, but that intrusion had never
altered the basic relationship one St Kildan had had with another.

The islanders showed themselves indifferent to the jobs they
were given on the mainland. The labours asked of them were
menial contrasted with the spectacular feats they had once performed in order to kill seabirds. Moreover, the slaughter of fulmars
and gannets directly determined whether the community on Hirta
had enough food to survive. When they worked on the mainland,
the St Kildans realized that the tasks they performed did not supply
them immediately with what was needed to keep them fed and
warm. On the mainland, the islanders worked for money. Money
was necessary in order to purchase from others the things necessary
to life. Between the employment of their skills and survival came
a state of affairs that we all take for granted.

The history of the St Kildans after the evacuation, of their
inability and lack of resolution to fit into our urban society, makes
sad reading. If St Kilda had been an isolated home, the islanders
were to discover that the remote district of Argyll in which most
were settled was even more alien. On Hirta at least they had formed
a tightly-knit community with a common purpose. When they
were resettled on the mainland, the St Kildans were forced to live
in homes miles apart from each other, in a society whose values
were unacceptable if not incomprehensible to the majority of them.

The history of the St Kildans shows the folly of thinking of the
islanders as similar to ourselves, and their community but a distant
cousin of our vast urbanized society. The death of St Kilda was to

prove the most important in the history of island depopulation in
Scotland. The publicity the evacuation received brought home to
government and public alike the hazards involved in seeking to
solve the problems of isolated communities by simply evacuating
them.

When, in 1936, a government committee examined the economic
conditions of the Highlands and Islands, the members concluded
'that in view of the present trend towards concentration of population in the larger cities and industrial centres, the full development
of an area such as the Highlands for the building up of a strong,
healthy, virile race must be regarded as being of vital importance
to the nation, and for this reason, if no other, we feel justified in
making recommendations involving expenditure'. During the last
world war, in fact, the county of Inverness provided more soldiers
than any other county in Britain. It was not unemployment alone
that forced men into service: the battle honours of both world wars
read like the roll-call of the Battle of Culloden.

To this day, however, a large and often influential section of our
society demands that communities which cannot support themselves should be similarly dealt with. The history of mankind, it
seems, must of necessity be a continual process of the inhabitation
and evacuation of areas that for a time suffice man's needs. In terms
of Britain, the Highlands and Islands of Scotland have been
sacrificed in order to advance civilization.

The story of the life and death of St Kilda is perhaps more
pertinent today than it has ever been. Our industrial society has
forced people to contract relationships with each other on the basis
of money. Money is what binds individuals together and fixes the
relationships they have with each other. Opulence in the modern
Western world has become the yardstick of human happiness and
it has been widely accepted that men should always strive in search
of economic wealth unless ignorance, poverty, or sheer habit
prevent them from doing so.

We are presently faced with the pressures and problems that
the money motive has helped create. The poverty of urban industrialized life and the human stress that is now showing itself in
practically every Western industrialized society call into question
the basis upon which our society is founded. More recently, the
energy crisis, problems of pollution and monetarism have altered the
rate at and method by which society seeks to advance itself. Given

our present crises, however temporary they may prove to be, it is natural that we doubt the goal of our endeavours. The story of St Kilda may be a small human tragedy, but the study of the islanders' former ways and the reasons why the people were forced to evacuate their island might provoke some to question our future.

Introduction to the 1988 Edition

Since *The Life and Death of St Kilda* was first published in 1975, much has happened not only to St Kilda; but also to the St Kildans who left in 1930. Since 1957, the island has been occupied, rather than inhabited, by men from the military, visiting National Trust for Scotland volunteer work parties and scientists from the Nature Conservancy Council. Many from the mainland have now experienced what it is like to live on Hirta and it is interesting to compare and contrast our modern reactions to the problems posed by nature. Men now live on St Kilda for different reasons and in a totally different way; but their experiences, nevertheless, and the draw that the archipelago has on our minds and hearts, are worthy of investigation.

1
Exodus from St Kilda

Wednesday 27 August 1930 was overcast for most of the day on St Kilda. Shortly after dawn a raw mist slowly rolled over the Atlantic from the nearby island of Boreray and spilled over the cliffs on Conachair like a waterfall. By the afternoon a thick, grey blanket hung low over the village. It was cold and damp – so unlike the summer days of the previous week. Few on the island, however, had time to notice that the weather had changed. The St Kildans had much to do if in two days' time they were to leave the island for ever.

In house Number Five, Main Street, St Kilda, Annie Ferguson was busy at her spinning wheel. She was preparing yarn for a length of cloth that a tourist from the mainland had asked her to make. She would not finish the work, that she knew; but she would take the yarn to the mainland with her and in the coming winter months her husband would weave the tweed on the old loom they were taking with them.

In the other room of the house a young newspaperman was finding it difficult to pen his copy. Alasdair Alpin MacGregor, then thirty-one, had been sent all the way from London by *The Times* to report on the evacuation. As he sat close to the small window to catch the falling light, the paper he was writing on became wet in the heavy atmosphere. He struggled on, knowing he would have to wire his story as soon as he boarded the SS *Dunara Castle*.

On the advice of Nurse Williamina Barclay, the St Kildans had decided to take with them only those few possessions that could be of use to them in their new life. All through the day, heavy bundles were carried from the houses to the jetty. The women were busy packing kists with the few clothes and heirlooms each family possessed. They were also packing the wool taken that summer from the island sheep. It would be a waste to leave it behind; it could prove to be a useful source of income. Even in their new homes the St Kildans could knit and weave as they had done for generations to help supplement the new reward for their labour called wages.

Down by the old storehouse, used for over a century by the St Kildans to lay aside the produce they had bartered with those on the mainland, a few of the men were busy sawing up bits of wood. They were concerned to protect the few pieces of furniture being taken away from becoming damaged in transit. With battens and rope they made safe the tables and chairs that were to be transported to Lochaline in Argyll. Others were occupied at the back of the Manse, sifting through the driftwood that had been cast ashore over the years. Much of the wood was the cargo of a freighter torpedoed off St Kilda in 1917. The big planks of timber, the men agreed, might be of use; they too would be loaded on to the *Dunara Castle*, due to arrive at St Kilda that day.

To the right of the schoolhouse, about a hundred yards from the jetty, the remainder of the St Kildans' sheep were bleating in the calm air. Six hundred and sixty-seven sheep had already been transported by the SS *Hebrides* to the marts of Oban on 6 August. In July the Scottish Department of Agriculture had sent out an official and two shepherds from Uist along with their dogs to help the islanders round up their sheep. The task had not been an easy one. Many sheep had gone over the steep cliffs rather than be captured; many like those on Boreray had to be left undisturbed because taking them off proved impossible, given the time and manpower resources available.

To begin with, the St Kildans had stubbornly refused to help gather their scattered flocks. It had been suggested that the money obtained from their sale should go towards paying for the evacuation of the community. The islanders felt that if the government wanted to remove the sheep, they could do the work. One islander, old Finlay Gillies, had gone as far as to take to his bed the day before the rounding-up was due to begin, claiming that he was too sick to get up. The missionary Dugald Munro suggested to Macaulay, the Department's representative, that the situation might be eased if the government offered the St Kildans money in exchange for their help. When the islanders heard that they would be paid a pound a day, even Finlay Gillies was seen catching sheep along with the rest of the men among the cliffs. Removing the sheep from St Kilda proved a costly business. It cost the government over £240 to transport twelve hundred sheep to the mainland, plus £143 in wages and expenses for the shepherds. By the time the sheep had been dipped and penned at Oban until their sale on 3 September, the total cost was £506 0s 4½d.

At five o'clock in the afternoon the island dogs announced the arrival of the SS *Dunara Castle*. As she steamed like a ghost ship through the heavy mist into the bay, the islanders dragged their boats down the slipway into the water to go out and meet her. There was the hope of a last letter from friends on the mainland, eager to wish them well, and the chance to sell to the thirty or so visitors on board the few remaining socks and scarves the women had knitted. The last tourists to visit the island inhabited hoped to buy a spinning wheel or some other relic of life on St Kilda from a people only too eager to be rid of them. They were to be unlucky. The island had been stripped of most souvenirs in the few weeks since the world had got to know that St Kilda was to be abandoned. When the visitors had been rowed ashore, the St Kildans returned to the most pressing business of the day – the transfer of the sheep.

They had arranged the sheep in groups so that they could be loaded more easily into the boats that would take them out to the *Dunara Castle*. There were over five hundred sheep to put on board. It was a slow, tiring business; to and from the steamer, the islanders plied boats that could hold no more than a dozen sheep at a time. It was not until after nine o'clock in the evening that the majority of the sheep were safely on board. By then it was getting dark and dangerous to do much more; the few lanterns cast little light on the operation and the jetty was crowded with tea chests and bits of furniture. But work continued, and it was not until one o'clock in the morning that the nine fit men on the island struggled for over an hour to pull the boats up the slipway clear of the high-water mark.

At approximately three o'clock in the morning 'The Books' were brought out, and in the house of the Fergusons, Alasdair Alpin MacGregor joined in the day's last act of reverence to the Almighty. After a few verses of a psalm to the tune 'Wiltshire', 'The household', wrote the man from *The Times*, 'was so tired that we contented ourselves with a short reading and a shorter prayer. In the small hours we dragged ourselves to bed knowing that at daybreak we had to resume the shipping of the sheep'.

At first light the St Kildans were awakened by the siren of the SS *Dunara Castle*. The crew were anxious to complete the work and return to the mainland. After breakfast and family prayers, the St Kildans once again pushed their little boats into the water and took the last of the sheep on board. Then came the turn of the cattle, which had to be enticed down to the jetty with handfuls of soda scone. The four young calves were rowed over to the waiting ship in one boat, whilst the cows, tethered to the tail of the small craft in case they drowned, had to swim. The last ten cows of St Kilda were taken over to the *Dunara Castle* and hoisted aboard.

At approximately seven o'clock in the morning of 28 August, HMS *Harebell*, under the command of Captain Barrow, steamed into the bay. She had been sent by His Majesty's Government to carry out the evacuation of the islanders. The *Harebell*, the senior ship of the Fishery Protection Squadron, had spent the summer months touring the fishing ports of the British Isles. The ship had left Oban and crossed to St Kilda during the night. 'We knew we were due for this,' recalls Commander Pomfret, then medical officer on board, 'so we had fitted it in.'

In the corrugated iron shack that served as a post office, Neil Ferguson was busy getting ready the last mail bags to leave St Kilda. It was the largest mail ever to leave the island. Many on the mainland whose interest had recently been aroused by the publicity given to the evacuation in the newspapers were eager to obtain a St Kilda postmark by way of the passengers on board the steamer. As the tourists crowded the small office they complained bitterly when Neil ran out of penny stamps and demanded that he supply them with two halfpenny stamps instead. When there were no more halfpenny stamps Neil could only offer them three-halfpenny ones. Tempers became frayed.

The mailbags taken aboard the *Dunara Castle* that day were not the only mail sent from St Kilda. Three days earlier, Alasdair Alpin MacGregor and Neil Ferguson had despatched the last traditional St Kildan mailboat. Within its wooden hold was placed a solitary postcard addressed to the island's owner at Dunvegan, in the Isle of Skye. The wooden vessel, attached to an inflated stomach of a sheep, had been cast into the sea. 'This,' read the postcard, 'is the last mail from St Kilda.'

Meanwhile, the Master of Reay was being persuaded at great length by Alasdair Alpin MacGregor not to try to remain on the island. The Master, heir to the Chief of Clan Mackay, had come ashore from the *Dunara Castle* with the intention of remaining on St Kilda for a few weeks to do some exploring. He had even gone as far as to bring a load of provisions with him to last him throughout his period of isolation. The *Dunara Castle*'s sister ship *Hebrides*, he thought, was to make yet another trip that summer and he was relying on that to take him off before the winter. But Dr Shearer, sent by the Department of Health to carry out the evacuation, put an end to the young Robinson Crusoe's plans by saying no.

The Scottish Office and the proprietor of the island had already turned down hundreds of requests from people wanting to live on St Kilda. The government received more than four hundred enquiries and pleadings from those eager to accept that which the St Kildans were abandoning.

Sir Reginald MacLeod of MacLeod, the proprietor of the island, had told the *Glasgow Herald* in an interview, 'I am sorry to lose a population that has down its generations been tenants of my family for a thousand years. But they themselves have elected to go, and I cannot blame them. The life is one of hardship and inconvenience.' Sir Reginald played a minor role in the decisions that had to be made at the evacuation but was determined, as was the government, that no one should live on St Kilda after 29 August 1930. 'At all events,' he told the *Herald*'s correspondent, 'I am strongly opposed to the idea of new settlers. The present population have signed and sent a petition for removal which, at great trouble and expense, is now being carried out. In these circumstances it would be folly to remove one lot of people who know the island, and replace them with a group of strangers.'

The last thirty-six St Kildans on the island were sad but not sorry they were leaving. They had been convinced by the nurse and the missionary that they were leaving for a better land. The experience of living on St Kilda in the last few years had shown them they could not be leaving for a more inhospitable world.

The *Dunara Castle* had brought not only tourists and journalists, but also various officials who had work to do on St Kilda. The Examiner of Registration Records came ashore to check the island's entries of births, deaths and marriages with the missionary, Dugald Munro, who had been responsible for keeping them. Nurse Williamina Barclay told the Examiner that she had not had to assist with the birth of a single child since she came to St Kilda over two years before. No one had been born on St Kilda since 1927, when the youngest of the Mackinnons, Neil, was born. The books duly checked and signed by the Examiner were transferred to the vaults of Register House in Edinburgh. No further entries would be made.

At noon the *Dunara Castle* sailed for Oban. The journey would take seventeen hours and the skipper was anxious to be safely through the dangerous Sound of Harris in daylight. Together with the beasts and belongings went the last outsiders – the journalists, photographers, and visitors. No one but a few government officials was to be allowed to remain on the island until the end. Alasdair Alpin MacGregor had gone as far as to petition the Prime Minister to allow him to stay and witness the evacuation, but the reply from the Scottish Office had been definite: 'The Admiralty are naturally hostile to the idea of publicity and Mr Johnston himself is strongly of the opinion that the utmost effort should be made to avoid the miseries of the poor people being turned into a show. . . . The Scottish Office are endeavouring to carry out the evacuation with as little publicity as possible out of consideration for the feelings of the St Kildans themselves.' Tom Johnston, then Under-Secretary of State for Scotland, had decided there would be no cinema newsreel cameras present, no press photographers to capture for publication the first tears of sadness, no witness of any description to the emotions that were felt by the St Kildans between noon on 28 August and eight o'clock on the morning of the 29th. The officials even rejected a request from a former islander, Donald MacQueen, who wished to see for himself the removal, as he put it, 'of the last remnants of my race'. He had asked if the Department could help him get to St Kilda because, he wrote, 'owing to having to exist on seventeen shillings a week, I could not manage home to my people'.

One of the first tasks that had to be carried out once the sheep had been taken off was to deal with the island's numerous dogs. They were no longer of use to the St Kildans, and despite the pleadings of the National Canine Defence League and numerous offers from people on the mainland to adopt them, the dogs were put to death. Dr Shearer, assisted by Commander Pomfret of the *Harebell*, was able to destroy only two dogs with hydrocyanic acid in a room in one of the empty houses. The St Kildans stubbornly demanded that they drown the rest. A stone was tied round the neck of each dog and they were thrown off the end of the jetty. Weeks later, when the *Hebrides* paid a visit to the island, the bay was still full of dead dogs.

It seemed to the St Kildans that everyone had been interested in their island during the past few weeks. But it was their home and they would not be badgered, bribed, or bullied into doing things they did not want to do. Offers of help were made, but few were taken up. The afternoon of the 28th was spent ferrying out the islanders' belongings to the *Harebell*, and the work went on well into the night. As the women carried the last few bundles down to the pier, the men of the British Navy looked on. They were prepared to help, but the St Kildans did not want to be assisted in these last hours by representatives of a society that had ignored them for centuries. The sailors could only stand and watch, and the islanders were heard to murmur to one another that they would not be rushed should the entire navy come out for them.

By seven o'clock next morning, there was little left for the St Kildans to do save board the *Harebell*. The islanders put on their best clothes. If they did not feel a desire to impress their new neighbours on the mainland upon arrival, they were certainly determined that they would not be the subject of ridicule. The family prayers were said for the last time and, as was the custom among Gaelic people, a Bible was left open in each house, along with a small heap of oats. In one house the exposed text was Exodus.

In each of the eleven inhabited cottages, the fire was built up with fresh coal and turf. When they were burnt out some hours later, it was probably the first time there had not been a fire on St Kilda for a thousand years. Lachlan Macdonald, then a young man just turned twenty-four, recalls: 'I mind of everyone closing the door of his house and some of them read a chapter of the Bible before they left, and put up a prayer.'

Neil Ferguson, son of the postmaster, and the last male islander to marry and set up a home of his own on St Kilda, remembers those last hours well. 'You had a bed and chairs and them old-fashioned chests and all that stuff. All that stuff was left on the island when we left. Most of the furniture was left in the houses – dressers, and even pots and pans and stuff like that – all left. And all them pots they used to have in the old days with three legs, they were all left. And all the fishing gear was left, lines and boats. Oh, we never took much away, we were just running away and leaving everything.'

His father took a last walk round the village. In many respects he had been the most important man on the island. Not only had he been sub-postmaster for many years but he had also been the Factor's representative. If the St Kildans had ever allowed one of their number authority over the rest, Neil Ferguson Senior was that man. He was the one who had called the men together when important decisions had had to be made. He had taken the church services when the missionary was absent from the island. He was the only islander to have planted as much as a plot of potatoes that year, and was leaving the island with a heavy heart.

The corrugated iron shack bearing the crudely lettered notice 'St Kilda Post Office' was Ferguson's first port of call. The target of visitors to the island eager to prove to their friends they had been to St Kilda would no longer sell the famous St Kilda postcards. Inside, papers and postcards lay strewn over the floor. On one wall was pinned a notice headed 'What the disabled soldier wants to know' and dated 'War Office, August 1915'. Ferguson had often wondered why he had been sent the notice. The men of St Kilda had never in recorded history taken up arms against anyone. On 10 September 1930 the Post Office Circular announced: 'The St Kilda Post Office was closed on 29 August, the date of the evacuation of the island. Official Records should be amended where necessary. Any letters or parcels which may come to hand for St Kilda should circulate as for Oban, where arrangements have been made for their redirection to the addressees.'

In the little schoolroom where Ferguson had received an education forty years before, a piece of linoleum still served as a blackboard. The walls were of unvarnished matchboarding. There were two school pews that could seat fifteen scholars. In each pew were mountings for inkpots. On the wall was a map of Great Britain – a map which included England at the expense of Scotland. It did not even show where St Kilda was. On the same wall was a notice that proclaimed: 'Any scholars between the ages of three and fifteen will be exempted from payment of school fees, Harris, 14 October 1904.' The school calendar for the year 1930 had been torn off to September. The ten schoolchildren of Hirta had had their last lessons in this small, damp room. The St Kilda School Log Book's last entry, filled in by the missionary, was for June, and read: 'Attendance perfect for last week (Eight). School closed today with a small treat which the children seemed thoroughly to enjoy. Today probably ends the school in St Kilda as all the inhabitants intend leaving the island this summer. I hope to be away soon.'

A door from the schoolroom opened directly on to the Church, a high-ceilinged room with windows pointed at the top in the Gothic manner. Outside the Church, from a rough wooden scaffold, hung the Church bell, salvaged from the wreck of the *Janet Cowan* which had come to grief on the rocks round St Kilda on 7 April

1864, while on a voyage to Dundee from Calcutta with a cargo of jute. The interior of the church was filled by two rows of varnished deal benches with an aisle down the middle. The missionary's pulpit was the largest to be found in the Western Isles. The previous day, when the visitors had gone, the islanders under Dugald Munro had had their last service. The St Kildans left their bibles at their places in the pews, and the missionary left on the lectern an English and Gaelic bible. In the shadow of the pulpit, Norman Mackinnon, the precentor and head of the largest family on the island, had led community worship for the last time.

Like all the male islanders Neil Ferguson Senior had been offered a job with the Forestry Commission. He had never seen a tree growing in his life, there being none on St Kilda; but he had agreed to go to the Tulliallan Estate and was still wondering whereabouts in Scotland that was. Some days earlier he had asked some of his fellow islanders if they knew. Someone had thought it was near Fife. As he looked at the deserted village, he remarked 'it is like a tomb'. He closed the door of his own home. Like the other St Kildans he could not lock it. In a community in which everyone knew everyone else it had been sufficient just to shut the door against wind and rain.

The crossing to the mainland was a calm one. For as long as St Kilda could be seen on the horizon, the islanders stood silently at the stern of the boat. As the *Harebell* drew away from Village Bay, they showed the first signs of emotion. 'It was really quite sad', says Flora Gillies, then a ten-year-old schoolgirl, 'to see the chimneys and knowing we would never be back again.'

On board the islanders were fed on salmon, beef, bread, and butter. It cost the Navy £2 2s 6d to provide them with a meal – a sum which they insisted on recovering as soon as possible from the Scottish Office. While the islanders ate heartily, George Henderson of the Department of Health went below to send a telegram to Tom Johnston, who was spending the weekend at his country home, Monteviot, in Kirkintilloch. 'Evacuation successfully carried out this morning,' wrote Henderson. 'Left St Kilda 8 a.m.'

There was one further matter for Henderson to sort out. At the time it had not been resolved who was going to foot the bill for the evacuation. The head of every family, therefore, was obliged to sign a declaration over a sixpenny stamp, witnessed by Dr Alexander Shearer of the Home and Health Department and a representative of the Inverness County Council. By signing, the

St Kildans agreed to repay the Department of Health such sums as 'may be incurred by them regarding the removal of family, goods and effects (other than sheep), temporary accommodation in the course of removal, the purchase of furniture and furnishings for the new houses and execution of minor repairs required; also sum paid by way of maintenance until wages due to the islanders had been paid'. The sole qualification was that the total sum repayable should not exceed the money owed to the islanders by the Department of Agriculture for Scotland regarding the sheep. The authorities had thus, on the advice of the Treasury, covered themselves should questions be asked regarding the spending of British taxpayers' money.

The feelings of the little party of civilians on board the *Harebell* were mixed. Some left the island gladly. Norman Mackinnon, head of a family of nine, was among those eager to leave. The previous winter the Mackinnons had almost starved, and he had told the nurse he would remove his family to the mainland that summer regardless of what other St Kildans wished to do. In so deciding, he had forced the others into petitioning the government to evacuate the whole population. Support for the evacuation had come from the other young men on the island who, like Mackinnon, were weary of the hard life on Hirta.

For Nurse Williamina Barclay, 29 August represented a small personal victory. She had been instrumental in getting the St Kildans to agree to the evacuation, and had put in three months' hard work as the Department of Health's official on the island. As the ship steamed towards Lochaline, her greatest reward was to feel that at long last the little children of Village Bay would have a future in life. For her work she was to be later awarded the CBE.

The elderly of St Kilda left with the saddest hearts. Many of them had never left the island before and could speak no English. As Commander Pomfret remembers, they were the only ones to show outward signs of emotion as they left behind the one way of life that they were ever to understand. 'Nothing at all happened until they left *Harebell*, and then finality was reached – they had to go. Then one or two of them were weeping.' One of the most tightly-knit communities in Britain found itself split up when the fishery cruiser arrived at Lochaline. The government had been unable to find sufficient accommodation for the thirty-six islanders in Argyll, so some had chosen to make their homes elsewhere in Scotland. At a time when few words were said, Finlay Gillies was heard to mutter to himself in Gaelic, 'God will help us.' Finlay MacQueen, then in his late sixties, turned to the young Neil Gillies bound for Glasgow and beyond, and said, 'May God forgive those that have taken us away from St Kilda.'

The next day the nation's newspapers told their version of the day's events. In bold, black type one newspaper announced 'EXODUS FROM ST KILDA! ISLANDERS LEAVE THEIR HOMES WITHOUT TEARS'. For many who wrote and read the morning papers on Saturday 30 August, the evacuation of St Kilda represented a victory for their society. The social anomaly in the Atlantic that had been an embarrassment to progress made elsewhere in Scotland had at long last been eradicated.

2
A world apart

Until the evacuation St Kilda was the most remote inhabited part of the United Kingdom. It had been so for at least a thousand years, and as such the place fascinated those on the mainland. 'It seems almost beyond credence', wrote an astounded correspondent to *The Globe* newspaper in the middle of the nineteenth century, 'that such an interesting little colony, such an exclusive commonwealth exists as part of this busy kingdom. Beyond the whirl of commercial life, untroubled by politics, completely isolated from the rest of the world, the St Kildan lives his simple life. When death comes to him he is quietly buried in the little paddock which does duty for "God's acre", among the familiar crags and hills; the wild sea birds sing his *requiem* and the Atlantic surges toll his funeral knell.'

St Kilda is the name not of one island but of an archipelago which lies in the Atlantic Ocean about 110 miles west of the Scottish mainland. The nearest island is Uist in the Outer Hebrides which is about 45 miles east of St Kilda. The nearest port from which boats are able to sail is Lochmaddy, some 65 miles from the group. Dunvegan on the Isle of Skye is 80 miles away and Castlebay on the island of Barra lies some 90 miles from St Kilda. The origin of the name 'St Kilda' is the subject of controversy. A Dutch map of 1666 is the first to refer to the little archipelago west of the Sound of Harris as 'S. Kilda'. There is no reason to believe a saint called Kilda ever lived, and the islanders rarely referred to their home by that name. To the St Kildans the island of their birth was Hirta, and there is a map, issued in Italy in 1563, that plots an island called 'Hirtha' to the west of the Scottish mainland. But even this old Gaelic name is subject to scholarly debate. Many say it is derived from the old Irish word 'Hiort', meaning 'death' or 'gloom', a reminder of the old idea that the land of spirits lay beyond the sea. According to the Reverend Neil Mackenzie who was minister on St Kilda for fourteen years, the name was derived from the Gaelic '*I*' (island) and *ard* (high). Perhaps, however, the origin of the name Hirta comes from the old Norse for shepherd –

Hirt, a reference to the fact that the island almost rises perpendicular from the sea and overlooks the Western Isles.

The origin of the name St Kilda might also be found in the way in which the islanders pronounced Hirta. The natives pronounced an 'r' like an 'l', so that Hirta sounds like 'Hilta', or almost 'Kilta', as the 'h' had a somewhat guttural quality.

Hirta is the largest island of the group. The coastline measures some eight and three quarter miles and the total land area is 1,575 acres. It has two bays: Glen Bay lies to the north-east of the island and Village Bay, where the people of documented history lived, lies to the south-west. The two cut deep into the land and shape it into a rough letter 'H'.

Hirta can only be thought of as stupendous. In parts only one and a half miles long, and at no point more than one and three quarter miles across, the island has five peaks over nine hundred feet high. Of these, three – Mullach Mor, Mullach Bi, and Conachair – are over a thousand feet above sea level. Conachair rises to 1,397 feet, and its awe-inspiring cliffs are the highest in the British Isles.

Of the three other islands in the group, the island of Dun lies nearest to Hirta, to the western side of Village Bay. It is separated from the main island by a narrow channel, only fifty yards wide. Dun is a long, narrow finger of land which rises to over 570 feet above sea level as it stretches out into the Atlantic. The island is rocky and precipitous on its western side, grassy on its eastern flank, and in winter it was not unknown for the spray from waves to crash over the top of the island into Village Bay below.

Soay, the second largest island of the archipelago, lies to the north-west of Hirta. Abrupt on all sides of its two and a quarter mile coastline, Soay has a land area of 244 acres. Rising to 1,200 feet Soay, like Dun, is separated from Hirta by a narrow passage of ocean. Three needles of rock, Stac Donna (87 feet), Stac Biorach (240 feet), and Soay Stac (200 feet), stand in the sound.

Boreray, the remaining island, lies four miles to the north of Hirta. It has an area of 189 acres and is surrounded by a wall of rock which climbs from 300 to 1,245 feet above sea level. Lush grass grows on the steep south-westerly slope of Boreray facing Hirta.

The archipelago includes other giant rocks, called stacs, that rise out of the Atlantic like the tips of icebergs. Stac Levenish

(203 feet) lies outside Village Bay; Mina Stac (208 feet) and Brada-
stac (221 feet) lie at the foot of the cliffs of Conachair. Stac an
Armin, which rises to 627 feet and is the highest stac in the British
Isles, and Stac Lee, eighty-three feet shorter, rise from the waters
round Boreray. Stac Lee is the more impressive of the two, rising
like a great tooth of solid rock out of the ocean. Together with
Boreray, from which in ages past they broke free, the two stacs
have frequently aroused comments similar to that made by R. A.
Smith when he sailed to St Kilda in the yacht *Nyanza* in 1879.
'Had it been a land of demons,' he wrote, 'it could not have
appeared more dreadful, and had we not heard of it before, we
should have said that, if inhabited, it must be by monsters.'

Until the coming of steamships in the nineteenth century, the
journey to St Kilda even from the Hebridean ports was slow and
perilous. In 1697, when the island's historian Martin Martin visited
the people of Village Bay, the voyage took several days and nights.
There was only one type of vessel available – an open longboat
rowed by stout men of Skye. It took sixteen hours of sailing and
rowing before the crew caught their first glimpse of Boreray.
'This was a joyful Sight,' wrote Martin Martin, 'and begot new
Vigor in our men, who being refreshed with Victuals, low'ring
Mast and Sail, rowed to a Miracle. While they were tugging at the
Oars, we plied them with plenty of Aqua Vitae to support them,
whose borrowed Spirits did so far waste their own, that upon our
arrival at Boreray, there was scarce one of our Crew able to manage
Cable or Anchor.' It was left to the following day to row the few
miles to Hirta.

The prevailing winds helped further to cut off the people of
Village Bay from would-be visitors. On the northern, uninhabited
side of Hirta, Glen Bay is exposed to northerly gales, while on the
other side of the island Village Bay is open to winds that blow
from the south-east and the south-west. Because of steep rock faces,
Glen Bay was rarely used as a landing-place, except by a few stray
trawlermen running before a storm. The majority of landings
throughout the island's history were confined to Village Bay.

Wind and tide frequently prevented a landing. A sudden storm
could lash the sea into waves forty feet high and make dis-
embarkation impossible. To add to the difficulty, any vessel larger
than a longboat could not come close enough to enable people to
be put ashore on the slippery rocks that were the only possible
landing place.

Around 1877 a simple jetty was built on Hirta to assist the landing of people and stores. Two winters later it was swept away in a storm. In 1901–2 a small concrete jetty was built by the Congested District Board at a cost of £600. It proved less than adequate. Its size was governed less by the needs of the St Kildans, and more by the money available at the time. Although well constructed it was little improvement on the previous state of affairs. It made for a more graceful landing but did not significantly increase the number of landings possible. Even to this day, only the four months of summer – May, June, July, and August – hold out hope of a landing for visitors. To set foot on Hirta depends to this day upon small boats and calm waters.

For at least eight months of the year St Kilda, whose annual rainfall is about fifty inches, is subjected to frequent and severe gales and storms. Sudden and vicious, these storms are most common from September to March. Mary Cameron, daughter of one of the island's last missionaries, remembers a storm that literally deafened the people of the village. 'One particularly severe storm', she writes, 'left us deaf for a week – incredible but true. The noise of the wind, the pounding of the heavy sea, were indescribable. This storm was accompanied by thunder and lightning, but we could not hear the thunder for other sounds. Our windows were often white with salt spray, and it was awe-inspiring to watch the billows and flying spindrift.' On one occasion the entire village was destroyed in a gale, and sheep were frequently blown over the cliffs into the sea below. After a single night of rain, the island is literally running with water, and because of the steepness of the hillsides and the shallowness of the soil, the run-off is extremely destructive to crops.

Stormy weather inevitably meant privation to the St Kildans. 'Their slight supply of oats and barley', wrote Wilson in 1841, 'would scarcely suffice for the sustenance of life; and such is the injurious effect of the spray in winter, even on their hardiest vegetation, that savoys and german greens, which with us are improved by the winter's cold, almost invariably perish.' Somehow the St Kildans survived that year as they had done in the past and were to do in the future. They placed little reliance on the scant crops the weather would allow them to grow. Their main source of food and income remained the sea birds that were gathered in the few summer months.

Winter on Hirta was less cold than might be expected. The

archipelago lies in the path of the Gulf Stream and the sea helps keep the temperature higher. According to Wilson in 1841, the winter was mild and when ice formed it was little thicker than a penny. The St Kildans, however, claim that snow lay thick on the ground and there were often drifts deep enough to bury their sheep.

What was of greater concern to the people of Hirta was the rapidity with which the weather can change. The islands make their own weather as well as receiving the brunt of what rolls over the Atlantic, and within a period of twenty-four hours sunshine can make way for rain and rain for a storm. The St Kildans became weather forecasters *par excellence*; what to the outsider seemed a perfect day was frequently not a time to risk work either at sea or on the cliffs. 'The islanders in general', wrote the Reverend Kenneth Macaulay in 1765, 'possess the art of predicting the changes of the weather perhaps in much greater perfection than many of those who are beyond doubt superior to them in some other branches of knowledge . . . The St Kildans owe much of their knowledge to the observations they and their predecessors have made on the screamings, flight, and other motions of birds, and more especially on their migrations from one place to another.'

To an outdoor race like the St Kildans, weather was all-important. The summer months on Hirta frequently made up for the misery of autumn, winter, and spring. June, July, and August were months of much sunshine. When John Mathieson, the geographer, was on St Kilda in 1927, he kept a complete meteorological record of the months April to October. During that time there were 627 hours of sunshine and eleven and a half inches of rain. In Edinburgh during the same period there were 644 hours of sunshine and fourteen inches of rain. The average day temperature was 63 degrees Fahrenheit, compared with 67 degrees Fahrenheit in the capital city. On many days, however, the weather was too hot for comfort, and because the island offers little shelter the St Kildans worked stripped to the waist. In the spring and summer months it was occasionally very humid. George Murray, the schoolmaster, claimed that the atmosphere was often so heavy on the island that it was difficult to keep awake, and Mathieson and Cockburn also found summer days far from invigorating.

But the St Kildans rarely left their sea-girt home and had little idea what it was like to live elsewhere. Only the occasional visitor gave them an insight into the affairs of the outside world. Not only did the islanders know nothing of what the weather was like in other parts of the United Kingdom, throughout most of their history they were blissfully unaware of the troubles of the people who lived there. Only on a few occasions did the affairs of the nation beyond involve them.

St Kilda's reputation as the most isolated spot in the United Kingdom was quick to become widespread. As such it was suggested many times that the owner of the island, MacLeod of MacLeod, should offer the place up as a prison. For one woman the proposal became a reality. In the early eighteenth century Rachel Erskine Grange was virtually held captive on Hirta.

Lady Grange, as she came to be styled, was a bad-tempered woman totally opposed to the politics of her husband James Erskine of Grange, the Lord Justice Clerk, who was the brother of the Earl of Mar, leader of the 1715 Jacobite Rising. One night in 1731, when Jacobite sympathizers met at Lord Grange's house in Edinburgh, Rachel listened in to their conspiratorial talk from beneath a sofa. After a time she could take no more, revealed herself and threatened to denounce her husband and his friends.

The assembled nobles realized that they would have to get rid of her. MacLeod of Dunvegan and MacDonald of Sleat agreed to secrete her in the remote parts of their island possessions, and that night she was quietly removed from the city, bound for the Isle of Skye. News of her death was spread in Edinburgh and a mock funeral at Greyfriars Church was arranged. Her relatives attended, wept, and tried to accept that she was no more.

MacDonald looked after Lady Grange for two years on the lonely island of Heisker, off North Uist. MacLeod of Dunvegan then took responsibility for her and had her deported to St Kilda. There she remained a virtual prisoner for eight years, from 1734 until 1742. On the island it is said that she 'devoted her whole time to weeping and wrapping up letters round pieces of cork, bound with yarn, to try if any favourable wave would waft them to some Christian, to inform some humane person where she resided, in expectation of carrying tidings to her friends at Edinburgh'. The St Kildans were very hospitable, and put one of their houses at her disposal. She habitually slept during the day and got up at night throughout her period of exile, such was her dislike of the natives. The St Kildans, however, bore no malice and waited upon her royally. She was given the best turf on the island for her fire, and although food was scarce she never went without.

When it was thought that the danger had lessened, she was

brought back to Uist, then to Assynt, and then to Skye where she was taught how to spin. She worked alongside the local women who regularly sent their yarn to Inverness, and on one occasion she managed to hide a letter in the yarn sent to market.

Months later the letter reached her cousin, the Lord Advocate. He was appalled by her harrowing account of her adventures and persuaded the government to send a warship to search the coast of Skye for her. But the men of the British Navy could find no trace of her, and MacDonald had her swiftly sent to Uist and then on to the Vaternish peninsula, where she died in 1745.

To this day, Lady Grange is the only woman in Scotland to have had three funerals. The conspirators were still afraid that their evil deed would be discovered, so they filled a coffin with turf and staged a second funeral in the little churchyard of Duirinish, while her body was secretly buried at Trumpan, above Ardmore Bay, on the Isle of Skye. Lady Grange stayed longer on Hirta than any outsider before or since, save the occasional minister sent by the Free Church of Scotland.

After the defeat of his army at Culloden, Charles Stuart and a number of prominent rebels were thought to have escaped to St Kilda. On 10 June 1746, General Campbell of Mamore's intelligence services reported the rumour to him, and a grand expedition was swiftly mounted to go to St Kilda.

In the afternoon of 19 June soldiers and levies were ferried ashore at Hirta. The islanders had noticed the ships approaching several hours before and had taken to hiding-places in the hills. Forever in dread of being robbed and attacked by pirates, they had centuries before carved out small caves in the scree slope to the west of the village. Totally invisible to the naked eye from village level, the caves provided perfect cover. After searching the village the soldiers finally came across a group of men. The St Kildans had no idea what the soldiers were talking about. The islanders did not know of the existence of a Young Pretender, let alone of King George himself.

The people were to remain totally ignorant of the defeats and victories of a country fighting for an empire until the First World War broke out. In 1799 they had not heard of General Howe's illustrious crushing of the army of George Washington, and in 1815 knew nothing of Napoleon's Hundred Days that ended at Waterloo. When George Atkinson of Newcastle-upon-Tyne visited the island in 1831, the first question he was asked was 'Is there any war?'

It was traditionally the first question asked of any stranger, not that the St Kildans had any idea of what fighting was like. They took part in no war and never lost any of their number in battle. In a description of the islands for the period 1577 to 1595 in which each parish of MacLeod of MacLeod's empire was allocated the number of men it was expected to put into the field of battle, St Kilda was said not to supply any men because it was inhabited by poor folk who lived too far away. The same attitude of mind found expression in more modern times. St Kilda remains one of the few communities in the British Isles that has no war memorial. 'Safe in its own whirlwinds and cradled in its own tempests, it heeds not the storms which shake the foundations of Europe,' wrote Dr Macculloch in 1819, 'and acknowledging the dominion of MacLeod and King George, is satisfied without enquiring whether George is the First or the Fourth of his name.'

In 1836 when the island was cut off from the mainland for nearly two years, the minister found, when a passing ship dropped anchor in the bay, that he and his congregation had been praying for King William months after his death. The minister changed his prayers to 'His Majesty'. It was not until the spring of 1838, by which time Queen Victoria had been on the throne for nearly a year, that to his embarrassment he finally got wind of the sex of his new monarch.

Few on the mainland were prepared to take on any responsibility towards the people of so isolated an outpost. When James IV of Scotland passed an Act stating that islands were in future to be under his rule, he excluded St Kilda because it was so remote that he could not guarantee the people living there his protection. In more modern times, the existence of a community on the island was completely unknown to the Poor Law Commissioners. It was not until 1851 that the first official census was taken on St Kilda – fifty years after the first had been carried out on the mainland. The St Kildans never paid income tax because the Inland Revenue did not bother to send them forms to fill in, and they never paid rates. They never cast a vote in either a local or a general election. No aspiring politician ever sought to solicit their support, although a few Members of Parliament used St Kilda as an example when they wished to complain about the treatment of impoverished areas of Scotland by the government. The islanders never needed to call a policeman. No crime has been recorded in four hundred years of their history. 'If this island', wrote Macculloch, 'is not the Eutopia so long sought, where will it be found? Where is the land which has neither arms, money, law, physic, politics, nor taxes? That land is St Kilda . . .'. Neither *Times* nor *Courier* disturbs its judgments . . . No tax-gatherer's bill threatens on a church-door, the game laws reach not gannets . . . Well may the pampered native of the happy Hirta refuse to change his situation.'

A few departments of state showed an occasional interest in the people of St Kilda. The Registrar of Births, Deaths, and Marriages periodically checked the books, and the Receiver of Wrecks at Stornoway on the isle of Lewis claimed half the flotsam and jetsam that drifted ashore on St Kilda, if ever the islanders saw fit to tell him about it. Reports on the physical and economic situation of the islanders were made to the Scottish Home and Health Department in Edinburgh, particularly in the latter years, and a police constable from Harris was sent to make notes.

Nor were the people deprived of official proclamations. On 2 April 1901, the *Westminster Gazette* announced: 'His Majesty's ship *Bellona* left Greenock yesterday for St Kilda. The captain will land with a party of marines and bluejackets and announce the death of Queen Victoria and read the proclamation of King Edward's accession. Under the British Standard, the party will present arms, and the band will play "God Save the King".' The British monarchs have visited practically every corner of the globe, but it was not until August 1971 that Queen Elizabeth II became the first to set foot on what is the most westerly point of her kingdom.

Isolation makes for limited knowledge. In 1697, the St Kildans were intrigued by the samples of writing shown to them by Martin Martin and were amazed that people could express themselves and communicate with others in such a way.

When a St Kildan was taken to Glasgow in the early part of the eighteenth century, he was worried by the patches worn by the ladies of fashion because he thought they were blisters. He was astounded and frightened that there could be so many people in the world as were to be found in the city, and when some big loaves of bread were placed before him he could not make up his mind whether they were stones, pieces of wood, or made of the flour and water the local inhabitants told him they were. Another islander was shown St Mungo's Cathedral in Glasgow at about the same time. He remarked that the pillars and arches of the church were the most beautiful caves he had ever seen. He was taken aback by the size of Glasgow and was surprised that people could move about from place to place in carriages pulled by horses.

Even knowledge of things natural, like animals and plants, was limited on Hirta. The islanders were never to know what a pig, a bee, a rabbit, or a rat looked like. They never saw an apple until 1875 when John Sands took three with him to the island. They had no idea what a tree looked like, for no trees grow on St Kilda. It was not until a few of them began to venture forth to the mainland before the evacuation – some for a holiday, others in search of work – that they first saw and then came to know the hundreds of objects that are part of everyday life on the mainland. For centuries the St Kildans measured time by the motion of the sun from one hill or rock to another and by the ebb and flow of tides. Even in 1909, the Old Style Calendar still operated on Hirta. Unlike Scots anywhere else in the world, the St Kildans celebrated New Year on 12 January.

The fear of the incomprehensible and unknown made for a deep attachment to their island home. Even as late as 1875, John Sands discovered, 'All beyond their little rock home is darkness, doubt and dread – incomprehensible to us.' The physical size of their world and the small number of persons involved in it made for the existence of strong relationships within the community. St Kildan was inextricably bound to St Kildan. All of them were tied emotionally as well as physically to their desolate rock in the Atlantic. Even if it had been possible, few islanders ever wished to leave St Kilda. Ewen Gillies was one of the few who ventured forth into the big world that lay beyond Hirta.

Born in 1825, Ewen spent all his childhood on the island, and when the time came to settle down he married the daughter of one of the elders. At the age of twenty-six he decided to leave the island and seek his fortune in Australia. He sold up his croft, furniture, and unwanted effects for £17, and with his young bride decided to go to Australia, where he was first employed as a brickmaker.

After six months he became bored, left his job and took to travelling. For two years he explored the virgin lands of Victoria digging for gold. He had luck and bought himself a farm. Owing to a lack of capital the farm proved an unwise investment, and within two years he was off to New Zealand to dig again for gold, leaving his wife and children at Melbourne. In less than two years he was back again in Australia to find that his wife, thinking she had seen the last of him, had married someone else. Disillusioned but not dismayed, Ewen packed his bags and sailed for North America.

Like many penniless immigrants, Ewen Gillies joined the Union Army. After getting some money together he deserted the ranks when word got round that gold was to be found in California. For six years he worked in the gold mines with considerable success. With his fortune, he decided to return to Australia and claim his children. Reluctantly, his wife finally agreed to surrender them, and not wishing to stay in Australia any longer than was necessary, Ewen packed up his belongings and set sail in 1871 via London and Glasgow for St Kilda. He was welcomed enthusiastically by the islanders, but to a man who had been round the world St Kilda offered little, and after only four weeks Ewen and his children set sail for America.

Eleven years later, after he had settled his family in the New World, Ewen again found the call of St Kilda too strong to resist. Yet again, he set out for the isle of his birth. This time he proved too much for the St Kildans, and after a short stay he found himself no longer welcome on the island and set sail once again for Melbourne. He had, however, stayed long enough on St Kilda to fall in love with a local girl. His second bride found the Australian climate little to her liking and was homesick. Eight months later the couple were again on St Kilda.

The St Kildans, distrustful of his wisdom and overpowering self-assurance, finally forced him and his wife to leave. Ewen boarded the first boat to reach St Kilda in the summer of 1889, and made his way to Canada where he spent the remainder of his life.

The hospitality of the people of Hirta, however, was normally something that visitors could not easily forget. 'The people', wrote a former schoolmaster, 'were exceedingly kind to me, quite a different character they had to what was presented to me on landing. One has to stay some time amongst them to know them thoroughly.' Nor was their concern confined to those who chose to live amongst them.

The St Kildans frequently had to play hosts to unfortunates who found themselves stranded on the island. On 17 January 1876, some of the crew of the 880-ton Austrian ship *Peti Dubrovacki* were shipwrecked. Three of the crew, including the captain, stayed with the minister while they were on the island. The remaining six were quartered with the islanders, each home taking in a man or two by turns for a few days at a time. The St Kildans showed themselves to be generous to those in distress. 'I myself', wrote Sands, 'saw a man take a new jacket out of the box into which it had been carefully folded, and with a look of genuine pity, gave it to the mate to wear during his stay, as the young man sat shivering in an oilskin.' The St Kildans had not only studied the parable of the Good Samaritan, but throughout history followed it. A people used to deprivation, they could feel for those forced to accept the same condition. But nine sailors were additions the people could scarce afford to feed. It was mid-winter and the owner's boat was not expected until the spring. John Sands realized that contact with the mainland must somehow be made before the St Kildans as well as their uninvited guests starved.

Sands first got an idea when he observed that the St Kildans used reeds in their looms. He was told that they were salvaged from the beach, and deduced that the currents of the Atlantic, namely the Gulf Stream, must have brought them to Hirta. He decided that the same currents could be used to send a letter from St Kilda to the mainland. In January 1877 he set about constructing a vessel to convey a message that would inform the mainland of the existence of the band of shipwrecked Austrians.

'On the 29th, the captain and sailors called on me and felt interested in seeing a canoe I had hewn out of a log,' wrote Sands. 'I had written a letter and put it into her hold, enclosed in a pickle bottle. The sailors, glad of anything in the shape of work, helped me to rig her and put the iron ballast right, and to caulk the deck. We delayed launching her until the wind should blow from the North-West, which we hoped would carry her to Uist or some other place where there was a post. A small sail was put on her, and with a hot iron I printed on her deck, "Open this".

'The captain brought me a lifebuoy belonging to the lost ship, and said he intended to send it off. I suggested that another bottle be tied to it with a note enclosed to the Austrian Consul, and that a small sail should be erected. This was done and the lifebuoy was thrown into the sea and went away slowly before the wind. None of us had much hope that this circular vessel would be of service. She was despatched on the 30th and strange to say, reached Birsay in Orkney, and was forwarded to Lloyd's agent in Stromness on 8 February, having performed the passage in nine days.

'On 5 February we sent off the canoe, the wind being in the North-West and continuing so for some days. She went to Poolewe in Ross-shire where she was found lying on a sandbank on the 27th by a Mr John Mackenzie who posted the letter.'

In fact, it was the first mailboat that was to bring help. On 22 February HMS *Jackal* arrived at St Kilda and took the nine Austrians and John Sands back to the mainland. By that time, the St Kildans had already given up eating porage and bread. This continued for three months, until the factor's smack visited the island and took grain, sugar, tea, salt, and other foodstuffs to them. The foodstuffs were paid for out of a donation of £100, made by the Austrian Government to the people of Hirta in recognition of their kindness.

The St Kildans were greatly amazed by such a crude method of communication as the mailboat of John Sands. It was thenceforth thought a useful way in which contact could be made with the mainland. The earlier mailboats were usually of a common construction: each consisted of a piece of driftwood, the centre of which was hewn out sufficiently to hold a letter and some money for postage, and then sealed with pitch. In later models, an inflated sheep's bladder was attached to the block of wood, together with a rude flag to make the mailboat more conspicuous at sea.

Around 1900, cocoa became popular on Hirta. Instead of wood, an eight-ounce tin that once contained Van Houten's chocolate was thought to be an admirable carrier of a message. The mailboats, with a penny enclosed for postage, were normally put out to sea from the rocks of Oiseval and, depending upon the North Atlantic Drift, occasionally turned up as far away as Norway. They were used by the St Kildans as a last resort in times of emergency, but more often than not as tourist attractions.

To the end, mailboats were a romanticism introduced to St Kilda by people from the mainland. The islanders preferred their age-old method of attracting attention if faced with a problem. Bonfires were lit on the hilltops, which in clear weather could be seen on the horizon by the inhabitants of Lewis or Harris.

For the greater part of St Kilda's history, however, communication with the mainland was as sporadic as it was unnecessary. The community was self-sufficient, relying only upon the visit once or twice a year from a representative of the island's owner to collect rent and deliver a few essential supplies, such as salt and seed.

3
The paternal society

Feudal society existed in Scotland centuries after it had disappeared
elsewhere in Britain. The Celtic people who inhabited the most
northerly remote parts of the British Isles were thought to be of
little consequence by the Anglo-Saxons who dominated British
society. The Celts were therefore allowed to carry on living the
way they had always done. In most of northern Scotland the social
system was ruthlessly destroyed after the 1745 Jacobite Rising, but
in the more remote parts of the Highlands and in the Western Isles
the old order lived on.

Enlightened paternalism was the basis of the society of the Gael.
The chief who owned the land also ruled over the people who lived
upon it. As long as the chief acted as a good and wise father and
the crofters settled on his estate were respectful children, feudalism
proved itself to be a successful as well as convenient way of
managing society. If the critics of the more 'civilized' South thought
the feudal system of the Celt was primitive, it could at least be
seen to be a social organization that worked and worked well
for hundreds of years. In the words of Dr Fraser Darling in
West Highland Survey, gaeldom is 'an example of a culture finely
adjusted to an environment which placed severe limitations on
human existence'.

The people on the lone isle of Hirta were throughout their
history part of the old order. Until the evacuation in 1930, the
proprietor of the island group, MacLeod of MacLeod, not only
owned St Kilda but held sway over its inhabitants. He was father
as well as landlord, and as such received for himself and his house
the greatest of respect and affection. 'Their Chief is their God, their
everything especially when a man of address and resolution', wrote
Lord Murray of Broughton in a report on the Highlands he drew
up in 1746 for the London government. The duty of the Chief was
to protect his clan, administer good and impartial justice when
settling disputes that might arise among his people, and above all
hold his land so that his people might live and prosper upon it.
In return the crofters would offer their services to fight for any

cause deemed just by the Chief, and give him absolute claim over any produce deriving from the croft.

Although the Gaelic word *clann* means 'children', the system did not depend upon the people working the land being of the same family or even the same name as the owner. On St Kilda no inhabitant was related to MacLeod of MacLeod by ties of blood near or remote. The few families whose surname was MacLeod were like all the other families – they were descendants of the poor from other parts of the Chief's estates who were encouraged to take up crofts on St Kilda. The concept of kinship played little or no part in the clan in the wider sense. What bound the people together was a shared feeling of loyalty to the chief whose land they held, and mutual understanding between him and his people.

MacLeod of MacLeod, Chief of Clan MacLeod, owned St Kilda throughout most of its inhabited history. When and how the family gained possession are questions the answers to which are lost in time. Legend has it that at one time both Harris and Uist disputed ownership of St Kilda. Even in ancient times the island group was regarded as a jewel in the Atlantic that any laird would be proud to own.

A race was planned to settle the question of ownership. Two boats representing the contending interests were rowed out to the island by crews of equal size. It was agreed before the start that the first crew to lay a hand on Hirta would claim it for his Chief. The race was extremely close, and as the two boats neared the island the stout men of Uist were ahead. Colla MacLeod, head man of the Harris boat, cut off his left hand and threw it ashore in a last desperate attempt to win the island for his master. The loss of a hand was not in vain, and St Kilda was won for MacLeod of MacLeod. This noble deed, some would have it, is recorded for posterity by the red hand on the clan coat of arms.

The MacLeod of MacLeod was an island Chief with an island empire. As such he tended to be too remote to become involved with the politics of the mainland to the same extent as the Campbells or MacDonalds did. Although many MacLeods, for instance, fought at the battle of Culloden, they did so against the wishes of their Chief who had little heart for the Jacobite cause.

After Culloden, the policy adopted by the Hanoverians was aimed at obliterating the Celtic way of life. 'In Scotland more than elsewhere,' wrote Grant, 'into the purely feudal relationship had crept something of the greater warmth and fervour of the ancient bond of union of the clan (or family)', and the government was determined to put an end to such dangerous feudalism. The Disarming Act was revived and important additions made to it. The wearing of Highland dress and the use of tartan were prohibited, and the playing and even carrying of bagpipes was forbidden. The bans were to last thirty-six years and dealt a damaging blow to a people's culture. In 1747, Parliament passed an Act for the Abolition of Heritable Jurisdictions which took away from the Chiefs their legal powers. After Culloden many Highland estates were forfeited.

The victors, however, did not take vengeance upon the laird of Dunvegan. He had played a passive part in the rebellion and, besides, his estate was remote and fragmented. MacLeod of MacLeod held on to his lands and the patriarchal rule of Dunvegan was allowed to continue well into the nineteenth century.

The economic buttress of the Chief's hold over his people was the system of trading by barter. Every year a representative of the Chief would visit St Kilda to claim the rents in kind. Often the 'tacksman', as he was called, was related if only distantly to the Chief. He leased the island from the proprietor for a sum of money or was given the revenue of the island as a reward for performing some special service.

When Martin Martin visited St Kilda in 1697, he did so in the company of MacLeod of MacLeod's representative. While on the island the steward and his retinue, which often numbered forty or fifty people, were housed and fed at the expense of the islanders. He would go once a year to the island in the summer and stay for anything up to two or three weeks. The ancient Gaelic due of free hospitality to the Chief or any of his household was known as *cuddiche* and was exacted in St Kilda when it had long disappeared elsewhere. *Cuddiche* was similar to the right to hospitality demanded by medieval and Tudor monarchs in England when they made their royal progresses.

At the end of his stay on St Kilda, the steward or 'tacksman' would take back to Skye the oils and feathers of the sea birds and the surplus produce of the islanders' scant crofts. The goods would either be sold to tenants who lived on other parts of the Chief's estates or else sent south to the commercial markets. Part of the proceeds of their sale would go towards the St Kildans' rent, and part would be retained by the tacksman as profit. But he had to fulfil his obligation to the islanders. A good part of the money obtained by the sale of the island produce was used to purchase commodities such as salt and seed corn which the St Kildans had need of. Supplies of essentials that the island could not provide were normally transported to St Kilda the following summer, or else delivered later the same year should the people be in dire need of them.

For centuries the system worked admirably. Hirta's exports were in much demand on the mainland, and the island was a source of profit for the tacksman and proprietor alike. According to Lord Brougham in 1799, the tacksman paid £20 a year to MacLeod of MacLeod and reckoned to make twice as much himself. The barter system, however, benefited the people of Hirta. No one would have claimed that the islanders received a true market price for their goods, but on the other hand they did not need to bother themselves with finding outlets. In bad years they never went without essential supplies. It was in no one's interest that the St Kildans starve. A loss to the tacksman one year would no doubt be turned into profit the next.

An islander, called the ground officer, was appointed by the Chief to speak for the community should differences of opinion arise with the steward. If the difference was serious, it was the ground officer's duty to make a personal appearance before MacLeod of MacLeod himself to air the complaint. 'He makes his entry very submissively,' wrote Martin Martin, 'taking off his bonnet at a great distance when he appears in MacLeod's presence, bowing his head and hand low near the ground, his retinue (usually the crew that had rowed him over from St Kilda) doing the like behind him.' MacLeod of MacLeod would then listen solemnly to the evidence and pass judgement. Few disputes, however, came about regarding the management of St Kilda. The tacksmen for the most part were 'Gentlemen of benevolent dispositions, of liberal education and much observation'. (John Knox)

The Chief rarely failed to exercise what was seen as a moral responsibility towards his people. During the last quarter of the eighteenth century, MacLeod of MacLeod ceased to receive any money from his estates for a while. 'This estate', wrote Knox in his *Tour Through the Highlands of Scotland and the Hebride Isles*, which was published in 1787, 'has been greatly diminished of late years on account of debts, and much remains to be discharged. Notwithstanding this circumstance, the proprietor raised no rents, turned out no tenants, used no man with severity, and in all respects maintained the character of a liberal and humane friend of mankind.' In 1780 the proprietor supplied the St Kildans with a new boat, and although salt was heavily taxed at that time and was virtually unobtainable in many districts of the Highlands, the people of St Kilda still received their more than adequate supplies.

Life on the mainland, however, was changing, and MacLeod of MacLeod suffered drastically from the changes, being forced to sell much of his estate. Tacksmen became people of the past, and what remained of the estate of the Chief of Clan MacLeod was henceforth managed by his factor at Dunvegan. St Kilda forever held an affectionate place in the history of the MacLeod family and was not sold.

The last factor was John Mackenzie of Dunvegan, an amiable man fond of St Kilda and its people. Once a year it was Mackenzie's duty to go to Hirta and collect the Chief's rents. Dressed in a long tweed trenchcoat and rarely seen without a gamekeeper's deerstalker hat, Mackenzie was much liked by the islanders. He would spend most of his time on St Kilda having long conversations with them, listening to their problems and attempting to solve them while on the island. If that was not possible, he would see what could be done after he had returned to Dunvegan. To the St Kildans, the factor was the go-between. He was their real link with the outside world.

One of the major tasks of his visit would be the landing of the stores he brought with him on board the *Robert Hadden*. Such work was normally done by the women, supervised by the men of the island. One of the most important things he took with him was a cask of paraffin, which was invariably given to the islanders as a gift.

The ceremony attached to the annual payment of rent always remained the same. The St Kildans would gather outside the old storehouse down by the shore, and once their produce had been inspected by the factor the bartering would begin. As fair a price as possible would be bargained by both sides – in later years it proved less and less favourable to the islanders. During the twentieth century the payment of rent was less a reality and more a symbolic act. During the thirteen years prior to the evacuation, the islanders failed to raise enough produce to pay rent due on their crofts. In John Mackenzie's day, the only produce of any real value was tweed, a few stones of dried ling, and perhaps a sheep or two. The end of the annual rent ceremony was marked by the factor presenting sweets to the St Kildans, instead of the traditional presentation of Highland whisky with the receipts. The St Kildans never kept account of what they handed over to the factor: there was trust on both sides.

The introduction of money, however, did more than all the vengeance exacted after Culloden to destroy traditional Gaelic society. Crofting, the most prominent feature of the Highlanders' way of life, was proving to be extremely uneconomic. The coming of the Industrial Revolution and the payment of money in exchange for labour was drawing people away from the country. It was no longer possible to think in terms of payment in kind. The barter system was no longer relevant or tenable. Money was required for the purchase of foodstuffs and materials essential to the maintenance of life upon the island and the cost involved in the transportation of those goods; both factors conspired to render a fatal blow to the old social order. The St Kildans, like other Celts, were forced to accept modern society and its values or else be condemned to oblivion.

From time immemorial the men and women of Hirta governed their lives as best suited their lonely predicament. 'Their government is strictly a republic,' wrote George Atkinson in 1831, 'for though subject to Great Britain, they have no official person among them; and as they are only visited twice a year for a few days by the Tacksman, who is referred to as a sort of umpire or settler of disputes, their knowledge of our laws must be very trifling and of little use or importance in their system of economy.'

The community as a whole shared the responsibility for the two major tasks: to ensure that every islander was fed, clothed, and housed as was thought proper, and to provide sufficient wares to pay the proprietor his rent. All possessions, such as boats and ropes, upon which the safety and prosperity of the community depended, were therefore held in common. Authority over the actions of every islander was vested in what tourists were later to call 'Parliament'.

Every morning after prayers and breakfast all the adult men on the island met in the open air to discuss what work was to be done. In latter years, the men met outside the post office, every day except the Sabbath. In so small a community, where the normal pursuits of its members were so fraught with danger, it was important that all knew what was planned, and a meeting was a sensible way of letting everyone know where members of the community could be found during the rest of the day. 'It wouldn't do to go away on your own,' recalls Lachlan Macdonald, 'and the other fellows didn't know where you were going. So they always decided where they were going and what they were going to do that day.'

It was a simple way in which a people who thought and acted in terms of each other could communicate as a group. The St Kildan parliament, however, came in for criticism from outsiders. 'The daily morning meeting', wrote John Ross, the schoolmaster, 'very much resembles our Honourable British Parliament in being able to waste any amount of precious time over a very small matter while on the other hand they can pass a Bill before it is well introduced.' But the islanders themselves would have been the last to think of their assembly as capable of great, philosophical thought. As far as they were concerned, the morning meeting was the only way, in a land that lacked telephones and newspapers, of letting others know what was planned, what was believed, and what was to be done.

If it was a 'Parliament', it was one that perhaps met the needs of those it served better than any other. There were no 'headmen' in parliament. Every islander had an equal right to speak, and to cast an equal vote. It was an assembly that had no government. There was always a total lack of distinction upon St Kilda. No islander held sway over his fellow islanders. Equally, no rules governed the conduct of the morning meeting. The men arrived in their own time, and at the meeting, according to observers, everyone appeared to talk at once.

If the proceedings of the day were important, the morning meeting would waste little time. If a visit to one of the neighbouring islands or stacs to tend the sheep or kill the seabirds was in order, the men would be quick to get to the work at hand. If, however, there was little of urgency that required to be done, the meeting could and would often sit all day in discussion. A break for lunch would be taken as and when the proceedings allowed, but otherwise talk would be the work of the day. 'Upon the whole,' wrote John Ross, 'the St Kildans are just as much engaged as their crofter neighbours in the Outer Hebrides and although they do at times spend much more time than is necessary over "parliamentary" affairs, they often derive benefit from it inasmuch as any stray piece of useful information picked up by a single individual is imparted to the whole.' The adventures of those who had had the opportunity to visit the mainland were related in great detail to the assembled throng. Information such as the cost of buckets and spades in the great metropolis of Glasgow and what wonderful shops were to be found there were not the only subjects of great interest. The most important function of the morning meeting was the exchange of views and the sharing of experiences.

The St Kildans never regarded themselves as individuals. Each and every one was a component of a community. The daily meeting was that which held them together, even though 'parliament' was often the market place of gossip. 'Very often,' said Ross, ' "my neighbour" and anything he has done out of the way, whether it is right or wrong', were matters to be examined by the assembled islanders. Discussion frequently spread discord, but never in recorded history were feuds so bitter as to bring about any permanent division within the community. Perhaps the fact that criticism was aired so readily ensured that gossip was never allowed to get out of hand.

The laws that governed the island were equally of the people's own making. Although formally subject to the law of the rest of Scotland, there was never an instance when those laws were either enforced or needed to be. 'Murder, of course, from the impossibility of escape and the absence of the usual causes of incitement is unknown in their traditions,' wrote George Atkinson, 'and dishonesty from similar causes very nearly so; a case of adultery has never been known among them, and as no fermented or spirituous liquor is made on the island, and they only receive a trifling half-yearly supply from the Tacksman, they are of necessity sober.'

The St Kildans looked to the Bible for their laws. In most respects they abided by the laws laid down by Moses in the Old Testament. How such a corpus of law became embodied in the community is unknown, but Macaulay in 1758 probably correctly believed that missionaries must, at an early date, have converted the St Kildans to accept such a code of behaviour.

Only the elders of the Church had authority over the rest of the community. They were responsible for sharing out the produce of the islanders' labours equally. Should there be any difficulty, the distribution would be settled by lot. The division of native labour was always carried out to the satisfaction of all concerned. After the harvesting of the seabirds, the catch of each day was placed in one great heap, usually on the foreshore, and was then divided out according to the number of households on the island. 'At the

end of the day's fowling,' wrote Christina MacQueen at the time
of the evacuation, 'the sharing began. Grouped around the large
heap of slain fulmars stood the representatives of every family.
In the rear the women and juveniles waited; waited to carry their
portion to the cottage, where the plucking would immediately
begin. The larger the family, the bigger the share. There was no
such thing as payment by results. Such a practice is only necessary
where the thing, miscalled "civilization" has blunted the natures of
men, and made them selfish and callous, and brutal to their fellows.'

The sick, the young and those who were old and lived alone were
always cared for. 'The St Kilda community', remarked Wilson in
1841, 'may in many respects be regarded as a small republic in
which the individual members share most of their worldly goods in
common, and with the exception of the minister, no one seems to
differ from his neighbour in rank, fortune, or condition.' The
St Kildans throughout their history never included either ministers,
missionaries, nurses, or schoolmasters in the sharing out of their
food, be it the carcass of fulmar, gannet, or sheep. They were
always regarded as outside the community. All received a part of
the community's produce as a gift; none of them ever received a
share as a right.

Like every system of sharing, there were exceptions to the
general rule. Any St Kildan, for instance, who killed a young fulmar
or gannet 'out of its nest' was allowed to keep the bird for himself.
The justification for such an exception was that if he had not taken
the bird, it would either have died a natural death or have been
swallowed up by a raven or a crow. By 1880, the fulmar and the
puffin were the only birds subject to equal division. By that time,
apart from homespun tweed, their feathers and oil were the only
staples used to pay the rent, a concern always regarded as the
responsibility of the community as a whole.

All the grazing for the sheep that each St Kildan kept was held
in common. The island of Dun was the only grazing that was
subject to conditions. The lush clover grass that covered the island
was strictly reserved for wintering the young lambs, and because
of the island's size, only a certain number of sheep could be
accommodated. An islander was able to keep as many sheep and
cattle as he was able to pay rent for, and the number of lambs
that could be transferred from Hirta to Dun every year was decided
equitably by the morning meeting.

A mutual insurance scheme operated in St Kilda. Any islander

who had the misfortune to lose sheep during the winter or during
the time when they were rounded up for shearing was reimbursed
by his fellow St Kildans in proportion to the number of sheep the
latter possessed.

The island's boats were throughout history owned and maintained by the community at large. Boats were essential to the
island's way of life: it was only right, therefore, that everyone be
concerned with their condition. Each islander was made responsible
for the upkeep of a section of the boat, and its use was determined
by the morning meeting. No islander or group of islanders was able
to make use of the craft unless everyone had given his permission.
Should foolhardiness mean the community lost its boat, then life
would be impossible. It was only right, therefore, that its employment be decided by consensus.

The St Kildans carried equality into every aspect of their lives.
When the Highland and Agricultural Society sent out meal and
flour to the people every year, the distribution of the supplies was
always strictly regulated. Each male and female over eleven years
of age on the island was entitled to a full share; islanders between
the ages of nine years and eleven were entitled to three part of a
share, and from cradle age to under nine every St Kildan was
entitled to a half share.

A man's share equalled one boll, which was the equivalent of
140 pounds of flour or oatmeal. After the supplies were distributed,
anything left was given out to each household in shares applicable
to smaller quantities.

The supplies of tea and other commodities brought to the island
by the factor were distributed in a similar way. Potatoes, for
instance, were shared on the same basis as meal and flour. Only
sugar was an exception. An equal share was given to both young
and old, and if preference was ever exercised it was in favour of
the younger members of the community.

In later years, the division was calculated more simply. One share
was allotted to each adult islander and a half share was given to
children of sixteen years and under.

The islanders were equally equitable when it came to sharing
gifts donated by tourists and well-wishers. All that arrived on the
island was divided, just as every St Kildan was prepared to
distribute domestic wealth. If the St Kildan sought anything in life,
he sought to be fair.

'The mental constitution or social polity of the St Kildans', wrote

Wilson, 'consists in their tenacious adherence to uniformity – no man being allowed, or at least encouraged, to outstrip his neighbours in any thing leading rather to his own advantage than the public weal.' In some respects, the communal system stifled initiative. 'I myself', wrote John Ross the schoolmaster in 1889, 'heard one man expressing a desire to have one end of his house floored with wood so as to make it more comfortable, but he had to give up the idea, some of the others coming down on him with most peculiar arguments leading him to understand the folly of his plan.' The wife of the last missionary sent to St Kilda recalls : 'When the St Kildans started doing something, they all did it on the same day. If they killed a sheep, it wasn't enough for them to kill one sheep for maybe the whole community. No, every house had to kill a sheep. So there was a piece of mutton landed from each house at the manse. You had mutton till you were fed up with the sight of it.'

The socialist system, whatever its faults, was the direct result of the condition in which the St Kildans found themselves. Common survival was the prime concern and although many from the mainland saw fit to criticize the islanders in latter years because, they claimed, the St Kildans lacked initiative, such a human quality was alien to a people who always thought in terms of the whole rather than the part. It was not that the people of Hirta were ignorant, it was simply that the concept of individualism was not applicable, as far as they were concerned, to the set of circumstances they faced.

In the careful ownership of the MacLeods the social and economic structure changed little for over six centuries. But people may have lived on Hirta for possibly two thousand years. The beehive-shaped stone and turf structures in Glean Mor suggest that in prehistoric times a pastoral people may have lived there. Possibly as a result of changes in climate and the lie and content of the soil, they found it necessary to abandon the settlement. Perhaps those early St Kildans were wiped out by disease or forced off the island by those who at the same time or at a later date chose to live in Village Bay. Whatever happened in those early times is unknown, and it is unlikely that the thin, stony soil has many secrets to give up when archaeologists ultimately dig.

In the eighth century the Norsemen invaded Scotland. For four centuries they ruled the islands of Scotland, and lone St Kilda may well have been part of their empire. In 1886, Richard Kearton and his brother Cherry found earthenware pots similar to those used for cooking purposes in Viking times. Many St Kildan place-names, moreover, have their origins in Norse. Oiseval is derived from the Norse *austr fell*, meaning 'east hill'; Soay gets its name from *Saud-ey*, Norse for 'sheep isle'. In practically all cases, however, the Viking names apply only to landmarks that can be clearly seen from the sea.

The names of those places the discovery of which requires a landing on Hirta are mostly Gaelic in origin. The names of streams and wells, for instance, derive from the ancient language of the Celts. It could therefore be argued that although the island group was known to the Norsemen, they did not permanently settle on St Kilda. It seems likely that the islands were known to them as a place of shelter in a storm and as a source of supplies of fresh water.

The rule regarding place-names, however, is not a hard and fast one. Many names, such as Mullach Bi and Dun, both easily visible from the sea, are Gaelic; one of Hirta's fresh water wells, Tobar Childa, gets its name in part from Norse. All that can be deduced with certainty is that St Kilda was known to the Norsemen.

Whatever the origins of the early peoples of Hirta, by the middle ages feathers and the oils extracted from sea birds were valuable commodities. To the owner of St Kilda, therefore, the repopulation, or perhaps population of the island, was the result of economic considerations.

The inhabitants of documented times were descended from those who had been born on the adjacent isles of Lewis, Harris, Skye, and North and South Uist. They were, without doubt, Celtic in origin. Although it seems unlikely that the St Kildans were the descendants of 'pyrates, exiles or malefactors who fled from justice', as was thought by the Reverend Kenneth Macaulay in 1758, it is probable that MacLeod of MacLeod occasionally sent the discontented to the most remote part of his territory.

The community must have had several injections of new blood during its long history. Some were necessary, others were totally unexpected. Disease practically wiped out the population twice in the history known to us, and the proprietor, anxious to have such a profitable outpost of his estate inhabited, must have encouraged or cajoled crofters from less remote parts of his empire to populate the archipelago. Many ships were wrecked around St Kilda, more visited the islands whilst fishing the rich waters that surround the group and sailors must have taken a fancy to local girls, jumped ship and settled upon the island.

Many writers tried hard to discover physical peculiarities that would illustrate the difference between the St Kildan and the generality of mankind. 'As a race', wrote the Reverend Neil Mackenzie in the nineteenth century, 'the natives now are undersized and far from being robust or healthy. They are generally of slender form, with fair hair and a florid complexion.' There is little real evidence, however, that the islanders differed from their neighbours on the Long Island, or that they were less strong. If the St Kildans exhibited any characteristic worthy of note it was that, from an early age, their faces were quick to show the harshness of life on the island. Towards the end of the community's history, the people seem to have become more susceptible to cuts and grazes, colds and headaches, but their physical prowess did not appreciably decline and any physical deterioration must be attributed to the general decline of the St Kildan way of life.

The personal qualities of the people of Hirta attracted even more attention than their appearance. Apart from their ignorance, which bemused many a visitor, the St Kildans were thought by many observers to be stubborn, superstitious, lazy and greedy. 'A total want of curiosity, a stupid gaze of wonder, an excessive eagerness for spirits and tobacco, a laziness only to be conquered by the hope of the above mentioned cordials, and a beastly degree of filth, the natural consequence of this renders the St Kildan character truly savage,' was Lord Brougham's conclusive description of the average islander in 1799.

The people of St Kilda, however, like those of many primitive communities, possessed remarkable qualities. They were strong of character, and the unique way of living that evolved reflected to a great extent their almost inexhaustible fund of common sense. 'They are at heart a kindly disposed people', wrote Nicol, 'who mean well, and while you are with them you are one of them. They are extremely solicitous for your welfare; indeed those who have lived for some time in their midst say that it is almost embarrassing when they call each morning to ask if you are well, if you have had a good night's sleep, and if they can do anything for you.'

Like many Celts, however, they were dreamers rather than men of action. They much preferred to talk and could, to the observer at least, always give better reasons for not doing something than they could acquiesce. Many writers took their lethargy to be laziness. 'I fear', wrote John MacDonald in 1822, 'they cannot be exempted from the charge of almost habitual indolence. They are seldom wholly idle; but when they are at any work, one would think that they are more anxious to fill up than to occupy time.' To the St Kildans, however, the pace of work was dictated by their needs. Time to them was an immaterial dimension divided more into seasons than into months and days. The men in particular saved their energies for the capture of sea birds and did little to help around the croft.

'The men I always thought might have done more work,' wrote the missionary's wife in 1909, 'although once properly started they worked well. I used to find fault with them for allowing the women to do all the work they themselves ought to have done. It was no uncommon thing to see the young men helping to rope the bags on to the women's backs. Sheep, coal, or any burden was carried from the pier by the women as a rule – very occasionally the men. I thought it very funny on one of my visits to the village to see the wife digging the ground, preparatory to planting the potatoes, but the good man of the house was seated at the door sewing a Sunday gown for his wife.' Life on Hirta was such that women were never allowed much leisure. Apart from the routine household chores, the women were responsible for bringing water, fuel, and provisions into the house. Every summer, knitting as they went, the women used to walk over two miles twice a day to milk the cows and ewes in Glen Mor. Whilst boys were soon taught the art of talking much and doing little, the girls were accustomed to carrying heavy weights on their backs from a very early age.

The morals of the St Kildan and his spouse, however, could not be faulted. Crime was virtually unknown on the island. In a society in which each and every member had to get along with his neighbour in order to survive, crime could not be tolerated. Moreover, there was a distinct lack of motive – each islander was the same in terms of both wealth and status as his fellow St Kildan. 'I held, along with Mr McLellan and the Gaelic teacher,' wrote John MacDonald in 1822, 'a meeting, something like what might pass in St Kilda for a justice of peace court, in order to settle little differences that might exist among the people; and was pleased to find, much to their credit, none of any consequence, except one relating to a marriage.' St Kilda was totally free from the 'bend sinister', the morality of the men being even more unimpeachable than that of the women. There was little drunkenness. When a St Kildan had whisky to drink, it was reserved for medicinal purposes, or put away in a cupboard to celebrate a marriage. Their morals', concluded the Reverend Macaulay in 1758, 'are and must be purer than those of great and opulent societies, however much civilised.'

The islanders were intensively religious. Their fervour was in part induced by their physical situation. A sea-girt isle, rising almost perpendicularly from the sea, with nothing save the often fierce Atlantic in sight, St Kilda presented man with almost insurmountable odds. Under such conditions of geography and climate, Man became even more infinitesimal before the Infinite. The people took for their own a harsh, puritanical religion, which gave them a peace of mind and offered them, if not a future on this earth, at least a pattern which they could follow and a promise of a more certain life in the next world.

As contact with the mainland increased during the nineteenth century, the St Kildan character developed in some respects detrimental to the reputation of the people. 'A St Kildan woman', wrote Kearton in 1886, 'always regards everybody with suspicion, and does not hurry over a purchase, thinking that she is being cheated.' The islanders were a simple, honest people: the tourists were more sophisticated and from a society in which it was the common thing to seek to take advantage. The St Kildans were incapable of adapting to a more complex set of rules of behaviour and became introverted. Nor did they distinguish between tourists and those who came to their island to do genuine good. Doctors found themselves faced with resolution and stubbornness. 'There is no need', wrote Norman Heathcote in 1900 of the St Kildans, 'for them to go through the form of saying that they are conscientious objectors. They simply refuse to allow their children to be operated on, and there is no more to be said.'

To the end, the St Kildans possessed a simplicity that was at once attractive, if infuriating. When Emily MacLeod, the sister of the then proprietor, told the St Kildans in 1877 that she like Queen Victoria was a plain old woman, she was sternly rebuked by the islanders, who informed her that she must not refer to Her Majesty in such a way, as the Bible said that subjects must honour their monarch. When a supply of cement was sent to St Kilda so that a proper aisle could be laid in the Church, the 'bags of dust' as the islanders called them were stacked outside the Church to await a time when the men could see their way to doing the job. The following summer a friend of the proprietor arrived to ask how the work had gone. The 'bags of dust', said the men, had by a miracle all turned into lumps of rock before they had got round to using them.

Whatever their faults, the St Kildans led an unenviable way of life. The provision of food was their major concern year in and year out. They were forced to make good use of everything that their poor island could offer them in the struggle for survival. Moreover, they lived in the knowledge that any part of the provisioning process could be disrupted at any time by weather and illness. Isolated from the rest of humanity, only the laird of Dunvegan was there to protect them from starvation.

4
Bird people

Boys on St Kilda were taught to climb cliffs as soon as they were able. 'The first thing to attract our notice', wrote John Ross the schoolmaster of an August day he spent in a boat at the foot of the cliffs of Conachair, 'was one of the men and his little boy on a rugged but fairly level piece of ground rather down near the sea. One end of the rope was tied round the father's waist while the other was tied round the boy's waist. Most probably, lest he being young, rash and inexperienced, might slip into the sea. There they were all alone then, killing away at a terrible rate, for the boy was collecting while the father kept shaking and twisting.

'The man removing himself from the rope shouldered a burden of dead fulmars and made for a cutting in the rock, too narrow one would think for a dog, and too slippery for a goat. Along this he crawled on hands and knees. A single slip in the middle would have hurled him at least eighty feet sheer down into the sea. But he landed his burden safely and returned for the boy. The rope was tied as before, but only about a yard was left between them this time and that brave little fellow of only ten summers fearlessly followed his father and reached safety without a hitch. This is how the St Kildans train their young to the rocks and what a dangerous life it is.'

The St Kildans learnt how to climb from childhood. Most of them remember playing on the cliffs of Conachair when they were young and thinking nothing of it. They grew up to be short, stocky, agile men, natural climbers. The bone structure of their ankles differed from that of people born elsewhere. The ankle of a St Kildan male was practically half as thick again as that of a mainland person, and the toes were set further apart and almost prehensile.

The slaughter of sea fowl for food was essential to life on St Kilda. What the reindeer is to the Laplander, so the gannets, fulmars and puffins that each year made their nests on the cliffs of the rocky archipelago were to the St Kildans. Due to the poverty of the soil, other forms of subsistence were incapable, on their own, of maintaining human life on Hirta. The islanders had their sheep, a few cattle, and a meagre crop of potatoes, barley and corn, but without the flesh of the sea birds they could never have survived. Totally cut off from the rest of society, they were only able to live on their island by denying themselves the way of life common to crofters in other parts of Scotland and becoming, as Julian Huxley remarked, 'bird people'.

'The air is full of feathered animals,' wrote John Macculloch when he visited St Kilda in 1819. 'The sea is covered with them,' he continued, 'the houses are ornamented by them, the ground is speckled with them like a flowery meadow in May. The town is paved with feathers . . . The inhabitants look as if they had all been tarred and feathered, for their hair is full of feathers and their clothes are covered with feathers . . . Everything smells of feathers.'

The sea birds and their eggs were jealously guarded by the St Kildans. In 1695, a boatload of strangers attempted to steal some eggs from the cliffs. The St Kildans fought off the intruders and put the precious eggs back in their nests. For good measure the islanders confiscated the pirates' trousers before sending them on their way. During the nesting season, the single egg laid by the fulmar was not allowed to be removed for eating. Steps were taken to prevent the sheep and dogs from worrying the birds. Every June, the St Kildans fenced off the cliff tops with ropes made from hay with feathers stuck into them, so vital was it to the community that the eggs be allowed to hatch. When Parliament at Westminster passed an Act for the Preservation of Sea Birds in 1869, acknowledgement was made of the islanders' dependence upon their feathered itinerants. A clause was inserted excluding St Kilda from the provisions of the Act because of 'the necessities of the inhabitants'.

For nearly nine months of the year, the St Kildans were preoccupied with the killing of sea birds. 'From their dependency on the capture of sea fowl for their support,' wrote George Atkinson, 'all their energies of body and mind are centred in that subject and scarcely any of their regulations extend to anything else; from the period of the arrival of the fowl in the month of March, till their departure in November, it is one continued scene of activity and destruction.'

Puffins in their hundreds of thousands were the first birds to return in March after a winter at sea. Most of them made for the island of Dun, and the St Kildans lost little time in seeking out the first fresh meat they had had the opportunity to taste for nearly four months. The adult gannets would begin to come back at the end of January, but it was not until April that the islanders would launch the boats to go to Stac Lee and Stac an Armin to kill the birds. During the month that followed, gannets and puffins continued to provide the people with food, and the fulmars nesting on the ledges of the cliffs of Conachair offered a welcome change of diet. Although the fulmar eggs were never taken from the nest because the female laid only one, those of the gannet and the guillemot were taken in their thousands. The St Kildans ate them fresh, or preserved for consumption at some later date, in the knowledge that the female of those species would replace the stolen egg.

June and July were lean months as far as sea birds were concerned. The puffin was the only bird available for eating while the young gannets and fulmars hatched and grew. The harvesting of fulmars took place in August when the young birds would be killed in their thousands before they could leave the nest. The young brown-feathered gannets, or *gugas* as they were called, matured more slowly, and it would be a month later before the men would take to the boats and rob the stacs of the birds.

When Martin Martin visited St Kilda in 1697, he estimated that 180 islanders consumed 16,000 eggs every week and ate 22,600 sea birds. From Stac Lee alone, he reckoned, the St Kildans took between five and seven thousand gannets annually. A century later an observer calculated that nearly 20,000 gannets were harvested each year on Stac Lee and Stac an Armin. In 1786, over 1,200 *gugas* were taken from their nests in a single expedition.

In the nineteenth century, however, the number of gannets killed declined. No more than 5,000 birds were taken each year in the first half of the century. By 1841, the catch had dropped to an average of 1,400 a year, and after the turn of the century only about 300 young gannets were killed and preserved for winter eating by the St Kildans.

As early as 1758, the islanders claimed that the fulmar had begun to replace the gannet as the staple of their diet. The reasons for the change were probably many. There was a sharp increase at that time in the number of fulmars breeding upon St Kilda, and the feathers and oils of the bird were of great value to the proprietor. Until 1878, St Kilda was the only breeding colony of the fulmar petrel in Great Britain, and the MacLeods may well have wished their tenants to exploit the situation. Centuries of decimation, moreover, may well have laid the great stacs almost bare of gannets. Robbed of its eggs as well as its young, the colony of solan geese had probably decreased.

The ratio of fulmars killed per inhabitant remained fairly steady throughout the island's history. During the years 1829 to 1843 when the population of St Kilda stood at about 100, an average of 12,000 fulmars was slaughtered every year, which divided out meant 118 birds for every inhabitant. In 1901, by which time the population had fallen to 74, the harvest numbered some 9,000 birds, which meant that each islander was consuming some 130 fulmars annually. Even in 1929, the year before the evacuation, the last harvest comprised some 4,000 carcasses, an average of 125 per inhabitant.

The diet of the St Kildans was based on the flesh of these sea birds. Breakfast normally consisted of porridge and milk, with a puffin boiled in with the oats to give flavour. Until the end of the nineteenth century, the people disliked wheaten food and fish, and ate mutton or beef only as a last resort. The main meal of the day, taken at about lunchtime, comprised potatoes and the flesh of fulmars.

Nearly all food on Hirta had to be boiled or stewed. There were no ovens on the island, save the range that was the proud possession of the minister in the manse. To the outsider, food tasted rather bland, and a lack of proper fuel meant that it was usually under-cooked and never served very hot. 'When boiling the fulmar,' wrote John Ross, 'they sometimes pour some oatmeal over the juice and take that as porridge, which they consider very good and wholesome food which I have no doubt it is to a stomach that can manage to digest it.'

The flesh of the fulmar is white. In the older birds, it is a mixture of fat and meat, while the young birds are nearly all fat. When cooked, the fulmar tasted somewhat like beef, and Heath-cote, having eaten a meal with the St Kildans, remarked, 'I must say that we were agreeably surprised. We had expected something nasty, but it was not nasty. It was oleaginous, but distinctly tasty.

If the fulmar was tasty, it was also tough – good for the St Kildans' teeth and gums. Ross noted that at the time of the fulmar season, the whiteness and strength of the inhabitants' teeth improved. Dental care was never to be a problem worthy of note on Hirta, in spite of the fact that toothbrushes were non-existent.

Eating the flesh of fulmars, puffins, and gannets seems to have preserved the islanders' teeth.

In the summer months, the puffins were the main source of food. Mrs Munro, the wife of the last missionary, remembers how they tasted when she tried to cook them. 'The first lot of puffins (of the season) were brought by the postmaster. They were all dressed, ready for cooking. I asked Nurse Barclay how to cook them and she said put them in the oven and roast them. My husband was in school and came home to dinner and he said, "Try them". I said, "No thanks, I've had enough – I've roasted them." I went to empty the tin and each time I emptied it nothing but oil would come out till you got fed up with seeing it.'

'The gannets we ate', recalls Neil Ferguson, 'tasted fishy and salty.' Like the fulmar, the gannet was normally salted down for eating in winter. Ferguson recalls: 'You had to steep them in water for twenty-four hours to take the salt out of them, and then boil them with tatties for your dinner.' The *guga*, in fact, was not a food peculiar to St Kilda: the birds were regarded by some on the mainland as delicacies and were regularly served by ships' cooks on the steamers that plied the Western Isles.

The islanders also ate large quantities of eggs, which, one visitor remarked, 'they just eat as the peasantry eat potatoes'. Gathered in the spring months, the eggs were boiled and eaten immediately, or else preserved in barrels. The St Kildans were never too fussy about the freshness of the eggs, often keeping them for six to eight weeks before eating them because, they said, time added to their flavour.

The most important possessions on Hirta, used and maintained by the community as a whole, were the boats. Without them, the St Kildans could hardly have existed. They depended upon being able to make the frequently hazardous journey to Boreray and the great stacs to trap the thousands of sea birds that were their livelihood.

At the end of the seventeenth century, the community owned one boat only, sixteen cubits long. It was divided into sections, proportional to the number of families on the island at the time, and every householder was responsible for providing a piece of turf large enough to cover his section of the boat in summer to prevent the hot sun from warping and rotting the precious wooden shell. In winter, the boat was dragged up high above the water line and filled with rocks so that it would not be swept away in a storm or dashed against the rocks.

By 1831, the St Kildans were having to make do with an awkward ship's boat, weighing almost three tons. Although the boat had three oars either side, the St Kildans made a square mainsail out of their own cloth. Because each family had been responsible for making its share of the sail, the final product was made up of twenty-one patches of various sizes and shades, 'like what you would have fancied Joseph's coat to have been', wrote George Atkinson. The islanders had given their boat a nickname – *Iair-Dhonn* (Brown Mare).

Ten years later, there was still one boat on Hirta, although the advantages to the community of possessing a second were being talked about by philanthropists on the mainland. In 1861, at a cost of £60, the St Kildans were presented with a fine, new, fully equipped boat. The *Dargavel*, as she was called, was tragically lost at sea with all hands two years later.

By May 1877 there were four boats on Hirta. Two were given to the people by a wealthy visitor and the others, although almost new, were not thought by the St Kildans to be strong enough to withstand rough usage.

Never in their history did the St Kildans build a boat of their own. Although each household possessed a hammer, and one islander, it is said, had a complete set of carpenter's tools, there was no indigenous supply of wood on Hirta. It was just as easy therefore to transport a finished boat from the mainland as it was to bring over the materials from which one could be built. The men did their best to repair the boats they had, although many from the mainland thought they did so in a less than enthusiastic way.

Like their cousins in the Hebrides, the St Kildans regarded the sea as a spirit to be wooed rather than a challenge. Although not thought to be particularly good sailors, they did at least respect the Atlantic Ocean surrounding them. 'The St Kildans', commented Wigglesworth in 1902, 'are as expert in the art of managing their boats as they are in climbing the cliffs. I do not mean to say that they are specially expert sailors, but the skilful manner in which they bring their boats up to the rocks and land and re-embark in the face of a heavy swell, where few sailors would even care to risk their boats, is remarkable.'

Every year, the men of Hirta would make the dangerous trip to Stac Lee. It was agreed by the morning meeting that time and tide were right to risk a boat on the four mile crossing. While the little rowing boat rose and fell with the swell of the ocean, the man in the bows would throw a rope towards the giant stac. 'In the olden days,' remembers Lachlan Macdonald, 'there was a bolt put into the rock there. You'd be lucky sometimes when you were in the boat if you would see it.' Once the rope was secured on the steel bolt, those who were to land scrambled from the boat on to the rock. 'Everyone', says Lachlan, 'had to take an empty box. You'd carry it up to the top of Stac Lee and when you reached the top you would fill it up with gannets' eggs.' Several men would have to stay in the boat. There was no safe mooring by the rock, so they would try to seek as sheltered water as there was available and wait.

When all the St Kildans had filled their boxes, the most dangerous part of the exercise began. Carrying the boxes of eggs on their backs they would make the treacherous descent, 'which was a worse job than going up', recalls Lachlan. 'There would be anything in the box from half a hundredweight to a hundredweight. And you hadn't got to break them; you had to take them down whole. Maybe sometimes there would be an odd one broken, but there weren't many.' The boat, laden down with men and eggs, then returned to the safety of Village Bay. The women, by tradition, were always waiting at the landing-place to greet their exhausted men.

In the early days, eggs were rarely taken from Stac Lee. Most were removed from the nests of Boreray and Stac an Armin. The St Kildans reasoned that by leaving the eggs on Stac Lee, by autumn the young gannets would be more advanced there. A double crop of sea birds was thus assured. Should bad weather, moreover, prevent a crossing to Stac Lee at the appropriate time of year, there were always the birds on Boreray. At the time of the evacuation, Stac Lee was climbed for eggs and nothing else. By then it was too dangerous, given the number of men available, to risk a crossing.

The St Kildans took the eggs of some fourteen species of birds that bred on their archipelago. Some, like those of the gannet and the guillemot, were for eating, others were blown and sold to tourists in the summer months or sent to egg collectors on the mainland. The eggs of the starling, oyster catcher, tree sparrow, fork-tailed petrel, grey crow, raven, and eider duck were frequently asked for, but the greatest prize was the egg of the St Kilda wren – a species of wren slightly larger than the mainland varieties, that was found only on Hirta. After all the eggs were harvested, they were laid out in boxes on the grass and divided out among the islanders. Most homes owned a glass blowpipe brought over from Scotland which was used to remove the contents of the eggs.

Puffins, the major source of fresh food throughout the summer months, arrived in March and remained on Soay and Dun until the end of August. The birds made their nests in the turf. The female laid her single egg at the end of a burrow, usually three or four feet long, dug by both birds. Until recently, it was estimated that the puffin population of St Kilda was over a million; but in the past two years the number has more than halved, and there is some mystery as to what has happened to the birds that never returned. It is thought that oil pollution out at sea has claimed them.

The islanders trained their dogs to drive the birds from their burrows. Once they were forced into the open, the puffins were trapped by an ingenious method. The St Kildans laid a length of rope to which were attached anything up to forty little nooses made of horsehair upon a rock or patch of turf that the puffins frequented. The bird would catch its ungainly legs in the noose. The capture of a few would attract the inquisitive attention of others who, by investigating, got caught themselves. It was estimated that using a puffin gin (as it was called) on the slopes and rocks of Dun, an islander could kill fifty puffins a day.

The puffins were plucked and their carcasses split down the middle. They were hung up on strings outside the house to dry and were then ready for the cooking pot. Apart from eating the flesh themselves, the islanders gave it to their dogs and cattle. In the first half of the nineteenth century, between 20,000 and 25,000 puffins were killed every year. By 1876, more puffins were taken in the summer months than all the other birds put together – upwards of 89,000 birds were slaughtered. In later years when the population was smaller, the St Kildans were still catching 10,000 annually.

There was a time when the women and young girls went to Boreray to catch puffins, while the men saw to the sheep on the island. Before the snaring began, a curious rite was performed. A puffin was caught and plucked of all its feathers, save those on its wings and tail. It was then set free and, according to the St Kildans, immediately attracted other puffins around it. Mass slaughter would then begin.

On occasions, the frightened birds were dragged from their burrows by the dogs. 'While the sagacious animals pawed at one hole,' wrote Sands who witnessed the harvest in 1877, 'they (the women) kept a watchful eye on the burrows adjacent as if they expected the puffins to issue from them. Some of the girls at the same time were plunging their hands deep into the holes and dragging out the birds, and twisting their necks with a dexterity which only long practice could give.'

Guillemots were also killed in the spring and summer months. Their flesh was eaten by the islanders and their feathers kept to be exported later in the year. Stac Biorach was their main breeding ground. The stac was nicknamed the 'Thumb Stac' because on the needle of rock the only firm hold available was of the size of a thumb.

Apart from the brief three months September to November, the fulmar petrel could be found on Hirta all the year round. The St Kildans ate some adult birds in the early part of the year, but their main concern was to harvest the thousands of young fulmars in mid-August.

Similar in size to the common gull, the female fulmar lays a single white egg towards the end of May. Both parents take it in turn to incubate the egg. After some forty to fifty days the young bird is hatched, and after seven weeks or so is big enough and strong enough to leave the nest. The St Kildans surveyed the cliffs daily from the beginning of August to be sure that they would commence their slaughter before the birds had flown.

The fulmar harvest was the busiest, most exciting and most important incident in the St Kildan year. 'They catch the birds for the sake of their meat, oil and feathers,' wrote Norman Heathcote in 1900, 'and the act of catching them is their only sport. It is this that makes them love their island home. If it were not that they can rival one another on the rocks, they would be less unwilling to seek adventures in the outer world.'

In the weeks prior to the harvest, many preparations had to be made. The women brought the cattle back to Village Bay from their summer grazing in Glean Mor and made sure that they had ground enough corn to feed the family during the harvest period. The men meanwhile got out the old barrels that would be used to store the prepared birds for winter. The salt, used to preserve the birds and normally delivered to the island by the factor in June, was fetched from the storehouse and distributed to each householder. The stomachs of adult gannets caught earlier in the year would be inflated and dried out. They would be used during the slaughter to contain the precious amber oil of the petrels.

The talk at the daily meeting would be of fulmars. The men would discuss and decide what parts of the cliffs should be cleared first. Normally the harvest began where it was agreed the young fulmars were most advanced, for fear that the islanders might lose them forever. The weather was also an important consideration. Some areas of the cliff were notoriously more dangerous in damp or wet conditions than others.

The most important task was to test the ropes. A length of rope taken from the loft of each home was tested by the men in full view of the rest of the community lest it had rotted during the months of storage. The rope was agreed to be safe if it could stand the strain of being pulled by four men against the weight of a large boulder.

On 12 August the harvest began. Everyone on the island took to the cliff tops. The men had ropes slung across their chests and the women carried the empty stomachs of the solan geese. The children accompanied their parents to watch and learn and help the women carry the day's catch back to the village. Many women were capable of carrying as much as two hundred pounds of dead birds on their shoulders at a time.

In the early days, particularly when St Kildans went off singly to kill birds, an iron stake was hammered into the clifftop to secure one end of the rope while the fowler descended the face. By the nineteenth century such a practice had been done away with. Instead, an islander would fasten the rope round his chest, low enough to allow the maximum freedom of movement. His colleague would hold on to the other end of the rope while a descent was made. The men worked in their bare feet to ensure a firmer grip on the grassy cliffs that plunged a thousand feet into the sea. When the fowler had gained support for his feet, he would shout up to his friend, '*Leigas!*' ('Let go!'), at which command the man at the top would slacken the rope. Below, the slaughter could then begin.

On the cliffs of Conachair the fulmars were normally so dense that the fowler had to kill them in order to clear a way for himself along the ledge. Each young fulmar could weigh up to two or three pounds. The man who did the killing wore a belt, and as the birds were strangled, he slipped the head through the gap between the belt and his body. When he had killed twenty or so birds, or had cleared a particular part of the cliff and wished to move on, the bundle of birds was tied to the end of a second rope and pulled up by one of his companions at the top. 'And then maybe you go to another place', recalls Lachlan Macdonald, 'and do the same and then you maybe take thirty or forty of them on your back home. It's pretty heavy sometimes. Hard work in a way.' As little time as possible was spent in the actual killing of birds, and with the call of '*Tarning nard*' ('Pull up'), the fowler would be pulled up to the top of the cliff and safety.

Occasionally the thirty-fathom ropes that the St Kildans used would not be long enough to reach the lower parts of the cliffs. In such instances, three men would work together. The first would stay at the top, as before, and the other two would be lowered down one at a time. The second man, having found a secure platform, would then lower the third down to a position from which he could continue the slaughter.

The St Kildans always adopted the easiest method of killing the birds. In many parts of the cliffs, ropes were not needed at all as the nests were readily accessible. In other parts, rather than haul the birds up to the cliff top, the islanders tossed them into the sea, where a waiting boat would pick them up.

The most dangerous operation of all, however, was the ascent of the cliffs from the sea. An island boat would be taken round to the foot of Conachair and two cragsmen would climb by turns in true alpine fashion. In such cases an end of the rope was attached to both fowlers so that in the event of the foremost losing his footing, his companion would be able to break his fall.

The fulmar is capable of spitting the vile-smelling oil contained in its stomach some two or three feet. To the St Kildans, the oil was valuable. 'As you were going down the rock on the rope,' remembers Lachlan Macdonald, 'you try and hide yourself as much as you can. The young fulmars were just about the stage to fly, right enough, but if you don't get them quickly they'll make an awful mess of you. They'd spew that oil out on you.' The fowlers had also to be wary of being startled by such an action lest they be thrown off balance and fall off the face of the cliff. In order to retain the oil in the bird's stomach, the St Kildans gave the neck a twist.

Sometimes the fulmars nested in places out of reach of a fowler on the end of a rope. To capture them, the St Kildans used a fowling rod, which they made themselves. This was a bamboo pole about fifteen feet long, to one end of which was attached a thin strip of cane. A running noose, made of plaited horsehair or wire and stiffened with a gannet's quill to maintain a bow, was attached to the cane. With a fowling rod the St Kildans could easily lasso the unsuspecting, inaccessible bird.

The killing lasted a fortnight. Every evening the fulmars were laid in a heap by the shore in front of the village and divided out carefully and equally amongst the islanders. Although the cliffs themselves were divided out before the harvest began, the St Kildans also shared the final catch. 'You see, supposing you had a share in the cliffs,' says Lachlan Macdonald, 'you might have a lot more than the other fellow, so it was fairer to share them all when they came home so that there wouldn't be any difference.'

'They all put them in one place,' recalls Neil Ferguson, 'and they shared them out – so much for each house – and when they took them home they started plucking them and cleaning them. The old men salted them and the young boys cut their feet and head off and the women took the guts out, and that was the way of it. Next morning you went for another load. That went on until you had two big barrels of fulmars salted. They didn't get much sleep at all. They would be working till maybe two or three in the morning and away again at eight o'clock for some more.' Every islander was given an equal share of the harvest, whether or not he or she had taken part in the work. The only exceptions to the rule of absolute equality were those fulmars killed while out of the nest, which the fowler was allowed to keep for himself. The reason why was explained to John Ross by an islander. 'Should they be left out there all night,' he said, 'the ravens, hawks or crows would have eaten them up and they would do good to no one.'

The St Kildans had a use for every part of the fulmar. The feathers, a valuable source of income, were graded according to colour and put into sacks. The fulmar oil, of which every bird normally yielded anything up to half a pint, was poured out of the gannet stomachs into canisters to be bartered when the factor came. Those birds that were to be preserved for eating in winter were split lengthways down the back and filled with salt. They were then packed like herring in barrels. The entrails of the birds were often used as fishing bait, while the bones were condemned to the midden at the back of the house to become a good, rich fertilizer by the following spring. A large number of birds, of course, would be eaten fresh. The carcasses were boiled and the fat that came out of them, once cooled, could be skimmed off and used in the islanders' lamps. 'All this time there is nothing but birds, fat and feathers everywhere,' remarked the Reverend Neil Mackenzie of the village at the time of the harvest. 'Their clothes are literally soaked in oil, and everywhere inside and outside their houses, nothing but feathers; often it looks as if it were snowing.'

Traditionally, the St Kildans did not use salt to preserve the flesh of the sea birds. Salt was frequently scarce and to a poor people often expensive. The strong winds that are rarely absent from Hirta were used instead to stop the carcasses from going bad during the winter months. To be preserved by the wind, however, the birds had to be kept dry and the islanders built hundreds of little stone storehouses called *cleits* that allowed the wind to pass over the food, but not take with it any moisture.

Cleits are unique to St Kilda. Without them life would not have been possible on such a damp and wet island. They were constructed entirely out of stone and turf. The granophyre slabs that litter the eastern part of the island were admirably suited to the building of corbelled, dry-stone walls. Large, flat slabs covered with turf provided the structure with a roof. For strength as well as dryness, the little doorway was normally set in the end of the cleit facing the hillside. The cleits were usually about eight to twelve feet in diameter and four or five feet high. Those built by the St Kildans inside the wall surrounding the village were used mainly to store the carcasses of sea birds and were round in shape.

The greatest concentration of cleits lies in the Village Bay area, but the islanders built hundreds more on Hirta, some on the slopes of Conachair, others on Oiseval. Beyond the wall, cleits were used to store practically everything that had to be kept dry, like ropes, feathers and even clothing. High on the hill-slopes they were used almost exclusively to dry and store the lumps of turf for the fires of Village Bay.

At the end of the fulmar harvest, the St Kildans would take two or three days' rest. Exhausted by their labours, they could relax for a while in the knowledge that safely stored away were some of the food supplies that would keep them alive in winter. But another harvest still remained to be reaped, that of the young gannet, or *guga*.

St Kilda, then as now, could claim to be the largest gannetry in the world. A count of the colony taken in 1960 revealed that some 40,000 pairs breed on Boreray, Stac Lee, and Stac an Armin. Until the nineteenth century the gannet was the buttress of the community's economy : the oils and feathers of the bird helped pay the rent and provide the people with essential supplies from the mainland.

The gannet builds its nest on ledges of rock. The female lays one egg which is incubated by both sexes for anything up to forty-five days. When the chick hatches it is black and naked but soon develops a white down. By September, the down is replaced by brown feathers. It was then that the St Kildans would prepare for the most spectacular and dangerous task of their year, the hunting of the gannet.

The gugas had to be killed at night, when the birds would be on their nests. Usually a dozen men were involved in the trip – seven would land on Boreray and the other five would stay in the boat and row and drift round the island all night. 'This island', wrote George Atkinson, 'is more universally precipitous than St Kilda, and to a timid or awkward person would be really difficult to land on.' Before a landing was attempted each man would remove his boots and don a pair of heavy woollen socks.

'The St Kildans', continued Atkinson, who went with a party of islanders to Boreray in the summer of 1831, 'are very dexterous in landing or embarking on, or from, a rocky shore, where the long, heavy swell of the Atlantic keeps the boat rising and falling by the side of the cliff, a height of fourteen or fifteen feet, even when the sea appears quite calm. The boat is placed with her broadside to the rock and kept from striking by a man in the head and stern, each with a long pole for the purpose. One of their barefooted climbers stands ready in the middle with a coil of rope on his arms, and seizing an opportunity springs on the rock and establishes himself firmly on some rough projection. He then hauls on the rope, the other end of which, I should have observed, is held by some in the boat, or attached to it, and giving way when the boat falls, tightens the rope at its rising. Another companion joins him and standing three or four feet from him employs another rope in a similar manner, so that together they form a firm and safe gangway or railing, for an inexpert person to spring to land by.

'When this is attained, however, a most arduous ascent of the precipice is to be accomplished, which is here of the height of six hundred or seven hundred feet, and quite difficult enough for the most indifferent climbers, though unembarrassed by any load, and we were told the women often ascend and descend this with a sheep or a couple of lambs in their arms.'

The colony of gannets on Boreray would be asleep on their nests, but one bird would remain awake and would give the alarm as soon as his suspicions were aroused. The 'sentry' bird always had to be killed first, then the fowlers could slaughter the un-suspecting birds at will with the aid of a small club. 'After working for an hour or two,' wrote George Murray in 1886, 'we rested and three of us sat down on the bare rocks with the ropes about our middles, the cloudless sky our canopy, the moon our lamp, and had family worship. The scene to me was very impressive. The the ocean still and quiet far below, and offered praise and prayer to Him who was able to preserve us in such dangerous work.' Before catching a few hours' rest, some of the night's catch would be gutted and stored in the cleits built on Boreray, to be eaten on further expeditions to the island. At daybreak, hundreds of gannets would be loaded into the boat and the crew would return to Hirta. At the landing-place the women, relieved at the sight of their returning men, would carry the catch after it had been divided out to their cottages.

A large bird with a five-foot wingspan, the gannet could be ferocious when disturbed on its nest. Although the birds would not intentionally attack the fowlers, they could and did hit them a hard blow with their powerful wings and sharp beaks as they attempted to flee. On the great stacs, Stac Lee and Stac an Armin, there was always the danger, in the dark particularly, of losing footing and falling off. 'They used to go at night time', recalls Neil Ferguson, 'and climb the rock [Stac Lee] at night when the gannets were roosting. But there was always one on watch and that's the one they made for first in the dark and broke its neck. They then killed all the rest one after the other and left them lying there till daybreak and then threw them out to the sea for the boat to pick up.' On Stac Lee, the St Kildans stood on a promontory, called the Casting Point, to throw the gannets to the men in the boat below. The point overhangs the base of the rock, so there was little danger of the night's kill being blown and crushed against the rocks.

A landing on Stac Lee was always dangerous. 'As we approached the stacs,' wrote Lady Mackenzie in 1853, 'the gannets came to meet us in their thousands, and one could hardly see the sky through them. There is no possible landing place on the stacs where a boat can be drawn up, as they rise sheer out of the ocean.

At one place for which we steered, there had been an iron pin three feet long let into the rock perhaps ten feet above high-water mark, and from the boat a rope with a loop at the end of it was thrown over this pin and the boat drawn in near enough for some of the best of the St Kildan climbers to spring on to a small ledge. Then they ascended very carefully and very slowly with their rods, with the nooses at the end, and soon they had caught and killed a large number of the solans.' As with the fulmar, the St Kildans would use fowling rods to trap the less accessible gannets.

When the gannets had been killed, the ropes and rods could be put away for another year. The St Kildans could face another winter confidently. Supplies of food were assured and the feathers and oils extracted from the fulmar and gannet would pay the rent.

The feathers of both birds fetched a fair price on the mainland. Throughout much of the nineteenth century, the factor sold most of the fulmar feathers to the British government. Once fumigated, they were impervious to lice and bed-bugs, and as such were much favoured by the army. The amber oil of the fulmar was said to have many of the properties of cod liver oil. Rich in vitamins A and D it was sold on the mainland as a medicine. The St Kildans claimed it helped soothe rheumatic pains and in London and Edinburgh it was sold in bottles to the public as the perfect remedy for toothache. 'Can the world exhibit a more valuable commodity?' remarked a St Kildan in the eighteenth century. 'The fulmar furnishes oil for the lamp, down for the bed, the most salubrious food, the most efficacious ointments for healing wounds, besides a thousand other virtues of which he is possessed, which I have no time to enumerate. But to say all, in one word, deprive us of the fulmar and St Kilda is no more.'

From time immemorial people could only live on Hirta at the expense of the fulmar and the gannet. Year after year the sea birds managed to survive the massive onslaught made by the St Kildans upon their number. Despite the decimation, the colonies were never to desert the stacs and cliffs of the archipelago. St Kilda was first to be deprived of men.

5
Life on the croft

To all outward appearances, life on Hirta changed little over the years. 'If other countries are furnished with a variety of luxuries,' concluded the Reverend Kenneth Macaulay in 1756, 'St Kilda possesses in a remarkable degree the necessaries of life.' Sixty years later, MacCulloch wrote in a similar vein: 'The men are well-looking and better dressed than many of their neighbours of the Long Island; bearing indeed the obvious marks of ease of circumstance both in apparel and diet.' Even by the end of the nineteenth century, when times became harder for the St Kildans, John Ross wrote, 'On the whole the people live well, all that is wanted is a greater variety and more vegetable food. A Skyeman who had been often on the island for various lengths of time gave me his opinion in these terms. "They are the best fed people in Creation. I speak the truth, master".'

The St Kildans were cragsmen first, crofters second. The remarkably high standard of living they enjoyed was based primarily upon the sea birds which provided so many of the islanders' wants and supplied the proprietor with a profit that enabled him to be generous to his remote tenants. The scant land available to them on Hirta was never a source of wealth. The St Kildans worked hard to grow essential crops and probably put more hours into their crofts than they spent fowling, but the yield was slight.

Despite native prosperity the village on Hirta in the seventeenth century must have appeared very mean and small to the outsider. One hundred and eighty islanders, according to Martin Martin, lived in twenty-five black houses. The homes were of dry-stone construction, roofed with turf and hay and lay above the line of the later nineteenth-century village, to the west of Village Bay. The chief attraction of the site was that the homes received the most hours of sunlight and that the land was relatively dry and well drained. It was the most sheltered area available: the hills that surrounded the scattered houses broke the main force of northerly and westerly gales, and the southern shoulder of Oiseval deflected winds from the east.

Inside the houses, all was black with soot and the air hung heavy with the perfume of rough peat. There were no windows and no chimney: the fire smouldered in the middle of the floor and the smoke escaped by way of the door. The furniture of every home was sparse – the islanders lived most of their lives eating and sleeping on the floor. Each family owned a set of quernstones to grind meal, a hollow stone called a *clach shoule* which acted as a lamp, and a *cragan* which was a vessel of rudely baked clay that served as a cooking pot. The only form of lighting available was the *clach shoule*; the hollow in the stone was filled with fulmar oil and a cinder of peat acted as a wick. Each house also had a pitcher for water that was readily available from the numerous wells on Hirta, and a dish or two to drink from.

Life in the black house, however, had much to commend it. The sound of the ever-present wind on Hirta was greatly reduced by the thickness of the walls. The structure was warm and draught-proof and there was little chance of condensation forming. The black house, in fact, was a healthy home for people who were primarily outdoor folk.

In winter, living conditions were apparently less beneficial. The St Kildans, like their neighbours on the Hebrides, shared their humble dwellings with their cattle, so that the beasts would not perish from cold. Although unhygienic, the custom had its advantages. The presence of the cattle added warmth and the dung that was allowed to amass and dry on the floor was of inestimable value.

The Reverend Neil Mackenzie, who went to St Kilda in 1829, was distressed by the unhygienic conditions. He was influenced by the trend elsewhere in the Highlands and islands to improve the conditions in which people were living in the name of sanitation. A new village was planned. With financial incentive provided by a philanthropic Englishman, Sir Thomas Acland, who paid a short visit to the island, the St Kildans began to construct their new homes. Wood and glass – two alien materials – were incorporated in their design and were duly supplied by the proprietor. Between the years 1836 and 1838, twenty-five houses, barns, and out-buildings were constructed in a crescent one hundred yards above the shore at the head of Village Bay.

The new black houses, a great improvement upon those they replaced, were described in 1853 by Lady Mackenzie of Gairloch when, together with her young son Osgood, she paid a visit to

Hirta. She was 'surprised at the cleanly appearance of the walls and roofs of the houses, and the nice dry walk which went all along the sides of the houses. The walls of the houses are built just as they are in Harris – that is double, being very thick and the middle filled with earth. The roof extends only to the inner wall, and you can walk round the top of the wall quite easily. The form of the roof is oval, like a big bee-hive. They are made of wood covered with turf and then thatched with straw above, and on the outside are straw ropes like a network put across to keep the wind from blowing away the thatch. The houses have generally a sort of window with a tiny bit of glass, and they have a plan of their own for locking their doors with a wooden key made by themselves. It appears to keep matters quite secure. Osgood observed that the beaks of the solan geese were used as pegs to keep down the straw on the buildings.'

The cattle, however, still occupied one end of the house. 'The byre is on the left hand side as you enter,' wrote Lady Mackenzie, 'and above it is the only aperture for letting out smoke, which in fact they wish to keep in as much as possible for the sake of the soot, which they use to enrich the land for barley and the potatoes in the spring. I was told that they never clean out their byres at all till they take away the manure in April, and previous to that time it is almost impossible to get in and out of the door.' The fireplace still remained in the middle of the room and once a year the interior floor was dug up and the roof was stripped and the straw, impregnated with soot, spread on the ground. Every October, in preparation for winter, fresh thatch was laid on the roof.

In the 1850s, the Reverend Dr MacLachlan decided the time had come to present the St Kildans with a quantity of crockery. He was particularly concerned with the lack of sanitation on the island. There were no lavatories at all on Hirta and human functions were performed upon the ground. The kindly reverend saw fit to donate a chamber pot to each household. The islanders, however, had no idea what they were for and used them to eat porridge.

In each house was a box bed, a standard feature of rural life in Scotland and, like so many things, the product of common sense. In Hirta it was called a *crub*. A boot-shaped sleeping cell, the *crub* was sensible in a place where wood was scarce, as the alcove could be built into the house when originally constructed.

In the early 1860s, new cottages were constructed by the then proprietor, John Macpherson MacLeod. A row of sixteen modern cottages, measuring thirty-three feet by fifteen feet, was built under the supervision of John Ross, master mason of the MacLeod estate. 'The walls', wrote McDiarmid, 'are well built, with hewn stones in the corners and about seven or eight feet high.' There were chimneys built into each gable and every home could boast two hearths. Every house had two windows, one for each room, facing out into the bay. Each window was fitted with nine panes of glass and the door, fitted with good latches, was placed between the windows. The stone and mortar cottages were built fifteen to twenty yards apart, gable end to gable end, and formed a long street.

The street was the only one to be found in the Western Isles. It was even given a name, 'Main Street, St Kilda', and each house was given a number, Number One being the dwelling nearest to the manse. A stone-slab causeway was laid along the entire length of the street so that when it rained there was no risk of mud being carried inside the house.

The interior of each home was divided into two or three rooms by wooden partitions. Two rooms were fair-sized and the third consisted of a closet opposite the front door in which were built wooden box beds. When first built, all the houses had mud floors: it was not until the end of the century that cement was laid in each living room and a wooden floor put in the main bedroom. The walls were lined with matchboarding to serve as protection against damp, and the roofs were made of zinc sheeting. Heavy gales, however, soon swept the zinc away and the proprietor had to reroof the houses with felt, securely fastened to the masonry with wires and iron staples and then painted with pitch.

The home of each family was the same inside as outside, and furniture was functional if scant. Although there were places cut in the walls for fireplaces, no home had a grate. Each house had a large, rough wooden bed, a few boxes in which to keep valuables, and a barrel or two for sea birds. Each family owned a couple of small chairs which were sent from Edinburgh, and a dresser containing a few bits of crockery. The only article of native manufacture was the occasional chair made from straw. A table of sorts could be found in every home, although in most cases, as the schoolmaster wrote in 1890, 'painted with mother earth'.

The hours spent sleeping in a St Kildan house were not the most comfortable. Strangely enough in a land of feathers, mattresses were stuffed with straw, and the St Kildans used the few articles of clothing that they discarded at bedtime as a pillow. 'They lie down year after year', wrote Ross, 'on a hard bed of straw, placing part of their clothing under their heads for pillows. The other part they keep on, having for most part nothing between them and the straw and their only covering being a rough blanket. In this they appear to be quite comfortable notwithstanding that in many instances a number of all ages and sexes are huddled together in one place.' In a community in which families frequently numbered eight persons or more, the two-roomed cottage provided little space. During the winter months, particularly, when the family was confined to indoors for much of the day, the St Kildans must have become adept at cramped living.

The old homes of the St Kildans were not demolished. Instead they became byres and storehouses. In the Gaelic spoken on Hirta, in fact, no word existed for 'byre', which was always referred to as 'the outside house'.

From the middle of the nineteenth century, therefore, the St Kildans were housed in the most advanced dwellings to be found anywhere in the Hebrides. The generosity of the proprietor in building them was surely an example of the economic value he placed upon the most remote part of his estate.

But the new homes had their disadvantages. There was, of course, no lavatory or running water installed, and the relative thinness of the walls made for a constant high-pitched whine whenever the wind blew. The situation of the homes, with the hills behind, meant that frequently the smoke did not manage to escape from the chimneys. By 1875, John Sands remarked that the interior of the houses was blackened with peat smoke. The walls, he claimed, had never been whitewashed since the houses were built. A few islanders rejected their new homes. Rachel McCrimmon, for instance, preferred to spend the rest of her days in her old black house. Few of the St Kildans changed their accustomed way of living when they moved into their new houses.

The standard of hygiene improved little. Even as late as 1875, the minister was the only person on the island who used a fork for eating. The ash and refuse heaps were kept almost at the front door. 'It would not take long', wrote Ross, 'to scrub up everything they possess, but they never think of such a thing.' Plates, if used at all at meal times, were cleaned by the women wiping them over with a corner of their blue skirts. Knives and forks when used were cleaned by putting them in the mouth. Most visitors during the nineteenth century remarked upon the dirty appearance both of the St Kildans and their homes.

Emily MacLeod, a sister of the proprietor, did much at the turn of the century to improve the standards of cleanliness. The attempts to stamp out disease also did much to instil into the women the need to keep a tidier home. The last nurse to serve on St Kilda, Nurse Barclay, recalls that their homes were spotless, and that the people washed themselves and their clothes regularly once a week. 'The floors of their houses were well scrubbed,' she says. 'You could go in and sit on their chairs, in some of the houses on the mainland I couldn't. I had to put my *Glasgow Herald* down first. I always carried a *Herald* in the front of my bag when I was on the mainland and I had to put it down on the chair before I could sit on it.'

Clothing on Hirta was warm and practical. The St Kildans by design as much as by tradition never wore kilts. Instead they preferred to follow the example of fisherfolk on the west coast of Scotland. The trousers, shirts and woollen garments were worn loose to enable greater freedom of action and were hard-wearing. 'It is remarkable', wrote Sands, 'that in all their work there is no attempt at ornament in which they differ strikingly from the Highlander, who when he was at liberty to please his own fancy, decorated his person from top to toe and who . . . abhors everything that is plain and unadorned.'

The St Kildans made most of the clothes they needed. The men not only made their own trousers and shirts, but tailored the dresses of their wives and daughters. Accessories, such as bonnets, caps, scarves, and cravats, were imported from the mainland. There is a story told that on one occasion a certain type of shoelace found its way to the lonely isle of St Kilda barely a year after it had made its first appearance in London.

The men all wore homespun woollen shirts, sewn together with worsted yarn, and blue tartan checked trousers which were dyed with imported indigo. In winter, they were muffled to the ears with big coarse cravats, twisted round their necks roll upon roll.

The women made a much more picturesque group. They wore short petticoats and long dresses, which they hitched up to knee level when work had to be done. For head-dresses they were fond of bright, turkey-red napkins. The wives kept their gowns together with two strings around their bodies, one under the arms and the other nine inches below. Every woman owned a plaid shawl, which was fastened with a brooch or a pin of native manufacture. The brooch was beaten out of an old copper coin and the pin was made from copper nails taken from wrecks that chanced to come ashore. 'The women', wrote Macaulay in 1756, 'are most handsome; their complexions fresh and lively as their features are regular and fine. Some of them, if properly dressed and genteely educated, would be reckoned extraordinary beauties in the gay world.' The strain of hard work, however, was soon etched in their faces.

Wedding rings were never worn on Hirta. Married women, therefore, distinguished themselves from unmarried ones by a white frill which was worn in front of the headshawl or kerchief.

During most of the year, the islanders wore neither stockings nor shoes. When Martin Martin visited St Kilda in 1697, the 'turned shoe' was still being worn, made out of the neck of a gannet and employing the natural bend in the neck for the heel. Such footwear had to be kept in water when not worn, and even then lasted only a few days. By the nineteenth century, however, every woman had a pair of brogues, rudely fashioned from raw sheepskin thongs by the men.

During the summer men, women, and children worked in the minimum of clothing. The weather could become unbearably warm and the island offered little shelter from the sun. 'The women are often to be seen', wrote Sands, 'on the cliffs and in the glen without any clothing but a woollen shirt, whilst the men also strip to their underclothing when engaged on the cliffs.'

In later years, the standard of dress on the island improved immensely. 'When I first went out in 1903,' wrote Thomas Nicol, 'the men were dressed on weekdays in rough homespun trousers, very baggy and just a shade neater than those adopted by a famous English University, a sleeved waistcoat, and a thick red muffler twisted as a rule twice round the throat.' In a little less than twenty years, with the help of a mail order catalogue, the St Kildans looked little different from the people who came to visit them. 'In many respects the people have become wonderfully modern,' continued Nicol, 'and this is particularly noticeable in their Sunday dress. The young men now appear in well-cut dark tweed suits with collar and tie. Some of the women even wear hats.' But the St Kildans were never to concern themselves overmuch with appearances, and little distinction as to dress existed on the island.

Heating and lighting were obvious necessities of life. In the old black houses, lighting was traditionally supplied by a *cruse*, an oil-bearing container, first made of stone and later of metal, in which a wick floated. A turf impaled on a stick was used as a torch by the islanders when they were outside at night. The St Kildans used paraffin, in later years, given to them by the factor in exchange for tweed and feathers, or else charitably donated by passing trawlermen. Hurricane lamps were regularly in use by the twentieth century both inside and outside the home.

The St Kildans burnt turf to heat their homes and cook their food. The fuel was generally cut from Mullach Mor to Mullach Sgar and from the slopes of Conachair and Oiseval. The turf was stripped often wastefully from good pasture land and occasionally good arable land, but the islanders had little choice in the matter. There was peat available on the island and many visitors argued that it should be cut instead. 'It is not good moss and would never make fire', was the islanders' usual answer when questioned. Besides, it was more difficult to dig, harder to dry out than turf, and above all heavier to carry. The deposits were primarily confined to the top of hills, over three-quarters of a mile from the village.

As with the storing of seabirds, so with the turf: the cleits were of inestimable importance to the St Kildans. Those built beyond the village wall were used to dry and store turf. Normally they were constructed as near to the cutting grounds as possible; hence over the centuries hundreds of cleits appeared on the slopes. Although the men would help, the cutting and fetching of turf was a task for the women.

Hirta could boast a society that from time immemorial treated women as equal, certainly in terms of the work that had to be done. The peats were carried by the women and children on their backs in old plaids or pieces of canvas. 'It is astonishing,' wrote Ross, 'to see the burden even the children from six to nine years of age can take.' There was little room in the house to store the dry peat, so trips to the hills had to be made regularly. 'We helped too, young as we were,' remembers Flora Gillies, only ten years old at the time of the evacuation. 'I always carried for my grandfather. I don't know why, but I always seemed to carry it. My Aunt Mary, it was nothing for her to carry a bag on her back. She was very strong.'

The women also looked after the cattle, and cut all the grass required for their feeding during the winter months. Twice a day in the summer months they would make the long walk over to

Glean Mor to milk the cows and ewes. The first visit was made at daybreak and they would return to the Glean again at five o'clock in the evening. If necessary they would take a bundle of grass with them on their backs to keep the beasts happy while they were being milked.

All the fetching and carrying on the island was delegated by the men to the women. 'Goods from Glasgow', wrote Ross, 'are carried by the women from the shore to their houses and woe be unto them unless they are ready waiting when the men get the cargo to the shore.' In the landing of stores, the men were responsible for manning the island boats out to the ship and the transferring of goods from the factor's smack or the steamer to the rowing boat. On reaching shore, the men would tumble the supplies out of the boat. 'There being but little room,' wrote Ross, 'everything must be removed quickly or the place is blocked up. Such a block happened that day bringing forth a hurricane of yelling from the men but no assistance with it. This is always the case when a thing comes too hard on the men, they poke their hands down to the elbows in their trousers pockets and yell away whereas the poor women almost worry their lives out to avoid this. That day I noticed some of them literally groan under their loads without being offered the slightest sympathy or assistance.'

Occasionally the women had some time to devote to knitting. 'The stocking', wrote the schoolmaster Ross, 'is always carried about her person, ready to be taken whatever situation if she is idle.' Except for the winter months, however, the women found little time to knit. They were far more busy than the men, for there were always things to be done about the house, and in the summer months they had their part to play in the harvesting of birds. The only work specifically reserved for the men was the grand, heroic task of manning the boats and climbing the cliffs in search of birds.

By the nineteenth century, the St Kildans had little faith in the value of their crofts. From a barrel of potatoes, weighing about two hundredweight, McDiarmid reckoned in 1877 that the islanders would scarcely lift three barrels. Owing to a constant subjection to seaspray, the potatoes that were salvaged were soft and tasted more like yams. Although barley and oats were equally prominent features of the St Kildan diet, the yield was likewise small. Oats were generally sown very thickly, from ten to twelve bushels to every acre of ground, and the return was rarely above three times the quantity sown. The islanders attempted to grow a few cabbages and a few turnips, but on Hirta weeds grew more easily than crops. In season, the whole of the arable land looked more like a bed of marigolds than a provider of grain and vegetables.

The soil of Village Bay, however, had not always offered up so little to the St Kildans in return for their labours. When Martin Martin visited the island in the seventeenth century, the barley grown there was reckoned to be the largest produced in the whole of the Western Isles. It ripened earlier on Hirta and was so plentiful that the islanders exported some of the harvest to the mainland. Even in 1819, MacCulloch claimed that St Kildan barley 'is by much the finest to be seen in the whole circuit of the isles'. After 1830, under the supervision of the Reverend Neil Mackenzie, drains were introduced and walls built to keep the livestock away from the arable land. For a few years the yield doubled.

But many primitive methods of cultivation continued well into the nineteenth century. Not only did the islanders still use ancient implements, but they persisted in a system of agriculture that adequately divided out the work but was at the same time uneconomic.

Arable land on Hirta was divided out according to the number of families living on the island. In 1799, Lord Brougham wrote in amazement of Village Bay, 'The great bosom is divided into four hundred rips, or fields of barley, oats and potatoes – twenty five feet by three!' At that time, when the old village still existed, the islanders confined most of their agricultural activity to the area of land to the east of the island. Every household was responsible for the same number of strips.

When the village moved, so too did the land under cultivation. In 1841 Wilson wrote: 'The arable land within the larger enclosure and fronting the village, is chiefly laid out in small rigs of barley, and is subdivided into about twenty portions, belonging to a corresponding number of families. There are besides about eight smaller families who are not so portioned.' Under this system, which was to remain in St Kilda throughout the remainder of the island's history, the head of each household was responsible for about an acre and a half to two acres of land. The produce gained from working his allotment had to maintain all those who lived in his house, regardless of numbers, and also help towards providing a share given to those smaller families by the community as a whole. In ordinary years, the system enabled the people of Village Bay to grow sufficient grain and potatoes, but only as a result of much hard work.

Manure was a precious commodity on Hirta. When they shared their homes with their livestock, the St Kildans went to infinite pains to preserve every scrap that built up on the floor of the house. 'After having burned a considerable quantity of dried turf,' wrote Forsyth in 1808, 'they spread the ashes with the greatest care over the apartment in which they eat and sleep. These ashes so exactly laid out, they cover with a rich vegetable mould or black earth; over this bed of earth they scatter a proportionate quantity of peat dust; this done, they water, tread and beat the compost into a hard floor, on which they immediately kindle large fires . . . The same operations are punctually repeated till they are ready to sow their barley, by which time . . . their floors have risen about four or five feet.'

When the new village was built, the midden was transferred outside the house, but the collection of manure was still of prime concern. 'There are covered outhouses for such collections,' wrote Wilson in 1841, 'while animal garbage, such as viscera and heads and feet of birds, are thrown into a circular open pit, of which one is attached to each little group of houses.' When the proprietor built new cottages in the 1860's, the middens were continued.

When spring came it took days and sometimes weeks to prepare the soil for sowing. All the tilling had to be done by hand: the St Kildans of latter years had no horses to help them. The agricultural implements used on Hirta were crude but effective. The common spade was not used on the island until after 1877, although the Reverend Neil Mackenzie had attempted to persuade the St Kildans to adopt it fifty years earlier. The people much preferred the traditional instrument of the Highlander, called the *caschrom*, or 'crooked' spade. Work on the land would begin usually in April and, as John Ross remarked, 'due to the short days of spring and the little time that must have been left after parliament, the tilling of the two meagre acres of soil that each house possessed must have taken weeks.' Changeable weather, moreover, would frequently drive the St Kildans indoors where they would take up a needle to make or mend clothes, or else a hammer to make a new pair of boots for some of the family. With the coming of spring, there was always much to do on Hirta.

Once turned with the *caschrom*, the soil was harrowed with a strong, roughly made, wooden hand-rake. Great care was taken to remove every small stone, weed and vestige of old crops that might sap the land of its meagre fertility. A major problem for the men were the marigolds that monopolized the land every year. Once the ground had been carefully gone over it was ready for the manure which was carried to the fields by the women. There were no wheelbarrows and only two handbarrows on St Kilda, so the women had to manage with creels on their backs. (Twigs were imported by the islanders, from which the creels were woven.) The patch of land reserved for potatoes was the most backbreaking to prepare because of the amount of fertilizer that had to be dug into the soil. Once the barley, oats, and potatoes were sown, the hand-rakes were again laboriously employed. 'With these,' wrote Ross, 'they go over and over the ground until the seed is thoroughly covered from the eyes of hungry sparrows, starlings, crows, and gulls.'

'In the spring time they were all speed cultivating the croft — sowing the seed and that,' recalls Neil Ferguson. 'Well, if you were finished before your neighbour, you just went over with your spade and gave him a hand out. Then, perhaps, there was a widow who couldn't work the croft; well, when they'd finished their own, all the men went and worked the croft for the widow. They were all working hand in hand.' The principles of sharing and helping each other that governed the community were applied just as much to the work that had to be done around the croft.

If the work was hard, it proved worthwhile. 'It is certain', remarked Forsyth in 1808, 'that a small number of acres prepared in this manner must yield a greater return than a much greater number of poorly cultivated as in the other Western Isles. The inhabitants of St Kilda sow and reap much earlier than others in the same latitude.'

Once the crops were in the ground, the St Kildans could turn their attention to their livestock. The sheep proved the most important animal husbanded by the islanders. At the end of the seventeenth century it was estimated that there were some two thousand sheep on Hirta and the neighbouring islands of Soay and Boreray. One hundred and fifty years later, the number had dropped to nearer fifteen hundred. Half the sheep grazed on Hirta, nearly five hundred were on Boreray, and the remainder were on the island of Soay.

The sheep on Soay were the property of the proprietor, MacLeod of MacLeod. They were not of any domesticated variety, but of a primitive, native breed. They were small, brownish in colour and resembled goats rather than sheep. In all likelihood the Soay sheep, direct descendants of the moufflon, existed on St Kilda since Neolithic times. They were kept not for eating but for their soft wool from which the islanders knitted socks and wove tweed.

The rest of the sheep, owned by the islanders, were mostly white, although some black-faced tups were introduced into St Kilda in about 1872. They were famous on the mainland for living to a ripe old age, despite the obvious hazards of being blown or chased over a cliff top. 'One old man', wrote George Murray, 'brought home and killed a ewe sixteen years old. I was told that long ago, within the memory of the old people, they used to have sheep twenty years old.'

The sheep of St Kilda were not held in common. The most likely explanation for such an anomaly was that the islanders did not regard their existence as a community upon Hirta as being dependent upon the sheep. In 1877, the smallest number of sheep owned by an islander was eleven and the largest was one hundred and fifty. Twenty years later, it was estimated that there were about one thousand sheep all told on the islands of St Kilda. By the time of the evacuation, the number had risen to nearer two thousand. The government in 1930 took off over thirteen hundred sheep, while those on Soay and Boreray were left behind.

The first task of the year was to take stock. A number of sheep were invariably lost during the winter gales. The St Kildans, therefore, would round them up and count them. In May, the men would take a boat to Dun where the young lambs had wintered on the island's lush grass. Lambs and ewes would then be driven over to Glean Mor where they would stay throughout the summer. The women would be responsible for milking the ewes daily, and the old beehive structures in the glen would be used to separate the lambs from their mothers at night so that the St Kildans would not be deprived of milk. 'There is a fold for each family,' noted Murray, 'and it is the women's part to herd them all day, keeping them separate.' After the ewes had been milked in the morning, however, they were normally let out of the enclosure.

The St Kildans had also, of course, to tend to the sheep on Boreray. By 1889, the islanders made three visits to the island. In the spring they went to collect eggs and count the sheep. As on Hirta a number were usually blown over the rocks during winter. In June they went again to Boreray to take the wool from the sheep. The last visit of the year was in the early autumn to kill the young gannets. The summer visit, however, was normally the longest, lasting anything up to two weeks. It was the longest period that the men would be separated from their families. Not all of them went to Boreray in the summer. Only about a dozen men were involved in the expedition, and of them only half would land on the island. Those who made the crossing were chosen by lot at the morning meeting.

While on Boreray, the men lived in what was known as the Stal House – an oval, half underground hovel, no more than ten or twelve feet by six, with sleeping apartments off the main chamber that looked like rabbit warrens. A supply of turf was always kept cut for the fire and there was a fresh water well on the island. The islanders wasted little time in getting down to the work at hand, and the dogs they took with them were invaluable in tracking down the sheep.

The mongrel dogs that roamed Hirta in their dozens went everywhere with the St Kildans. Small, lean beasts of collie extraction, they appeared to the outsider to be owned by no one in particular. At an early age, each dog had his teeth either broken or filed down so that he would not tear the flesh of the sheep as he ran them to ground. When they were not being used, a rope was tied round each animal's neck and one foreleg passed through the noose so that they could not escape from the village area and worry the sheep and the nesting birds. The dogs exhibited an agility upon the rocks that made them invaluable to the St Kildans.

Once the fleece of the sheep had been taken, it was time for the party to return to Hirta. The men on Boreray used to cut out areas of turf in the grassy slope visible from the main island, and after the party had been on Boreray for a few days those on Hirta would go up daily to the Gap to look for the signal. As the boat bringing them back home returned, the women would run to the landing place to help land the wool. 'On their return,' wrote John Ross, 'the congratulations are as joyful as the parting was sad. They are never happy when any of their friends are absent. They are filled with forebodings of every description which is mainly due to the very limited knowledge they have of the ways of the world outside their own small circle.'

Most of the month of June was taken up with rounding up the sheep. The method employed on all three islands was the same, namely to chase them until they were trapped on some ledge.

Men, women, and children took part in this exhausting work, helped by their dogs. The St Kildans built numerous sheep pens on Hirta and, once captured, the beasts were confined to the enclosures to await shearing.

'Rooing', as it was called, frequently involved the loss of many sheep. 'The sheep, more like mountain deer, run as for their dear lives,' wrote John Ross. 'The dogs run determined to seize their prey before they get out of their reach over the rocks, and the man, poor fellow, tries to run also knowing the penalty if they do so. If the dogs are some distance behind when the sheep reach the rocks there is not so much danger of any being killed, as they have time to look where they are going; but if they are hard pressed by the dogs they will jump right before them with the result that some must be killed. This hunt goes on for about half a day, when the men, wearied out, meet at the fold and after telling any that were killed start counting their catch.'

The St Kildans had an insurance scheme to counter any losses. The other men involved in the 'rooing' would give compensation to the man who had lost sheep, either by way of beasts from their own flocks, or else in terms of money. Even if an owner lost sheep as a result of a storm his colleagues would compensate. Nor did the St Kildans merely catch their own individual flock. If one of their number was ill or perhaps away from the island at the time, his sheep would be collected and sheared by the others.

The sheep were deprived of their fleeces with penknives. 'Today the sheep are to be clipped,' wrote the schoolmaster George Murray. 'I clipped seven yesterday and I learned them the way to use the shears. Their shearing instrument is the common knife which of course makes work. One man last year got a pair of shears in a present and on my making use of it yesterday it became an object of wonder and was called a *great invention*. There was a crowd of about forty men and women in a circle round me with eyes full wide with astonishment at the strange operation which the beast was undergoing. Remarks such as the following were made: "Oh Love, don't cut the throat", "Don't take out the liver", while the owner of the beast said it would not stay on that side of the island after hearing such a *ghogadich* (noise) about its ears, meaning the sounding of the shears.' To the end, the St Kildans refused to use modern methods.

The Soay sheep, which were rounded up in the same way as the domesticated animals, were more easily dispossessed of their wool.

The St Kildans left the wool on the beast until the undergrowth of hair pushed it from the skin, so that there was little to do but gently pull out the soft, brown fleece. The major problem of gathering their wool was that Soay was probably even more difficult an island to land upon than Boreray, and the sheep were more agile than their domesticated cousins.

The summer months on Hirta were busy months. Apart from tending to the crops there were many other jobs to do around the croft. No St Kildan was ever formally trained to be a carpenter or a cobbler or a tailor – everyone was brought up from birth to turn a hand at most jobs. If the men and women of Hirta were no craftsmen, they were certainly competent workmen. During the dry days of summer, there were cleits to repair, sheep folds to rebuild, work to be done on the boats and on their cottages. Many who visited St Kilda thought the people idle, but they did not take into account the fact that everyone on the island purposely stopped work on days when there were tourists to entertain. There can have been few hours of rest for a community whose tasks were as varied as the St Kildans'.

In the evenings the men would often go fishing. In 1841, Wilson estimated that the 200,000 gannets which he reckoned nested upon the cliffs consumed the equivalent of 305,714 barrels of fish each year. 'Think of this ye men of Wick,' he exclaimed, 'ye curers of Caithness, ye fair females of the salting tub.' The St Kildans were not enthused by his discovery. The men had fished from time immemorial with nets and long lines for ling and cod, but always looked upon the work with disdain. After all, they argued, they could get all the food they wanted and pay the rent by fowling. 'They possess already as much food as they can consume,' wrote MacCulloch in 1819, 'and are under no temptation to augment it by another perilous and laborious employment, added to which they seem to have a hereditary attachment.' The St Kildans, moreover, disliked the taste of fish, claiming that it was not oily enough for their palate. They claimed that whenever they ate it, it caused 'an eruption of the skin'. In later years, however, they resorted to fishing primarily as a means of helping to pay the rent.

When the St Kildans went fishing for themselves, the catch was divided out only among those who were actively engaged in the exercise. If, however, they went to catch fish to give to the factor, as was the case with ling, the produce was divided out equally among the sixteen households, despite the fact that the fish represented the labours of only eight or nine of their number.

Hirta could always boast a healthy herd of cattle. In the seventeenth century, Martin Martin claimed the St Kildans owned some ninety cows – small, fat beasts renowned for their sweet-tasting flesh. The beasts were frequently remarked upon by visitors and were famed on Hirta and beyond for their rich milk, most of which was mixed with the milk of ewes to make cheese. When McDiarmid visited the island in 1877, he noted that at that time the herd comprised one bull, which was then eight or nine years old, twenty-one cows and twenty-seven young cattle. Some twelve calves had been born that year, which McDiarmid remarked were 'nice, lively, well-fed little beasts'. The women not only milked and looked after the sheep and cows, but were also responsible for mating the animals, a state of affairs that George Murray thought a little improper. 'I fell in with a young girl,' he wrote in his diary, 'who told me she was putting the sheep and rams together. Things would look better and leave a better impression upon a stranger, were the fair sex to leave these things to the opposite sex.'

At one time ponies could be found on St Kilda. They were imported from the mainland by the proprietor to help carry turf. By 1831 there were nearly twenty small, reddish-brown ponies, but within ten years there were only two or three left. The islanders argued that the beasts ate more grass than they were worth, so they sold them to the factor for twenty-five shillings a head. By 1870, the horse had been banished from Hirta for good.

The islanders tolerated only a few domesticated animals. The goat was also banned on St Kilda a few years after its introduction because, the islanders claimed, it interfered with the birds on the cliffs. There were few poultry on the island, probably because of the difficulty in stopping them being swept into the sea in a gale, and the fact that the St Kildans lacked the proper foodstuffs for them. The only animal other than the sheep, the cow and the dog allowed on St Kilda was the cat. Each household had at least one cat and they were thought useful in keeping mice away from the valuable supplies of meal and oats.

By the end of August, usually after the fulmar harvest and before that of the gannet, the time had come to harvest the crops. Everyone on the island worked from dawn till dusk, and often by moonlight, until the season's yield was gathered in. In a place where a sudden storm or heavy fall of rain could destroy the total crop, every other activity on the island was put aside when the barley, corn, and potatoes were ripe. 'The whole population old and young were out at once,' wrote John Macdonald in 1822, 'and every family engaged in cutting down its little croft.'

The barley on Hirta was ripe by 25 August and was pulled out by the roots. 'It is so short,' remarked the islanders, 'we would have nothing were we to cut it.' The women and children made small ricks, which helped the barley dry quicker, but they were not allowed to stand longer than was necessary in case there was a change in the weather.

Reaping hooks, however, were used to cut down the corn, which ripened later than the barley. Again the men were responsible for mowing the hay and the women and children helped stack it. Trawl nets that had been washed ashore or given to the islanders by generous trawlermen were used to hold the stacks secure. Even as late as 1926, the St Kildans managed to grow all the winter supply of hay needed for their cattle. There were a few harvests that did not suffice the winter, and in the spring one of the first tasks of the women was to go and pick grass from those ledges too inaccessible for the sheep to reach. It was extremely dangerous work, but at times had to be done to prevent the beasts from starving.

The grain was thrashed out with a flail. Then, according to John Sands, 'it is scorched in a pot or put into a straw tub and dried with heated stones'. Only then could the corn be ground in a *quern*, of which at least one was to be found in every home.

The quern consists of two circular slabs of granite, about fifteen to eighteen inches in diameter. In the centre of the lower stone, which was hollowed out to some five inches in depth, there was an iron pivot, on which the upper stone was turned with the aid of a wooden handle. 'The women', wrote Sands, 'sit on the ground half-naked and work at the mills like furies.' It was said that two women – for no St Kildan male ever deigned to grind corn except for the benefit of photographers – could grind a barrel of meal a day. Once ground in the quern, the meal was put through a sieve made from sheepskin stretched on a hoop and perforated with hot wire. It was then ready for baking.

Before it was ground, the meal looked more like chaff, and was like dust after it had been through the quern. Nevertheless, it was of inestimable value to the St Kildans. According to the Kearton brothers in 1898, the islanders consumed about 120 lb. of oatmeal and flour per head, per annum. As their crofts were overworked and little attempt was made to grow crops in rotation, the St Kildans were to become more and more dependent upon their proprietor for supplies. Such a dependency put great strain on the owner of the island and was constantly endangered by a lack of proper communications. It was, in fact, lack of grain that brought about the shock famines of 1885 and 1912. The islanders found it impossible to grow any vegetables save the potato, and an exhausted soil yielded few of these. In 1886, George Murray wrote in his diary, 'The potato crop is very poor, scarcely worth the trouble of lifting.'

The decline in agriculture and the constant threat of famine helped bring about the decision to evacuate. No one in 1930, save the postmaster, even bothered to prepare the soil for sowing: crofting, like many other pursuits, did not seem worth the effort any more.

As a result of scarcity of food the islanders of later years ate more mutton than their forefathers. Traditionally the St Kildans did not kill many sheep for winter. Despite the fact that they were numerous and extremely fat in the autumn, their slaughter was reserved for special occasions. Mutton was a delicacy on Hirta, served up fresh at weddings and funerals. At the end of the year, however, despite the snow which invariably lay thick on the ground at that time, the men would go to Soay to kill a sheep, which was eaten by the community to celebrate New Year's Day.

Just before New Year the *cardadh mor*, the big carding of the wool, took place. Since the summer the bales of wool plucked from both Soay and domesticated sheep had been kept by each family in the loft of the cottage. During the long, dark nights of winter, the St Kildans busied themselves spinning and weaving.

Like most jobs on Hirta, the carding of the wool was communal work. The people would gather in each house in turn. A mountain of wool stood on the floor. The islanders would sit round the room, and as each pad of carded wool was finished it was thrown into the centre. The wool was carded again more thoroughly and blended by colour and carefully fashioned into rolls for spinning. It was spun either by means of an ancient spindle or on a more modern wheel. By 1879 there were thirty-six spinning wheels on the island and every house possessed a loom made entirely of wood. The proprietor supplied both in an effort to stimulate the island's economy by utilizing a valuable indigenous staple.

'The dogs of each house hailed us with loud barking and when we were ushered inside, there would be the purr of a spinning wheel, operated by the woman of the house.' Mary Cameron, daughter of one of the last missionaries to serve on Hirta, recalls her childhood memories of those busy winter days. 'The men and boys and older girls', she writes, 'might be teasing wool, picking out rough bits and pieces of grass and preparing the wool for its next stage, the carding; or else working oil into it to make it easier to handle.' The oil for greasing the wool came from the fulmar. When the young birds were cooked a great quantity of oil came out of their flesh, which the St Kildans skimmed and put on their wool to grease it for spinning. 'There might be someone else', continued Mary Cameron, 'wielding a pair of cards – flat wooden brushes with steel teeth, which combed out the wool. The worker then with a deft movement, would fashion the combed wool into a soft roll, ready for spinning; or he might lay it aside in a flat pad to be blended later with another shade.'

Some of the wool, when spun, was put aside. This was used by the women for knitting articles of clothing for themselves and their families, such as socks, gloves and scarves. When the tourists came the St Kildans were to find a ready market for their hand-knitted goods. Most of the wool, however, was used in the manu-facture of tweed.

In early February, the looms were brought down from the loft, and assembled by one of the windows in the house. Every loom on Hirta was the same – a simple handloom with foot treadles for changing the warp. The men were the weavers and worked long hours. 'His loom is in operation', wrote Robert Connell in 1889, 'when the days are stormy and out-door work is suspended. It is a primitive looking machine, every portion of it home made. For two months the sound of the shuttle is heard in every house. The work is carried out with astonishing zeal, sometimes the dawn of day finds them sleeping at the loom. This period of unremitting toil is often put forward to prove the industry of the people. It certainly proves the capacity of the people for work.' When the weaving was finished, the looms were taken apart and returned to the loft for another year.

In the spring, the tweeds were waulked and shrunk. The women were responsible for waulking, and on Hirta the process was called *Shiord Thu*, which literally meant 'Over to you'. They would sit round a table pushing the woollen cloth round and round and across to those sitting opposite, chanting all the while a song that ended up with the phrase 'over to you'. The waulking was normally done in the early hours of the morning. Those doing the work would sleep during the evening in the house where the work was to be done. They would rise early, clear the living-room of furniture apart from a table, and waulk all the tweed made by that household during the winter. On another evening, they would do the same in a neighbour's house.

By the time all the cloth had been shrunk it would be daylight and the young men on the island would take the tweed to the burn and wash it. It was then stretched out over the drystone dykes. When dry, the bales would be rolled up tightly and taken down to the storehouse by the landing-place to await the arrival of the factor. Some of the tweed, however, was kept back to make everyday clothes for the islanders.

By the end of the nineteenth century, tweed was to be the only article of value the St Kildans possessed. Even then, the people got a poor return for their hard work. In a *Report on Home Industries in the Highlands and Islands* in the year 1914, it was estimated that the St Kildans earned only 1¾d an hour making tweed. It was reckoned that a man and his wife working together could make a web of tweed thirty yards long in five weeks. The woman would work twelve hours a day during that time, while her husband, who did all the weaving, worked approximately forty-eight hours throughout that time. On that calculation, even the manufacture of cloth, the last innovation to be made in St Kilda, was uneconomic. Even the cottage industry of the crofter could not support the community.

The St Kildans, it seemed, were doomed, and their demise was not of their own making. If the crops and the tweed were to fail them it was through no lack of effort on the part of the islanders. Life on Hirta was never easy, but for a thousand years it was possible. As the people became more and more disillusioned and perplexed they were to turn to religion for their salvation. They found little comfort.

6
God and the Devil

Ann Munro opened the letter addressed to her husband and having read it sat down and cried. It was 1926 and Dugald Munro was missionary to the people of Kilfinan in Argyll. The letter was from Dr Roderick MacLeod of the United Free Church of Scotland who wrote to offer Dugald the post of missionary to the lone people of St Kilda. Tears gave way to devotion. 'You know the old tradition, you had to go where your husband went,' she says. 'It never dawned on me to refuse. Mind you, I'd no idea of what I was going to contend with.'

For a salary of £190 a year Dugald committed his young wife to a degree of isolation she had never before experienced. Although the appointment was normally for a period of three years, Dr MacLeod agreed to allow Dugald Munro to take his leave of the island whenever he wanted to. 'Every missionary we send to St Kilda,' said MacLeod, 'we presume he'll be the last.' Dugald Munro was to be the last in a long line of ministers and missionaries sent to the island from the mainland to spread and administer the word.

Of all the influences brought to bear upon the minds of the people of Village Bay, that of religion played the greatest part in determining their destiny. For nearly five hundred years, the ministers and missionaries were the only educated people to live on the island for any great length of time. In their hands, therefore, lay the power to encourage good and create evil. After the Disruption in 1843 within the Church of Scotland, the stern faith of the Free Church, in the manner of its application and of its acceptance, made slaves of the people of St Kilda. The damage that was done in little over half a century of Free Church rule was to prove too great for the repairing zeal of latter-day missionaries like Dugald Munro.

Hirta was in all likelihood made Christian long before much of the mainland of Scotland. It seems likely that during the migrations of monks from Ireland to Iceland in the sixth century many of them may have settled on St Kilda to convert the people living

there, or perhaps even to form the nucleus of a community themselves. As Macaulay remarked in 1758, 'If Providence has ever
designed any man for Monkish austerities or if any part of the
globe has been destined by nature for hermits, undoubtedly
St Kilda must be one of these stations . . . Here all the pernicious
influence of evil company, all avocations from the great business
of the spiritual life, all the flatteries of sense and time, are almost
totally excluded.'

In 1697, Martin Martin, then tutor to MacLeod of MacLeod's
children, discovered people 'governed by the dictates of reason
and Christianity' upon Hirta. They were suffering from numerous
delusions, he thought, concerning religion, but he and his fellow
travellers attempted to dispel them. At that time, St Kilda had no
regular incumbent. Marriages and baptisms were postponed until
the Steward and his retinue, which invariably included a minister,
came to the island during the summer months. John Campbell, the
visiting minister from Harris in 1697, married fifteen St Kildan
couples, and the ceremonies were accompanied by much gaiety
and dancing to bagpipes. It is likely that the Reverend Campbell
was the first minister of the Church of Scotland ever to visit Hirta.
Martin Martin concluded that the islanders were amongst the
happiest people in the world. Totally unaware of the Seven Deadly
Sins, the St Kildans were a gay people, fond of song and poetry,
who enjoyed playing games on the summer sands of Village Bay.

In 1705, the Reverend Alexander Buchan became the first
missionary on record to be sent to St Kilda. His purpose, he said,
was 'to root out the pagan and Popish superstitious customs, so
much yet in use among that people'. He was sent under the
auspices of the Presbytery of Edinburgh, and during his stay did
much to help the community. It was he who constructed the first
manse, and under his care the children of the island were, to the
best of his ability, educated in the beliefs of the established church.
Using money donated by 'charitable christians', Buchan started the
first library on Hirta. His wife, who accompanied him, was
responsible for teaching the St Kildan women how to knit. In 1730,
Alexander Buchan died from a fever. He was the first of several
ministers who attempted, as Wilson remarked in 1841, 'to raise the
St Kildans in the scale of thinking beings'.

There were to be few ministers like Buchan, prepared to stay
long enough on the island to influence the community for the
better by passing on to the St Kildans the benefits both of personal

education and of the practical advances made by society on the mainland. The influence of most ministers worked in the opposite direction. Most saw fit to pass on to their remote island flock their own personal prejudices and bigotry. On St Kilda, religion in the hands of some was to help stifle what little initiative existed among the inhabitants.

In July 1822, the Reverend Dr Campbell of Edinburgh suggested, on behalf of the Society in Scotland for the Propagating of Christian Knowledge, that the Reverend John Macdonald should visit St Kilda and preach to the people there. 'From your well-known principle and feelings of love to our common Lord, and to the souls of men, and from your habits of itinerating,' wrote Dr Campbell to Macdonald, 'I would incline to think this proposition would not fail to be agreeable to you. It is that you yourself shall take a trip to St Kilda, along with the tacksman in August. The necessities of the poor islanders are urgent in the extreme; I should think that the cry of their distress must be heard as loud in the ear of a zealous evangelical minister as yourself as that of the men of Macedonia by Paul, "Come over and help us."'

Until that time, the religious supervision of the St Kildans since Buchan's death had been in the hands of the occasional visiting missionary. A farmer from the Outer Hebrides, it is said, was sent to the island during the summer months to make marriages and preach the Scriptures. He was eager if unordained: he had learnt the Scriptures by heart from his father. When he could manage no more to make the dangerous voyage to Hirta, one of four descendants carried on the good work.

On 16 September 1822, the Reverend John MacDonald, later to be given the title 'Apostle of the North', paid his first of many visits to St Kilda. When he landed at Village Bay, the islanders were busy reaping the harvest. 'That we will,' was the enthusiastic reply to the minister's request that they stop work and attend his prayer meetings.

. MacDonald found that there was no longer a church upon Hirta. 'During my stay in the island,' he wrote in his diary, 'the people assembled in a barn.' He was even more shocked at the state in which he found the Calvinist faith on the island. 'Swearing', noted MacDonald, 'is too prevalent among them and its common expressions, such as by the soul, by Mary, by the Book . . . and what is worse, by the sacred name seem to be quite familiar with them on every occasion.'

'It grieves me to say, and I took pains to ascertain the truth,' he wrote in his diary with a zeal that could only be sincere, 'that among the whole body, I did not find a single individual who could be truly called a decidedly religious person; that is one who has felt the influence of the truth on his soul, and who exhibits that influence in his life and conversation.'

The earnest man of God set about his work. During the eleven days he spent on St Kilda during his first visit, he preached to the inhabitants thirteen times. The natives were impressed. When MacDonald took his leave, he did so 'midst tears. All shook hands in bading their final adieux and begging him to return again to them.'

The following year MacDonald spent two weeks on St Kilda, from 14 May to 1 June. When he landed, 'They all pressed around me', he wrote, 'and grasped my hand each in his turn. Few, if any, words were said, but tears trickled from every eye.' In all, the Reverend John MacDonald paid four summer visits to Hirta before finally he took his leave of the people in 1830.

Under MacDonald the Church got converts to its ideology in this lone outpost of the British Isles. It was due to him that the foundations of a highly organized, strictly managed, puritan and often harsh religion were laid. He succeeded where others failed in arousing a religious fervour that had been unknown on St Kilda and had perhaps been absent from much of the mainland since the Reformation. 'Oh let me not despair,' wrote MacDonald while on Hirta, 'though I should not see instances of immediate, sudden conversion! The seed below the ground may be making progress though I see it not. Let me therefore sow in hope.'

From the time of MacDonald's crusade a marked change took place in the nature of the people of Village Bay. The St Kildans lost their sense of gaiety and their love of song and dance. Their way of life, previously governed solely by wind and tide, was thereafter subject to the demands of regular church-going. If the well-intentioned mission of the minister was a success, that success was due to the character of the islanders themselves. What MacDonald preached appealed to their superstitious nature. They believed implicitly in what he told them and a religion, the roots of which lay deep in the fear of the unknown, began its long domination over the minds of the people of St Kilda.

What Hirta lacked, however, was a proper place of worship. In 1827 John MacDonald decided he would try to raise sufficient funds to enable the SSPCK and the proprietor to build a church and a manse. The 'Apostle of the North' preached all over Scotland on behalf of the islanders and took collections for their little church. Enough money was raised on the mainland to build a church and a manse, and justify the sending to St Kilda of a resident minister by the SSPCK.

In 1829, the Reverend Neil Mackenzie became the first resident incumbent on Hirta for over a hundred years. His first concern was to supervise the construction of the new buildings by the master mason of Dunvegan and his men, who had been sent over that summer from Skye by MacLeod of MacLeod.

The manse was built on the north-east side of Village Bay, about one hundred yards from the storm beach and two hundred yards from the homes of the St Kildans. The minister's house was a one-storeyed building of stone and mortar with a small porch, and inside Mackenzie was to have four rooms. Protected on one side against wind and storm by a high stone wall, the manse also had an enclosed patch of ground in front where ministers and missionaries of later years were to grow for their personal enjoyment rhubarb and even strawberries.

The Church was built immediately behind the manse, at a cost of £600. A plain building of hewn stone, thirteen feet long and eighteen feet wide, the church had one main door, four Gothic-style windows and a slate roof. The minister was able to enter the building by means of a small door at that end of the church nearest his own house.

The building was as austere inside as the faith dictated. The walls were unlathed and damp. Mother earth beaten down served as a floor, and there was no altar, no crucifix and no pews for the congregation. Two wooden chandeliers, the only ornaments, were presented by Sir Keith Murray to be hung in the church. Each chandelier held three candles made from sheep's tallow. Only the heat from the few native lamps allowed to light the evening service in the winter months kept the worshippers warm.

In the summer months of 1830, Neil Mackenzie temporarily took his leave of the St Kildans to get married. With his young bride, Mackenzie then went back to the island that was to be his home for the next twelve years.

For Mrs Mackenzie in particular life on Hirta was one of extreme isolation. 'He introduced us to his wife,' wrote George Atkinson in 1831, 'who is a Glasgow lady and has not one word of Gaelic.

St Kilda from the air *Above* 1. Boreray (foreground), Stac Lee (middle), and Hirta (background) *Below* 2. *Left to right*: Stac an Armin, Stac Lee, and Boreray

Left 3. The soaring heights of Stac Lee

Below 4. Gannets over Conachair

Right 5. Until the middle of the nineteenth century, the St Kildans lived in black houses, common throughout the Hebrides

Right below 6. Inside the new houses, built by St Kilda's owner in the 1860s, furniture was scant, but to an outdoor people they provided sufficient shelter

Above 7. In such a small
community it was thought
essential that everyone should
be responsible for important
decisions. The men of the
island usually met every
morning in the village street to
decide on the work to be done
that day. This picture was
taken in 1927
Right 8. The hardship of their
lives shows in these faces
(1890). Women were
responsible for the day-to-day
work of the community

Above 9. The Church was the centre of their existence. On Sundays there were frequently three services a day, attended by everyone. A photograph taken in 1930

Below 10. The pulpit was the largest in the Western Isles. From the little desk below the minister, the precentor led the congregation in unaccompanied psalm-singing

Right 11. The Reverend John Mackay preached to the St Kildans for twenty-four years (1865–89), and reduced them to a religious orthodoxy that was to help determine the ultimate fate of the community. *Below* 12. In later years the spiritual needs of the St Kildans were served by missionaries. Some, like Donald Cameron who was sent to St Kilda in 1919, brought their families

Above 13. After the First World War the interior of the Church was renovated. The harsh religion of the Free Church of Scotland, however, offered the St Kildans little in the way of creature comforts

Below 14. The last wedding on St Kilda. Neil Ferguson Junior and the only remaining eligible spinster on the island were married by a visiting minister. The year was 1926

Above 15. The schoolchildren of Village Bay in
1927. The missionary sent from the mainland
was responsible for teaching the last generation
of native St Kildans to read and write

Right 16. Nurse Williamina Barclay was the
last nurse to be sent to St Kilda (in 1927). It
was largely due to her efforts that the islanders
finally agreed to abandon their island home.
For this she was later awarded the CBE

She has just been twelvemonth on the island and it is nine since she had exchanged a word with anyone but her husband.' While on St Kilda she was to raise a family of six children – 'Fine rosy-cheeked children,' wrote Wilson of them, 'with clean hands and well-washed faces . . . and little bare feet.'

More than any other churchman before him, Neil Mackenzie succeeded in raising the standard of living on St Kilda. He persuaded the islanders to put their arable land in order and tried to show them the advantages of personal hygiene. It was his doing, for instance, that legs appeared on tables in the St Kildan home, raising the occupants, if only physically, above the level of their animals. He also saw to the construction of dry-stone dykes around the arable land to stop the livestock on the island from spoiling the precious crops.

But for the St Kildans, conditions were still primitive. An Englishman, Sir Thomas Dyke Acland, visited the island and was so shocked by the state of the dwellings that he left with the Reverend Mackenzie a reward of twenty guineas to be given to the first islander to build a new home. The St Kildans were against the idea of demolishing their homes, but the minister finally persuaded one man to make the effort and the rest of the islanders began to build a new village.

At all times, however, the minister stood apart from St Kildan society. He was never included in the division of any of the island produce. He was not entitled to a share, although the islanders were normally generous to the occupants of 'The Big House', as the manse was called. Ministers and their dependants had to find their own provisions, most of which came from the mainland or were home-grown in the glebe.

The St Kildans, a simple, credulous people, came to rely upon their minister. For a long time, the ministers and missionaries sent to Hirta were the only people on the island who could speak and write English, and therefore the only people who could talk to visitors or send letters to the mainland. 'The good minister', wrote Wilson of Mackenzie, 'is teacher and writing master (literally prime minister) as well as priest, and seems to leave nothing untried to ameliorate the conditions of his flock.' Without doubt Mackenzie, ably assisted by his young wife, did much to improve the material lot of the St Kildans.

When the Reverend Neil Mackenzie and his family took their final leave of St Kilda in 1844, it was a sad day for the people of Hirta. Mackenzie went to take up a living the SSPCK made available to him at Duror, in Appin.

What little culture the St Kildans once possessed, however, had long since died. 'These spiritual songs', wrote Wilson, 'may even be said to be of ordinary use almost as the popular poetry of the day, and have in great measure superseded all ordinary vocal music of worldly character. The Irish melodies are unknown. Dancing is also now regarded by them as frivolous amusement, and has ceased to be practised even during their more joyous festivals, such as marriage and baptism.' When Mackenzie came to write up his impressions of his stay on Hirta, he noted of the people, 'Many of them were under very serious religious impressions, and were becoming more so each succeeding year.' The islanders who possessed a more than ordinary development of the religious instinct became an eager congregation.

The St Kildans became ardent church-goers. By the middle of the nineteenth century, they were going to church every day of the week, except on Mondays and Saturdays. On Sundays they went twice. Attendance at every service was compulsory for all islanders over the age of two, save those sick. For a people whose livelihood so depended upon the elements, such strict regulations and such time-consuming devotion was a danger to their survival. The Church services put a halt to all work not only for the hours of their duration but, to all intents and purposes, for the twenty-four hours within which they took place. The prayer meetings held every Wednesday put an end to evening fishing expeditions, as did the monthly service on Mondays.

The year before the Reverend Neil Mackenzie took his leave of the St Kildans, the Disruption, led by the Reverend Thomas Chalmers, took place in Edinburgh and the Free Church of Scotland was born. The highlands and islands of Scotland succumbed to its preaching. 'The great evangelical movement of the Free Church, after the Disruption of 1843,' noted Fraser Darling in *West Highland Survey*, 'was a glorious phenomenon, just as was the Oxford Movement at much the same time in England. An innately religious people responded, and as so often happens in the more drastic type of religious experience much of what went before was abhorred without discrimination, and there came about an almost fanatical condemnation of such spontaneous and proper social manifestations as music and dancing. Many a fiddle was dramatically broken across the knee, and gay voices and feet were stilled to conform to the gravity now thought to be desirable for salvation.'

In 1866, the Reverend John Mackay from Lochalsh in Ross-shire arrived at St Kilda to save Scotland's most remote souls. He was to live on Hirta for a quarter of a century, longer than any other minister before or after him. During his incumbency he introduced, with the obedient, silent consent of his parishioners, a religious orthodoxy unknown on St Kilda since the days of the 'Apostle'. Under Mackay, there were three services every Sunday on Hirta: one at eleven o'clock in the morning, another at two o'clock in the afternoon and the third at six o'clock in the evening. John Sands, the author, estimated that the St Kildans, in the care of Mackay, spent six and a half hours in Church every Sunday.

From Saturday night to Sunday morning no islander dared to indulge in conversation. All but the recitation of the Bible was thought sinful. No work was done – not even the drawing of water or the milking of the cows or ewes. 'When the women milk the cows,' wrote Ross of the last milking on a Saturday, 'they leave the pails with the milk in the *cleitan* on the Glen until Monday morning . . . If you are buying milk you get it sent you on the Sabbath as on other days, but it is not charged for.' 'The Sabbath is indeed a day of intolerable gloom,' wrote John Sands. 'At the clink of the bell the whole flock hurry to the Church with sorrowful looks, and eyes bent upon the ground. It is considered sinful to look to the right or the left. They do not appear like good people going to listen to glad tidings of great joy, but like a troop of the damned whom Satan is driving to the bottomless pit.'

Mackay demanded the full attention of his flock during the service. Should a child's attention wander, the minister would severely reprimand the parents. 'I have never seen a more earnest and attentive audience,' wrote Sands. Even the children were remarkably well behaved; they learnt while still babes in arms to remain silent and motionless throughout the long proceedings. On one occasion when Sands was visiting St Kilda, the service came to an abrupt halt when an old woman was observed to be asleep. The elder publicly reproved the woman, for whom, he said, there would be no sleep in the next world.

There was no organ or musical instrument of any kind allowed in the Church. The precentor, striking a tuning fork, would lead the congregation in psalm singing. Only psalms were allowed by the Free Church. Hymns were opposed to on scriptural grounds, it being asserted that the psalms are part of the inspired canon of the

Scriptures and as such they alone were fit for singing in church. With a total absence of any sense of harmony, the St Kildans would fight their way to the end of the psalm. 'I can compare it', wrote Connell, 'to nothing but the baying of a pack of hyenas . . . It pained one to be compelled to listen.'

The quality of Mackay's sermons left much to be desired. Surrounded by the small library he had brought from the mainland, and obsessed with 'the Evil One', he set about composing oratory that would lead his people along the path of righteousness. Among his favourite books were Smith's *Moral Sentiments*, Butler's *Fifteen Sermons*, Hervey's *Meditations*, and of course the volume that no Free Church minister would be without, namely the *Select Works of Dr Chalmers*, the man responsible for the Disruption. Sermons were about matters too serious and important to be treated briefly by Mackay. Services frequently lasted upwards of three hours, and more than half that time was taken up by the minister talking to his flock. For the most part, his sermons preached hell, fire and damnation to all who sinned. They were delivered in a monotone that inspired few. Usually they were laced with a comment or two from the learned minister on the state in which the world found itself, and the relative merits of its leaders like Bismarck, Gladstone and Disraeli.

The story of the Prodigal Son was basis of many a sermon. On Sunday 26 December 1886, Mackay preached at both services upon the parable. 'That,' wrote Murray the schoolmaster, on returning to his room in the Factor's house, 'being the third Sabbath and the sixth sermon on the same subject.' Two weeks later, Mackay preached his ninth sermon on the Prodigal Son and still did not feel he had fully exhausted the matter.

Under Mackay, each islander had to prove that he knew his catechism. Once a year, the minister would preside in the Church while the St Kildans, five families at a time, came before him to be tested. 'The weak-minded pope and prime minister rolled into one,' wrote Connell, the journalist, scathingly, 'who rules the destinies of the island has reduced religion into a mere hypocritical formalism, finding no place in his creed for self-reliance or any of the manlier virtues . . . It is nothing to Mr Mackay whether the poor people starve their crofts or neglect the fishing so long as his own silly fads are observed.' The schoolmasters sent to educate the people from the middle of the nineteenth century were able to do little to temper the bigotry of Mackay or exert restraint upon his commanding influence over the lives of the people.

On one occasion, in 1877, supplies without which the St Kildans would have starved arrived on a Saturday night on board HMS *Flirt*. McDiarmid wrote, 'They told us rather than land goods on Sunday, they would prefer sending to Harris for them, should we be compelled by stress of weather to betake ourselves there before Monday.' And yet, five days before, three St Kildans had risked their lives in an attempt to go to Harris in an open boat for the very provisions that lay a quarter of a mile out in Village Bay. 'As the people must be prepared for the devotions of the morrow,' the minister said, 'they could not think of encroaching on the Sabbath by working at the landing of the goods.' Nothing on St Kilda was allowed to happen between dusk on Saturday and Monday morning.

The St Kildans allowed their religious beliefs to dominate their entire way of life. Even when they went to the adjacent islands and stacs to tend sheep or catch sea birds, they always took an elder with them, for fear of being stranded over the Sabbath. 'The elder', wrote Connell, 'is a sort of ornamental man carried . . . for conducting the services on Sunday, without which no St Kildan would feel happy.' When on Boreray, the islanders would find time each day for morning and evening prayers. And at every evening service all the unmarried islanders had to recite from memory one of the Psalms of David.

Reading matter on Hirta was normally censored. When George Seton visited St Kilda in 1877, he took with him a supply of children's books, but Mackay refused to allow him to hand out such trivia. Young girls carried their bibles with them everywhere they went, and when asked if they would like to be sent some books to read, asked for theological works. Emily MacLeod read an old blind islander some stories on one occasion, but was reprimanded by the St Kildan who thought the stories were light and profane. He much preferred sermons.

The introduction of a permanent minister on St Kilda brought with it changes in the social structure of the community. For the first time, the organization of the Free Church gave some islanders positions of power over the rest. Elders were appointed by the minister, and for a people who thought and acted as one, such a state of affairs caused division. Mackay encouraged the elders to monitor and report back to him any deviation from strict observance. 'The stir these days', wrote Murray in 1886, 'is that the precentor in the church was seen several times to laugh on Sabbaths and they are threatening dethronement. His confession was that he was made to laugh when the steamers were coming here by some of the people (islanders) eating sweets in a curious manner. Most laughable.'

Critics upon the mainland thought the quality of some of the ministers sent to St Kilda was low. The Reverend Mackay in particular came in for searing criticism. Throughout most of his incumbency, he was attacked (perhaps with justification) by two authors, John Sands and Robert Connell. But it was difficult to find people to go to St Kilda: few were prepared to sacrifice themselves, in the name of God, before an altar as desolate and insignificant as Hirta, and to those who sought to maintain an organized Church on St Kilda, any minister was better than none. The ministers and missionaries who accepted the post did so out of extraordinary zeal. They were prepared to be cut off from the intellectual and cultural life of the mainland as well as leading a hard and uncomforting life. But those who went were perhaps motivated by more than a simple desire to preach the Gospel. St Kilda offered bigot and zealot alike a chance to instil into the people there a personal view of Christianity, without fear of the critical appraisal that might be made of their interpretation, were they confined to preaching on the mainland.

The St Kildans themselves never once voiced a complaint against the clergymen sent to their island, or against the dogma they were asked to accept. Physical isolation forced the people towards the easy acceptance of a faith, whatever denomination it represented. The St Kildans were sincere in their beliefs and true to them in their actions. Damage was done, therefore, not only by the ministers but also by those who in their desire to improve the lot of the islanders tried to modify the expression of that sincerity. The St Kildans were frequently criticized for the religion they believed in, rarely praised for the ways in which they practised it.

In October 1889, the Reverend John Mackay took his leave of St Kilda. He was then over seventy years old. Behind him lay the manse that had been his home for twenty-four years, and the little church which had recently been given proper pews for the first time, but which, like religious teaching on Hirta, was in a deplorable state of disrepair. The St Kildans wept as Mackay hobbled down to board the boat that would take him back to the mainland of his birth. As they helped him into the rowing boat that would ferry him to the steamer, he remarked, 'I think it is time I was leaving them now.'

Things changed very much for the better under his successor. The Reverend Angus Fiddes who arrived at St Kilda in the same year as Mackay left, was the first in a line of enlightened envoys of the Church. In the main, the improvement was due to much younger men being sent out and the fact that their incumbencies were short.

Under Fiddes the number of church services held on Sundays was reduced from three to two. The morning service was held from seven until nine o'clock and that in the evening from six until eight. His services, however, were of no set length in practice and often lasted anything up to three and three-quarter hours, which Heathcote in 1898 found 'rather trying to the patience'. But to the St Kildans religion was never trying. 'Little mites of five or six years old would sit through the whole performance', noted Heathcote, 'without even fidgeting, and even babies in arms seldom disturbed the peace of the congregation. I should say', he concluded, 'they are the most truly religious people I have ever come across, because they seem really devout and honestly believe their religion to be the most important part of their life.'

Fiddes was the last Free Church minister to serve on Hirta. His successors came as missionaries and were not ordained until after they had finished their tour of duty. Fiddes returned to the mainland in 1903, and first Lachlan MacLean and then John Fraser were sent by the Church. On 16 August 1906, Peter MacLachlan and his industrious young bride came to St Kilda.

Peter MacLachlan was an evangelist whose ideas were influenced by the work of Moody and Sankey. He was born on the Isle of Mull and had studied law. His first thought was to emigrate to Canada, but forces natural as well as supernatural made him change his plans and think about becoming a missionary instead. His wife, Ann, was a striking woman, tall with auburn hair and very blue eyes. Born in Haddington in East Lothian, she received her education south of the border at Lincoln and had spent several years teaching small children in York before at the age of twenty-five she met and married Peter.

Ann MacLachlan was the first wife to live in the manse since the days of Reverend Neil Mackenzie, and on taking up residence she soon found there was much to be done. She spent many of those first days making little white curtains for the dining-room in the manse. She brought to the house a feminine touch that helped drive out the bare austerity that had typified it in earlier days.

'We have been very busy', she wrote in her diary, 'unpacking all our boxes and getting things into order. We have people coming to see us every day and all who come bring as a pair of fulmars, plucked and ready for the pot.' As was customary, the new missionary and his wife were to be readily supplied by their congregation with what little produce was available. 'It was rather a puzzle to me before I went to know how the larder was to be filled,' she recalled in a lecture she later gave to the YMCA, 'but once there it was wonderful how, day by day, with ease dinner was provided. There were lots of sheep, which we bought for twelve shillings each, fine black-faced sheep. We could get these from September to New Year. We used as much as we could fresh and salted the rest for a standby.

'Then we had a lot of ducks and hens,' she continued, 'which came in nicely, and any amount of fish – the pick of the sea – halibut, turbot, soles, all sorts sent in by the trawlers and deep-sea liners, which were very often in the bay . . . Sometimes we too were able to help these poor men who perhaps had had bad fishings and had been unable through stress of weather to get home. They would come ashore and would have to get necessary meal, sugar, salt, mutton, etc., and which they would bring back to us on their return. Our groceries, of course, we had to take with us. We had a year's supply each summer as we went. Captains of vessels were often very thoughtful and would send ashore a supply of beef, fresh fruit or other dainties which one would not think much of on the mainland but which in St Kilda were luxuries indeed.'

Ann MacLachlan also made her own butter while on St Kilda. Peter had purchased a cow before leaving for St Kilda and had had it shipped over. The glebe, attached to the manse, was worked by the missionary himself and when the grass was cut, it was stored in a nearby cleit for the winter. There was much besides religion to keep a young couple busy.

The St Kildans in the beginning were somewhat wary of their new missionary. 'Children fearfully stiff and shy,' wrote Ann in her diary on 26 August 1906. 'Good congregations and singing slightly better than on previous Sunday. Duine (Mrs MacLachlan's nickname for her husband) asked one man to pray and he wanted a tremendous amount of pressing. He refused three or four times, but he was pressed all round by his wife and several others and at last did pray. It seems he only wanted to be persuaded. It was too funny.'

MacLachlan held two services every Sunday, as the Reverend Fiddes had done. The only difference was that the morning service began much later, at eleven o'clock. The attendance of every islander was still demanded, and if any were absent they would be called upon by the congregation after the service to give good reasons for not attending.

From half past four until half past five, the missionary and his wife took Sunday School. On Sunday evenings after they had eaten, they took it upon themselves to visit the sick and elderly.

Ann, however, was frequently worried by her husband's narrow-mindedness. 'Cross with Duine as he slept all night in the chair,' she wrote in her diary, one October evening. 'I can't help getting cross with him. He seems to have *no* inclination to improve his mind, and he reads so little, which keeps him small in mind, but he can, or will, not see this.' The religion preached was nevertheless more enlightened and smiles once again came to the faces of the islanders. 'If Sands was correct in his statement, then things must have changed very much for the better,' wrote Nicol in 1903 of a St Kildan Sunday, 'for apart from the fact they will do no work on Sunday, I saw no trace of this wretched state of affairs. They walk to church in leisurely fashion like rational beings. When the service was over I photographed them leaving the church, and instead of scowls, I only received smiles and no one objected in the least.'

By the summer of 1909, Peter MacLachlan had completed his three-year term on St Kilda. His wife's first child had been born in April. It was the first child to live at the manse for nearly a hundred years, but by no means the last.

Donald Cameron, his wife and their children came to Hirta in 1919. Born in Argyll and brought up in Ballachulish, Donald had decided to become a missionary. He was sent first by the United Free Church of Scotland to the Hebrides. He met his wife, who was born on Uist, when he worked at the local Faith Mission.

After they were married, the Camerons moved to Stornoway, where Donald worked as a missionary assistant to the Reverend Roderick Morrison of the local United Free High Church. But when the authorities in Edinburgh asked him if he would be prepared to go to St Kilda, Donald and his wife, together with their two daughters, Mary, not yet six years old, and Christina, just four, agreed to go.

It had been decided before they left for St Kilda that it would be a dual appointment. Donald was made responsible for the islanders' spiritual welfare, and his wife, who had been a teacher before she got married, was charged with the education of the children of Village Bay. The authorities, however, had agreed that Donald Cameron would also be allowed to teach. As it worked out, it was he who regularly rang the school bell in the morning and led the class into the little schoolroom where he began the day with a lesson in Scripture.

The impressions of life at the manse proved lasting for Mary Cameron. 'The house was partly furnished,' she writes. 'I remember in the living-room some chairs, a gate-lag table, and an enormous horsehair covered sofa, which scratched the backs of one's legs, when one sat on it!' The room appeared to be full of books, most of which formed part of the library that the Coats family had given the people of St Kilda. Some bound volumes of the more popular periodicals of the time were also stored in the oak bookcase that practically covered one wall. Volumes of *Sunday at Home* and *The Quiver* helped pass the long hours of winter.

Above the mantelpiece there was a portrait of Queen Victoria, who had died eighteen years before the Cameron family went to St Kilda. On another wall hung a picture entitled *The Squire's Daughter*, which depicted a young lady in riding habit, clutching a horse's bridle. The living-room was one of only two rooms in the house that had wallpaper: the walls of the remaining rooms were lined with wood which was either painted or varnished.

There was a deep cupboard in the main room of the house that contained mysteries for Mary Cameron and her sister. Their parents kept the Christmas presents they purchased every summer on the top shelf. Here too was kept the store of sweets, of Mackintosh's Toffee-de-Luxe and Sharp's Super-Kreem Toffee, that would be strictly rationed out to last the year.

The kitchen was a small room at the back of the house. The manse had a cold water tap, one of two on the island. The other was in the factor's house. On one occasion, the pipe bringing the water from the well that lay a few yards away burst. There were no plumbers on the island, so the missionary had to roll up his sleeves and try to fix it himself. He dug a hole to expose the leak, and built a box of wood round it which he filled with cement.

In a cupboard off the kitchen were stored the supplies of food that would keep the missionary and his family alive for six months or more. 'This meant', writes Mary Cameron, 'several sacks of flour and oatmeal; a hundredweight bag of sugar; tea by the stone; dozens of tins of syrup, treacle, meat and milk; butter in large tins prepared for export; whole cheeses; hams and bladders of lard; tins of biscuits and quantities of dried fruit, jam, and so on.'

The missionaries of later years ordered their provisions from Coopers, the grocers. Orders were placed with the company's Export Department, a department which was primarily there to service the wants of Scots scattered round the Empire. Mrs Munro, who succeeded Mrs Cameron at the manse, recalls how she ordered her supplies. 'I think I got about ten bolls of flour and three to four of oatmeal. Nurse Barclay said to me, count how many breakfasts and dinners and teas and the rest of it, and then order accordingly. We had to get our butter in airtight sealed tins and you took your butter out the night before – so much for the day – and put it into a bowl of water.' Although there was always the possibility that a passing ship or trawler would be able to supply some food, a winter of total isolation had to be allowed for. 'You were told when you went there', says Mrs Munro, 'you had to take in your stores from August to do you till the end of May.'

The missionary was paid £190 a year by the United Free Church of Scotland. The sum was paid quarterly and the missionary left it to his bank on the mainland to see to paying the bills.

Missionaries' wives became excellent bakers. Mrs Cameron is remembered by her children for her scones and oatcakes. 'We had healthy appetites', says Mary Cameron, 'and I don't think we ever got tired of them. I can see my mother yet, with her white apron on, toasting the edge of the scones before a bright red fire, after taking them off the girdle.' Because it was difficult to make, bread was normally reserved for high days and holidays.

The manse had several outhouses which were used by the missionary to store fuel and foodstuffs. One was used exclusively for coal, another contained as many cans of paraffin as were needed in order to light up the manse at night, and a third was used to store carcasses of mutton, purchased from the islanders, and a barrel of herrings.

Every missionary kept a cow. Donald Cameron brought over his from Uist, and when she died he purchased a cow that at one time had belonged to a previous missionary and had been bought from him by one of the St Kildans. In addition, every missionary had to be able to work his arable land. Fortunately for Donald Cameron, he could employ a wheelbarrow to help him. It was the only one on the island, and apart from the toy pram that his little girls played with, was the only implement on the island that had a wheel.

'A Sabbath well spent brings a week of content, and strength for the toils of tomorrow,' claimed Donald Cameron. 'But a Sabbath profaned, whatsoever is gained, is a certain forerunner of sorrow.' The Sabbath on Hirta was never to change. Observance was still strict.

Donald Cameron continued to hold two services each Sunday, with a Sunday School for the children in the afternoon. Mrs Cameron took the younger children, while her husband saw to the teenagers. Hymns and psalms were sung in both English and Gaelic, but the children were taught to remember portions of Scripture and the Shorter Catechism in Gaelic only.

Every male communicant of over six months' standing was expected to attend the Wednesday Prayer Meeting and the Monday service held every month. 'Every member in the Church', recalls Neil Ferguson, 'had to take his turn for a prayer on a Wednesday or a Monday. The missionary, he read a chapter and then the precentor sang two or three lines and then he would ask more of the members for a prayer and then another two or three verses again. Another fellow, another prayer – and that's how it was carrying on.'

If spiritually things on Hirta changed little, the Church at least, damaged during the war, became a more heartening place of worship. The interior was lined with wood, walls as well as ceiling, and new pews were installed and varnished brown. A set of brass duplex lamps with tall chimneys and opal globes were fitted into wall brackets to throw light on the proceedings during evening services. The church was also presented with a pulpit (the largest in the Western Isles), and Donald Cameron himself made a desk and seat for the precentor. He even turned his hand to making a collection box, which was hooked on to a pew near the main door.

A special pew for the family at the manse was also installed, set at right angles to the others, from which the Cameron girls could observe the little congregation. The men and the boys of the island traditionally occupied the inner end of the pews, and the women the outside. When the service was over, the men remained seated until the women and girls had left the church. The girls on the island were made responsible for scrubbing the new wooden floor and keeping the place neat and tidy. 'It was a very simple place,' recalls Mary Cameron, 'rather austere, which matched the simple, robust faith of the folk who filled it each Sunday. There was no heating, but I don't remember that we ever complained of the cold. The St Kilda folk were grand churchgoers.'

The missionaries, of course, were not ordained. Every summer it was necessary for the Church to send a minister from the mainland to baptize, to marry, and hold communion. While he remained on the island he was a guest at the manse. When Dugald Munro was missionary, the minister held services every day for five days. 'It started at nine o'clock,' remembers Mrs Munro. 'That was a prayer meeting which was conducted by my husband. Each islander would get up and say something planned – a prayer, you see. There was another I think at twelve o'clock and another one in the evening. There were services every day until Monday. I think I counted fourteen, there were three or four a day anyway.' From the Thursday to the Monday, the usual preparatory and post-communion services were held. On the Friday, however, known as the Men's Day, the elders and other male communicants would speak on 'the Question', as was common in the Highlands and Islands. The meeting was held in the church, and each member would speak in turn, remarking on a text set by one of their number.

Before the visiting missionary arrived on the island, however, the missionaries normally took their leave of the St Kildans to return to the mainland for a short holiday. It was always a welcome, if brief, return, and gave the missionary and his wife a chance to purchase clothes and household goods as well as meeting up with friends. During the missionary's absence, the precentor took the pulpit. In the days of Donald Cameron, either William Macdonald or Norman Mackinnon conducted the services.

When Donald Cameron returned to the mainland for good in 1926, the Church sent Dugald Munro to replace him. Fifty years of Munro's life were spent preaching to those who inhabited the outer isles and other fringes of British society. 'The last one we had', says Neil Ferguson, 'was a nice wee fellow, but they were all the same. Come to church three times a day. If you don't turn up next Sunday, you'll be up – "What's wrong with you, are you badly?" and all this. You had to make an excuse. And the old folk, they wouldn't let you do a thing on a Sunday. My grandpa seen me picking up sticks – we were just wee laddies – out in the fields and he would shout at me to come home. You wouldn't get playing or doing anything on a Sunday. Nothing doing on a Sunday but the church.'

The old inherited ways were never to die out. While on St Kilda, the islanders never challenged the authority of either the belief or its numerous exponents. It would have taken more time than was to prove available to the St Kildans for the effects of over a hundred years of strict religious instruction to mellow, let alone fade away.

When they came to the mainland, the young St Kildans in particular were to abandon the fervour of their forefathers. When the islanders left behind their Bibles in the Church at the evacuation, all but the elderly turned their backs on a form of religion that had so blatantly restricted their happiness.

7
The far-flung dominie

There should be a school in every parish of Scotland. This idea was put forward as early as 1560 by John Knox and his fellow Reformers. It was proposed that an elementary education should be provided for children up to the age of eight and that a grammar school course in Latin be given until the age of twelve. The church revenues were to be used to build schools, pay the stipends of teachers, and provide bursaries for poor students. At the time little was done about it. The Scots nobles may have read the *First Book of Discipline* but were loath to part with any of the newly-won spoils of the old church for the sake of educating the masses. It was not until nearly a century and a half later that they were to think schools worth paying for.

In 1696 an Act of the Revolution Parliament of Scotland decreed there should be a school set up in those parishes that did not already have one. Under the Act, the chief landowners in the country were to provide accommodation suitable for use as a schoolroom and pay the salary of a schoolmaster. Despite the passing of an Act, many of the far-flung parishes of the Highlands and Islands were still denied a 'dominie'.

In 1701 a group of gentlemen met in Edinburgh to see what could be done. They established the Society in Scotland for the Propagating of Christian Knowledge and appealed to the public for subscriptions. Queen Anne looked favourably upon their purpose and eight years later granted the society Letters Patent under the Great Seal. With Royal patronage the SSPCK made rapid progress. By 1711, they were financing and managing a dozen schools in the Highlands and islands of Scotland. By the turn of the century more than three hundred schools were in their care. One of the first schools to be set up in 1709 was on St Kilda, and Alexander Buchan, already acting as missionary to the people, was appointed as schoolmaster of their children.

Alexander Buchan taught the children of Village Bay for over twenty years according to the principles laid down by the society. The Letters Patent of the SSPCK decreed he was on St Kilda 'To teach to read, especially the holy Scriptures, and other good and pious Books, also to teach Writing, Arithmetick, and such like Degrees of Knowledge, in the Highlands, Islands, and remote corners of Scotland, and in popish and infidel Parts of the World, and to use such Means for instructing the People in the Christian reformed Protestant Religion, as may be competent.' Although the society could not afford to provide Buchan with either a school or a home to live in during his stay, other than a cottage similar to that lived in by the St Kildans, they provided the schoolchildren with schoolbooks, Gaelic Bibles and paper. By 1727 the island possessed a library of fifty-six books 'gifted by the Society to the Church of St Kilda'. Nor did the children have to pay for their education – the society's reward was that they worked hard.

The children had to pray in the morning and in the evening. School began at seven o'clock in the morning and went on until eleven. After a break for lunch, lessons were taught from one o'clock in the afternoon until five in the evening. Such were the school hours between 1 February and 1 October. During the winter months the work day was limited by the daylight hours. If the children had to be diligent, and there were never more than twenty-eight at one time on the island, the schoolmaster had to possess a degree of calling rarely expected on the mainland. As the society's rules said, the teacher had to be 'a person of Piety, Loyalty, Prudence, Gravity, competent knowledge and Literature and endued with other Christian Qualifications suited to that Station'.

The society sent inspectors to examine the work done in their schools. In 1728, the Reverend Daniel Macaulay went to St Kilda and sent his findings to Edinburgh. 'I have heard Mr Buchan preach,' wrote Macaulay, 'and I found him pretty well read in the Scriptures but otherwise of low qualifications. He is fitter for this place than any other person I know.

'After the sermon I asked Mr Buchan and the people several questions, and got satisfying answers. There were only two persons that Mr Buchan had taught to read. But it would be a great hardship upon the poor people now in their dismal circumstances to take Mr Buchan from them. The said person is getting very old, and not every one will go there to succeed him. I suggest that Douglas Buchan, now in Edinburgh, should be bred to be a Schoolmaster in this island.' The society for some reason did not take up Macaulay's suggestion, and when Buchan died in 1729 they sent out Roderick McLennan the following year to replace him. When he left, the Reverend John MacDonald took upon himself the task of teaching Hirta's little children.

Under the guidance of the 'Apostle of the North' the principles underlying the education of the St Kildans were still dictated by the Church. As such the community was not unique, but perhaps the isolation of the island made the people more God-fearing and less sophisticated. Perhaps too, the challenge of educating so remote and so unique a people attracted missionaries with more zeal than was good for them.

In 1811, the Gaelic School Society was founded and took care of the education of the St Kildans until practically the turn of the century. In the care of the society's Gaelic-speaking teacher were forty-four scholars – twenty-six males and eighteen females. Not all were children : six of the male pupils were between twenty and forty years old, and three of them were married. Of the female pupils, six were between twenty and thirty.

But despite the numbers attending school, few learnt much. In September 1822, the Reverend John MacDonald on a visit to the island discovered that only one St Kildan, John Ferguson, could read, although a year later he was able to note with a certain pride, 'considering that the school commenced only in June last, the progress was truly pleasing . . . some of the grown up people . . . already read some Psalms and have begun the New Testament'. The St Kildans were eager to learn. 'The people', he wrote, 'seem to be sensible of his (the schoolmaster's) worth, and show him every due attention.' What learning the St Kildans possessed had up till then mostly been passed on by word of mouth from one generation to another. English, although taught by Alexander Buchan, still remained a language yet to be mastered by the generations of islanders following his tour of duty on the island. Those who had learned English in their youth rarely had a need to speak it, so they forgot it.

A comprehensive education was not to come to the islanders until the end of the nineteenth century. From the time of Mac-Donald until the advent of the first schoolmaster in 1884, the people of Hirta received a sporadic education wholly dependent on the attitude and interest shown in them by the minister. In 1830, there was only one woman on the island who could read and write a little. When the Census of 1861 was taken by Alexander Grigor, he found that only two islanders, neither of whom was a St Kildan by birth, could speak English. Only two men, apart from the catechist who also acted as registrar, were able to sign their names. In the various records which had been kept on the island since 1856 (when St Kilda became a registration district for births, deaths, and marriages), the islanders still signed by making a mark. Nevertheless, Grigor found that the catechist was trying to instruct the islanders in Gaelic reading and, to a lesser extent, writing. His niece was trying to teach the women sewing and knitting. No one up till that time had thought of teaching them how to hold a needle, let alone how to wash clothes properly.

Even as late as 1877, there was only one woman on the island, a married woman from Ross-shire, who understood English. All the adults, however, could read the Gaelic Bible, and one or two could repeat the Psalms by heart. McDiarmid wrote in 1877, 'They all have a pretty fair idea of number and dates in Gaelic, and know the value of current coins.' John Sands, in an earlier visit, had heard one old man mutter in Gaelic, 'Units, tens, hundreds, thousands,' as he deciphered the year 1875.

The main preoccupation, however, of those on the mainland who sought to improve the lot of the people on Britain's loneliest isle, was a desire to get rid of 'the Gaelic nuisance'. To the liberal-minded on the mainland, the fact that the islanders could speak only Gaelic was seen as the main obstacle that stood between them and their enjoyment of the fruits of progress. 'It is difficult to discover', remarked John MacCulloch who visited St Kilda in 1819, 'what countervailing advantages can arise from the cultivation of a rude language, now inadequate to the improved state of society, in which no books have been written, and of which the literary value is confined to a few traditional poems. For philological purposes, it is sufficient if it exists in the libraries of the grammarian and antiquary.'

'Probably the most beneficial influence', wrote George Seton in 1878, 'that could be brought to bear upon the St Kildans would be of an educational kind . . . An energetic effort ought to be made to introduce a systematic course of instruction in English, with the view of the inhabitants enjoying the vast benefits which would inevitably arise.' The St Kildans could then, according to the respectable advocate from Edinburgh, 'enlarge their minds and subvert their prejudices by the perusal of English Literature'. The aim of the SSPCK was to help crush the way of life of the Gael. It failed to do so, but it did damage that culture. Those on the mainland had to be satisfied with instilling a knowledge of English, while turning a blind eye to a continuance of the Gaelic language. 'The English tongue and the Gaelic bible', writes M. J. Jones in *The Charity School Movement of the Eighteenth Century*, 'suggested two ways of escape from conditions which were fast becoming intolerable. Far from undermining the characteristic independence of the Highlanders, the Charity Schools provided them with the only means of translating it into effective action. To men of vigour and courage, the English Language offered a new world across the seas; to those who remained behind, the schools made possible independent access to the consolation of the Bible.' At that time education was in the hands of the Reverend Mackay. In his care were the islanders' six or seven children who were of an age to learn.

'But the man is old and has a disordered liver,' wrote John Sands, 'and perhaps does not see the importance of giving the young a better secular education.' The people's knowledge of the Bible could not be faulted. Some St Kildans could recite whole chapters of it by heart. 'Their secular education has been less cared for,' continued Sands, 'and indeed the difficulties of imparting it are very great as there poor prisoners have no inducements to learn. Why should they trouble themselves learning to write when they are cut off from correspondence with all the world? Why should they learn English when in the course of a year, they may only see two or three strangers who use that language and then only for an hour or two?'

A formal education was not offered to the people of St Kilda until 1884. Although the Act of 1872 put an end to the parochial system of education throughout most of Scotland, and laid down that schools in future should be managed by school boards elected by those who paid rates and supported by grants from the Government, St Kilda was too small and too remote to be immediately catered for under the new Act. An application to educate the children of Hirta was lodged with Miss Abercrombie, Secretary of the Ladies' Association of the Highland Society, and in the summer of 1884 Mr Campbell became the first schoolmaster proper on St Kilda. A room in the factor's house was made available by the island's owner to be used as a schoolroom, and for the first time in the island's history education was removed from the iron grip of the Free Church of Scotland.

Each schoolmaster was contracted to serve a year on the island, from the end of one summer through to the beginning of the next.

Hugh McCallum succeeded Mr Campbell, and in 1886 George Murray was appointed to help break down the barrier of language that to many appeared to isolate St Kilda even more than geography. At three o'clock in the afternoon of 5 June 1886, George Murray received a telegram. He had recently graduated with a Master of Arts degree from Aberdeen University, and had returned to his native village of Rogart in Sutherlandshire to await instructions from the Ladies' Association concerning his first appointment as schoolmaster to the children of Hirta. The telegram informed him to leave as soon as possible for Dunvegan on the Isle of Skye, from where on the following Monday he would catch a boat bound for St Kilda. 'I felt not a little sad', he wrote in his diary, 'leaving home on that occasion as I did not expect being back for a twelve-month at least, nor did I know what might befall me on such a long and perilous journey.' Along with his books, he set off for St Kilda with enough clothes and food to last him until spring the following year.

One of George Murray's major tasks was to salt away the meat that was sent to him on the last steamer of the year from the mainland to see him through his period of exile. There were also the dried and tinned groceries. 'On counting,' he wrote in his diary on 25 September 1886, 'I found that between Mrs McKinlay (the housekeeper) and myself there are today in the house 22lb. of tea, 96lb. of sugar, 21lb. of coffee and 2 tins of cocoa. We trust we may have health to consume it during the next nine months.' Traditionally, the St Kildans supplied the schoolhouse with peats for the fire, and they were generous in sharing their mutton with the schoolmaster as well as the missionary.

Also to arrive on the last boat of the year were the books that would be given out to the most promising pupils as prizes on Christmas Day. Even as late as 1884, Christmas Day to the St Kildans was celebrated on 5 January and on that day, after the prize-giving, the children were given ten days' holiday.

Apart from teaching the children how to read, write, add, and subtract, Murray also started a singing school on the island, in an attempt to improve the quality of voices on Sundays. 'I intend holding it once a week,' he wrote in October, 'to learn them some tunes.' Among the hymns taught was *I love to think of the Heavenly Land*. As they struggled not only with the tune, but the thought behind it, he remarked, 'God grant that it may be blessed to them.'

Murray was one of the few educated people on the island. As such he not only saw to the needs of the children, but acted as letter-writer for the islanders who wished to communicate with friends on the mainland. He also helped them with their accounts as they calculated their rent in terms of cloth and feathers, and tried to work out whether they had got value for money from the factor for their produce. He was also a source of knowledge of the world beyond – a man from whose mouth came information and advice, and who could patiently correct the false impressions frequently left in the islanders' minds by tourists.

During the winter children kept proper school hours. The only exception was when someone died, when the school would be closed for anything up to a week. Although Murray himself occupied the factor's house, classes were held during the winter months in the 'Big House', the manse. Each morning, school was summoned by the ringing of a brass handbell donated to the island in 1832 by Peter Ewing of Glasgow.

There was little to stimulate the mind of a young schoolmaster on St Kilda. Thoughts of home were never very far away. Christmas Day on the island was a particularly thoughtful day for George Murray. 'Forenoon snowing heavily,' he wrote in his diary. 'It being Saturday I wished to exercise my limbs by taking a walk, for the "New Style" is not kept in St Kilda, so there was nothing out of the usual routine to take place. On reaching the tops of the hills, it was just the thing for Christmas, heavy flakes of snow falling fast and thick, while all around was already white and the small hamlet below seemed asleep under the thick atmosphere. What a contrast to the stir and bustle of a town on such a day as this.'

'I cannot help reflecting', he continued, 'upon the way and place I used to spend my Christmas holidays – in Ballater with my friends, how happy. This year I cannot as much as hear whether all my friends are spared to enjoy this season of the year as happily as usual. Now my thoughts turn homewards. How are they? May God bless them and all those who contributed to my happiness when with them.' By then, Murray had spent six months on St Kilda: he was to spend a further six months before a successor was sent from the Ladies' Association to relieve him.

In June 1888 John Ross was appointed 'dominie'. By then there were fourteen schoolchildren on St Kilda – ten boys and four girls. One boy and two of the girls had just begun the First Book of English. One boy had progressed to the Second Book, and three others were working with the Illustrated Third Reader. A boy and a girl had moved on to the Illustrated Fourth, while the remaining schoolchildren were either working with the Illustrated Sixth Reader or studying beyond that level. Besides grammar, the children learnt some geography, history, arithmetic and composition in the upper forms, and the one boy who had progressed beyond the Sixth English Reader was starting to learn some Latin – a language that had been banned on St Kilda since the Reformation under the strict orders of the SSPCK. With so few children on so many levels, it was a problem to teach them all. If at all possible the 'dominie' would divide his pupils into three classes – a Senior, an Intermediate, and a Junior class. Although the age-range of each class depended largely upon the progress of individual children, the Senior Class generally comprised the eleven- to fourteen-year-olds, and the Intermediate and Junior classes held within their ranks the nine- to ten-year-olds and the six- to eight-year-olds respectively. Some of the children, Ross found, had a very good ear for music, a result no doubt of George Murray's music classes. Some of the older children could speak English quite fluently, although with a slight lisp. 'One would be apt to suppose', wrote Ross, 'that they would be prejudiced against any foreign tongue but no, on the contrary, the success of the children in mastering the English gives great satisfaction to the parents. They are as bright as the children on the mainland, and do not take long picking up what is explained to them.'

'The school age in St Kilda was six,' recalls the Reverend Donald John Gillies, who himself was educated in Hirta at the turn of the century. 'You started at six and the standards, as they were called in those days, began at one and you could go as far as standard six . . . My parents were very anxious that all of us would get the education that was available at the school at that time, and they were very conscientious and saw that we went to school. I think that all the children went to school: there weren't many absentees in my day. You went as far as standard six, that was all that you could get. If you were able to assimilate it then that was your good luck.'

The children of St Kilda, however, had a lot to learn. Deprived of practically everything in the way of toys, all things were new to them. In 1888, Mr Campbell of Sunderland sent the children some toys – a few boxes of marbles, some tin whistles and some toy bagpipes. On first seeing them the children had no idea what

they were for. Dominie Ross had to show them how to play with
them. Slowly, and with a patience even greater than that expected
of a man of his profession on the mainland, the schoolmaster set
about his task of educating the little children of Hirta. But in
August 1889, John Ross's term of duty ended, and once again
education passed into the hands of the missionary. When he
boarded the steamer bound for his new appointment on the Island
of Uist, the children cried. 'Tears flowed copiously in all quarters,'
he wrote, 'and kerchiefs could be seen waving till the distance
became too great.'

In 1897 the masons and carpenters of Dunvegan came to build
a schoolhouse. The proprietor, MacLeod of MacLeod, and the
Church authorities had agreed that besides repairing the Church,
the time had come for the dominie to have his own domain. The
foundation stone for the building was laid with full honours, but
it was to take two summers before the schoolhouse was finished
and the little island kirk, with its floor levelled and boarded, had
been renovated out of all recognition. The schoolroom was a
bright, high-ceilinged room with large windows on two sides.
As the children had to do their work solely by the light of day,
it was essential that the windows should allow for the maximum
amount of light. The desks were of the old-fashioned long type,
and slates were provided for each child. 'There was always a big
coal fire on cold days,' writes Mary Cameron, 'and it was really
very cosy.'

By 1902 there were nineteen children attending school, of whom
all except eight were under fourteen years of age. By 1906, the
total number had risen to twenty-two and they were by this time
under the care of Mr MacLachlan, the missionary, and his wife.

With the arrival of Mr and Mrs MacLachlan, there began a new
era in the practical education of the people. The school opened
for the first time under their care on 4 September 1906. Under
their supervision, school began at ten o'clock in the morning and
went on until four o'clock in the afternoon, with an hour's break
for lunch. Mr, MacLachlan took the morning classes, while his
wife took those in the afternoon. Mrs MacLachlan's main ambition
was to teach the women to sew, and in the afternoon classes the
young girls and their mothers were taught how to make blouses,
undergarments, and dresses. Both found the islanders, especially
the young ones, quick to learn and keen for knowledge.

The schoolchildren of Hirta were subject to the same inspection of academic standards as was carried out in each school on the mainland. Every year, an inspector was sent to test the children. 'The inspector, Mr Beaton,' wrote Ann MacLachlan in her diary on 16 August 1906, 'came with us and inspected the school at seven o'clock in the morning . . . The children are very far back but answered fairly intelligently the questions about the poetry they had been learning during the year, *viz Waterloo* and *Lochiel's Warning*.'

By this time the responsibility for the education of the islanders had fallen to the Inverness County Education Authority. St Kilda's school was classed as the 'St Kilda Sub-School, conducted under Article 19 of the Scotch Code and is under Obbe Public School Harris for the purpose of that Article'. In the 1920s Murdo Morrison, then Director of Education for the County, made personal visits to the island to inspect the school. On one occasion, when the steamer bringing him to St Kilda arrived on a Sunday and the islanders refused to entertain an inspection on the Sabbath, the captain of the steamer, anxious to set sail from St Kilda as soon after midnight as possible, demanded of His Majesty's Inspector of Schools that he test the sleepy children of Hirta as soon as possible after the Sabbath had ended. The children had to be got out of their beds in the early hours of Monday morning.

Education was always a fairly haphazard affair on St Kilda. Not only did the children rarely obtain the benefit of having the same teacher year in, year out, but there were many years when there was no teacher at all. Similarly, school classes were always subject to the work that required to be done on the island, particularly in the summer months. When the crops had to be harvested or the sheep rooed, or the fulmars and gannets caught and prepared for eating during the winter months, school had to close. These were activities demanding the attention of the entire community: they were of more vital importance to survival.

The St Kilda School Log Book, now preserved by the Inverness-shire Education Authority, reads more like a record of the times school was closed than open. Whenever there was a death on St Kilda, school would close during the entire period of mourning. In October 1906 an entry in the Log Book reads, 'No school for three days owing to the sad death by drowning of Norman Gillies, one of the VI stream pupils. Great gloom over the island.' On 22 March 1909 the teacher noted, 'Great drowning accident: school closed for seven days.' During the First World War the school was closed for ten months. The entry for 10 December 1918 reads, 'School reopened today. No school had been held since the island was bombarded (by a German submarine) on 15 May. During most of that time the school had been occupied by a party from the naval station while their own premises have been repaired.'

In 1919, two new pupils joined the school desks of Hirta. They were Mary and Christina Cameron, the daughters of the then missionary, and hence teacher, Donald Cameron. At that time there were seventeen children on the school-roll, including the Cameron girls and Ian and Alexander Mackenzie, the two sons of the widowed district nurse on St Kilda. The Camerons were among the more enlightened educators of the people of St Kilda, and the girls received most of their 'schooling' from their mother, who did her best, by way of potted geraniums on the window ledges, to do away with the austerity forever associated with the St Kilda school-house. Mary remembers well that during gales on the island, she and her sister were not allowed to make the short journey from the manse to the school on their own. 'My father would wait', she wrote, 'for a lull between squalls then holding on to one another's hands we would run to the shelter of the school. Otherwise we would have been blown off our feet.' Owing to the mails to the island being delivered so erratically, Mary Cameron's papers of the qualifying and bursary examinations for Inverness Academy failed to arrive on time – a situation over which she lost little sleep. As the population of the island dwindled, so did the number of children needing to be educated. By the time the Camerons took their leave of the island in 1926, there were only eight attending school.

Education on St Kilda was limited, as was education at that time in most remote areas. The St Kildan children depended solely on the quality of the missionary sent out primarily to cultivate and stimulate the people's religious fervour. But the St Kildans were largely deprived of the more practical aspects of education. Although their knowledge of the English language proved of great use to them in their new tourist trade, enabling them to converse freely with visitors, learn about the mainland, and thus lose part of their feeling of isolation, their general education was typical of its age and of the minds of those who thought that the ability to read and write at once converted the ordinary man into an educated being, capable almost magically of improving his standard of living. Those aspects of education that might have improved their lot in real terms were never made available to them. They were taught nothing of how to improve their methods of spinning and weaving so that their cloth might be of better quality and hence find a more sure market on the mainland. The men were taught little of how to increase the yield of the small amount of arable land available to them, how to use fertilizers to improve their crops, or how to rear stronger cattle and healthier lambs.

The missionary and his wife occasionally attempted to teach the adults new methods. Mrs Munro, wife of the last missionary, taught new methods of knitting. 'It wasn't that they needed knitting,' she recalls, 'but the thing was that they only knitted gloves and socks, so that I thought it was time they started knitting suits.' The Mackinnon family at that time were short of clothes, so as well as the knitting of jerseys, Mrs Munro also encouraged the knitting of woollen trousers for the smaller children. She showed Mrs Mackinnon how to give the wool an extra twist in the spinning, because it was otherwise too soft for such garments.

As it was, the little education they received merely encouraged the St Kildans to take up employment on the mainland before and after the evacuation. If improvements were possible in the way in which they led their lives on the island, education did little towards providing them. Instead it showed the St Kildans that there were easier, perhaps better, ways of living elsewhere.

Ignorance may have bred bliss: education bred dissatisfaction. When questioned by the schoolmaster, even as early as 1888, the majority of those attending school were decidedly in favour of leaving the island as soon as they were able. Education continued to make the St Kildans, especially the young, think in terms of leaving home in order to better themselves. It undermined the struggle for survival on the island. It seems that St Kilda had to be abandoned before educationalists realized the mistakes that had been made, and themselves became enlightened by the experiences of those very people whom they had set out to enlighten. It was not until 1945, when the Alness Report on the Highlands was published, that the government ultimately accepted responsibility. 'Whether the system of instruction', concluded the report, 'which has proved satisfactory in other parts of the country is best suited to the specific circumstances of the crofting communities, it is difficult to say.' By then, much of the damage had been done.

8

A chance to turn a penny

It was the first steamship the St Kildans had ever seen. When the *Vulcan* from Glasgow steamed into Village Bay on Saturday, 28 July 1838, with a full complement of passengers and a brass band on board, the islanders rushed to the manse to inform the minister, the Reverend Neil Mackenzie, that a 'ship on fire' was approaching. When the brass band struck up, the St Kildans fled to shelter among the rocks. The ministers, missionaries and school-masters were not the only people responsible for bringing St Kilda closer to civilization. Many others, set alight by the discovery of a primitive society within the bounds of the British Isles, sought to visit St Kilda, and in a short space of time converted a quiet, lonely outpost into a national curiosity.

Only a few during the eighteenth and early nineteenth centuries, when travel was thought the best way of increasing knowledge and broadening the mind, made the often treacherous journey to St Kilda in open boats and private yachts. Set amid what must be the most fantastic natural spectacle to be seen in British waters, these fortunate early travellers found a unique human settlement, divorced for centuries from the progress of civilization. In 1838 for the first time a large number of people experienced for them-selves the sights and sounds of St Kilda. A passenger on board the *Vulcan* was moved to write to a friend, 'I am at length, thank God, arrived on *terra firma* in St Kilda, the place which of all other places within the British dominions, I longed most to see; and I had not certainly been led to form a false or exaggerated concep-tion on it; nay, the half had not been told me.'

St Kilda had stood still for centuries, a remnant of a feudal society that had long since died out on the mainland. The people themselves had stood still. They spoke a peculiar variation of the Gaelic tongue, and no one knew the reason why; they were a people who scraped a living from the sea birds that soared in the air above them. In fact, some of the birds were unique to St Kilda: the fulmar petrel was found nowhere else in the British Isles until the middle of the nineteenth century. The St Kildans lived on an iceberg of rock that was all that could be found in the great ocean dividing Britain from America. In the period of history following the publication of Darwin's *On the Origin of the Species*, the movement to seek out the natural and primitive gained added impetus. St Kilda became the Ultima Thule of Victorian and, later, Edwardian Britain, where lived the Noble Savage.

The discovery of such a place, besides being a personal revelation, was worthy of imparting to a public who knew increasingly of little else but their own unexciting, urban existence. The island, and above all the people who lived on it, began to receive far more attention than either properly deserved. Hardly a week went by without some piece of news or anecdote of a recent voyage being printed by some newspaper or learned journal. A glance at any bibliography for St Kilda is ample proof that the place and the people became not just a fascination, but an obsession to those on the mainland.

Up until the middle of the nineteenth century, most of the tourists were gentlemen of standing, who went to St Kilda in private yachts. A voyage to St Kilda was normally the highlight of a leisurely summer cruise round the Western Isles of Scotland. From about 1830, St Kilda was regularly visited in the months of June, July, and August.

In July 1860, the Duke of Atholl visited St Kilda in HMS *Porcupine*. Much to the amazement of his fellow travellers, the Duke insisted on eating St Kildan food and spent a night in house Number Nine, Main Street, the home of Norman Macdonald. Seventeen years later, the islanders still pointed out with great pride the house that once had sheltered a titled man.

Not all the visitors arrived in Village Bay aboard such glamorous craft as those transporting Dukes. When George Atkinson decided to visit St Kilda in June 1831, he and his eight companions made the journey in a three-ton, eighteen-foot yawl, crewed by three stout men of Harris. 'Our boat as I observed was a small one considering the distance she had to go in the open sea,' he wrote, 'but the fact is, the Atlantic comes so heavily in the bay at St Kilda if the wind has any south in it, that you must either go in a vessel large enough to ride with safety in any swell, or in a boat small enough to be hauled up on the beach while you remain there. We chose the latter.'

As suggested to him by a friend who had made the crossing before, Atkinson and his party took with them two or three heavy blankets and some pillows. They would have to sleep rough, in an open boat. Also taken on board were five bottles of whisky, a cask of water, a bag of oatmeal, and a selection of cold meats and oatcakes to feed them during their long voyage to St Kilda. 'We had the after part of the boat filled with straw for sleeping on', wrote Atkinson, 'and a fire in an iron pot forward. Thus provided we went merrily on our way to St Kilda, or Hirta as they call it; an island which by many has been described as all but un-attainable and attended with so many dangers and difficulties to reach, that our departure was looked on as a rare and memorable circumstance by the natives of Harris.'

The invention of the steamship changed all that. Boats could now go farther afield with greater surety. Steam, above all, brought travel and mobility to the middle-class Victorians at a price hitherto undreamed of. Even the lower classes who now, by law, were entitled to paid holidays for the first time, could venture forth and explore. The St Kilda tourist trade began when John McCallum welcomed people on board his steamship *Dunara Castle* for a voyage to 'The Romantic Western Isles and lone St Kilda'. A fare of £9 entitled the traveller to cabin-class comfort and full board for ten days, and for the first time the general public could make the perilous voyage to St Kilda in the reasonable comfort afforded to them by a 240-ton ship. The *Dunara Castle*, with some thirty passengers on board, left the 'Tail o' the Bank', just outside Glasgow, on her maiden voyage in June 1877. Having called in at Oban, Dunvegan, and several other places on the way, the steamer dropped anchor in Village Bay on 2 July.

But even for the steamer tourists, a landing on Hirta was frequently impossible because of heavy seas. Many were to be disappointed, although the challenge made for determination and added to the allure of the place. For those who were able to get close enough to land, it was always a difficult business. The rocks were so slippery at the landing-place that visitors had to scramble ashore. Lady Mackenzie of Gairloch who went to St Kilda in 1853 found landing on the island a somewhat disconcerting experience. 'I had been told there was but one small flat stone on which one could land,' she wrote, 'and that the natives would pull me up from it. This is not quite the case. There are twenty to thirty yards of shore on which you might put foot, but there is one spot more convenient than the rest and yet not altogether good, for the rock is covered with seaweed of the most slippery sort and you are almost sure to tumble on your nose.'

There was no jetty on the island until 1906, and even then the steamers were too large to come any nearer than a quarter of a mile from the shore. The St Kildans soon saw a financial advantage in ferrying visitors to and from their ships by charging them a shilling each. The journey in a small rowing boat from the steamer to the shore was frequently hazardous, but even more dangerous was landing, which in an age of long skirts and demure manners was often less graceful an exercise than the ladies of the party might have wished.

'It frequently happened, if the sea were choppy,' writes Mary Cameron, 'that passengers being ferried ashore in the small boats were drenched with spray; and my mother would have to come to the rescue with dry clothes.' For the missionary and his wife, it was an exciting day when the steamer came into the bay. There would be the chance to get the news from the mainland. 'On one occasion', she recalls, 'an elderly lady appeared at the door, very wet, and my mother took her in and lent her garments until her own were dried. It had been a rough crossing, she said. She had got into conversation with the captain who had enquired if she were a good sailor. She had answered, airily, that she had sailed round the world. "Ah, yes, madam," he had remarked, "but you haven't been to St Kilda yet!" '

'The first thing to be done', advised John Ross to those contemplating visiting St Kilda, 'after getting fairly balanced, is to shake hands right and left with all you meet.' The women would be lined up on the shore by the landing place on one side of the pathway, the men lined up on the other. 'Pay no attention to the welcome of the army of dogs', continued Ross, 'with which you are escorted up the bank. Their bark is certainly worse than their bite.' The St Kildans were very reticent. 'They didn't talk,' remembers Willie Clelland, who worked as purser on board the *Dunara Castle*. 'You had to speak first. They were very, very shy, particularly the women and the children.'

The *Dunara Castle* was later joined in making regular summer trips to St Kilda by the *Lady Ambrosine* and the *Hebridean*, both of which belonged to Martin Orme. In 1898, the *Hebridean* was replaced by the SS *Hebrides*, and from that time, both she and the *Dunara Castle* paid regular visits to the island until 1939. At the turn of the century, the two shipping firms came together to form 'McCallum Orme'.

Of all the steamers to ply the Western Isles of Scotland, the *Hebrides* was perhaps the least pleasant on which to travel. She quickly acquired the reputation for rolling and pitching, and few passengers managed to complete a cruise without being sea-sick. But if the weather was good, the passengers enjoyed a very leisurely sail. The accommodation was adequate and although those who could only afford steerage found conditions a little cramped, people in those days travelled rough and thought little of it. The food served on board was plain but good, and there was much to see as the steamer leapfrogged the outer isles, calling in at various harbours in order to unload cargo and a few passengers on its way to St Kilda.

The day the steamer arrived was one of great expectation and excitement on the island. The St Kildans would don the clothes otherwise reserved for Sundays, so that they might look their best. 'On a steamer day', wrote Ross the schoolmaster, 'the village will be found to be a "deserted village" as the entire population crowd to the shore, some carrying eggs and others cloth, stockings or other articles to be offered for sale to visitors.' While the men rowed out to meet the ship, the women and children would get their native wares ready.

What the tourists wanted was a souvenir. 'When we were boys' recalls Neil Ferguson, 'we used to sell egg shells. The guillemot, the fulmar and the puffin and all them wee birds – we got their eggs and blew them and we used to sell them for a penny each to the tourists.' The shells of the numerous varieties of bird on St Kilda would be gathered by the men in the spring. With the money obtained from the tourists the children and men could buy biscuits, sweets, or tobacco on board the steamer as she rode at anchor waiting for her passengers to return. The women of the island would meanwhile be selling the gloves and stockings they had spent the long winter months knitting. 'When the tourists came in summer', recalls Flora Gillies, 'we used to put them over our arms – socks and gloves and we used to try and sell them. It was quite an experience for we young ones trying to sell them. We were quite lucky, we used to get some sweets from the tourists and we used to see who could keep them the longest, for it was a treat for us then.'

Because of wind and tide the tourists normally had little time ashore. At most, they were allowed five or six hours before the captain, anxious to seek the shelter of the Long Island while it was still daylight, would sound the ship's siren and demand that the passengers return at once. Meanwhile, there was much to do: Apart from the village area which could take upwards of an hour to see, tourists would venture forth to explore the rest of the island. Perhaps, if they were willing to part with their money, they could persuade some of the men and boys to put on an exhibition of cragsmanship that would take the breath away. The tourists were on holiday and St Kilda was a novelty. 'It was the same as somebody in London wanting to see Stonehenge or the Tower of Blackpool,' says Willie Clelland. 'It was the novelty of going out there.'

Apart from souvenirs, the tourists were eager to purchase picture postcards, which were available on Hirta from about 1900. The first series featured photographs taken on the island by the naturalist Cherry Kearton in 1896, and had a space on the picture side of the card for a brief message, while the back was reserved for the address.

The more famous series of postcards, however, introduced on St Kilda later, consisted of photographs taken by George Washington Wilson, a photographer from Aberdeen who made many brilliant studies of the more out-of-the-way areas of Scotland, and whose collection is now preserved by Aberdeen University. Originally, many of his studies were sold to tourists as full-plate sepia prints mounted on pasteboard, and available not only on Hirta but also on the steamers.

Edwardian globetrotters sent postcards by the score. In an age when cameras were not common it was the only way of maintaining a record of their travels. In August 1906, the last summer mail taken off St Kilda included nearly 800 postcards, and in the tourist season August 1907–8 over 1,400 left Hirta's shores.

St Kilda became possibly the most photographed island in the world. For a small payment, many of the women would bring their spinning wheels out into the open so that visitors could watch wool being spun, and perhaps take photographs. It was not long before the St Kildans regarded photography as a source of income. Photographers, amateur and professional, wishing particular poses, could be satisfied on payment of a few shillings. On their return to the mainland, visitors used them to illustrate books written about the place, or to adorn their family albums with views of the remarkable that lent credence to their adventures, or else had them made into lantern slides to illustrate a winter lecture to a local club.

The tourists played a great part in improving the island's

economy. They paid cash for the community's produce. For instance, when tweed was sold to the tourists it made a greater profit for the islanders than it did when exported to Glasgow or given to the factor in lieu of goods provided. The St Kildans had fortunately found a new source of income at a time when they were running into financial difficulties.

But together with their money the passengers left in their wake an evil which was to play a far more important role in determining the destiny of the people of Hirta. 'One cannot be long on the island', wrote Robert Connell in 1886, 'without discovering the great moral injury that tourists and sentimentalists and yachtsmen, with pocketfuls of money, are working upon a kindly and simple people.' The introduction of money into a community which previously had not known what money was, did great harm and converted the St Kildans into what George Seton called 'the most knowingest people I have ever come across'. The islanders were quick to take from the tourists as much as the latter were prepared to give up. A sense of charity, coupled with the desire to possess something truly St Kildan and therefore unique, made many tourists part with more cash than they would have been prepared to give up elsewhere. Once the St Kildans had extracted high prices for their scant wares from the occasional wealthy tourist, they demanded the same from all. 'Possibly you may at times make a Glasgow merchant reduce his price,' wrote Ross, 'but the St Kildan stands to his price firm as the rocks that surround his island home. Once his price is set you must either pay it or want the article.'

With the money they obtained from the visitors, the St Kildans could purchase goods from the mainland. The steamers were invariably used, even by the factor, to transport stores from the mainland. Willie Clelland, who at one time worked as purser both on the *Hebrides* and the *Dunara Castle*, remembers the quantity of stores on board the first ship to visit the island each year. 'On the first trip of the season,' he recalls, 'we took out a lot of stores. There was an exceptional welcome for the crew of the first ship, which was usually the *Hebrides*.' Each year, the first ship took flour, groceries, and usually the first mail of the year. The crew of the steamer used to take back to the mainland with them several ten-gallon cans from the island. When they returned to Glasgow, they would go to the local grocer's shop and get the cans filled with paraffin to take back to the island. The islanders relied on the steamers to provide them with paraffin. Occasionally they offered the sailors money, but the crew usually refused to accept any payment.

'The St Kildans', proclaimed Ross, 'are spoiled children. This is the only opportunity afforded them of "turning a penny", and they are just overpressing in taking advantage of it. A few years back, visitors there used to scatter money right and left, and the poor natives expect that it should run a little more freely now.'

The St Kildans were not so much becoming greedy – they were simply assuming that charity should continue as charity. If some from the mainland wished to be free with their money and gifts, why not all? 'We came to the conclusion', wrote R. A. Smith, who went to St Kilda in 1879, 'that the people were quite as independent in spirit as other men, and perhaps more so than the same class elsewhere, but they had no idea of their true position, and finding tea, tobacco, etc., coming from the east, they have imagined that we could send them abundance without any trouble.'

To the islanders it was difficult to see some of those who came ashore as more or less wealthy than others. Those who visited them from the mainland were seen as one class: they were all outsiders, who spoke differently, dressed differently, and spent money because they were used to it. The St Kildans lived in a classless, moneyless society. They were never to realize, let alone accept, the values of a society based upon distinction.

The 'steamer season', as it was known on the island, was the one novelty in the people's lives. Given a more frequent contact with the mainland, it was only natural that the St Kildans should take an interest in what was happening in the world beyond their own. 'The excitement caused by the entrance of one steamer', wrote Ross, 'occupies the minds of the natives until the approach of another.' Although the visits were short, a feeling of friendship was always present. 'The visitors', wrote George Murray in 1886, 'had a proper day of it. They bought a deal of cloth and stockings from the natives. Before they parted with us, they and all the inhabitants of St Kilda assembled outside the minister's garden just as it was getting dark. The whole together constituted a small congregation. Three Gaelic tunes were sung at the request of one of the strangers. Then in English we sung the Hundredth Psalm and the Hymn "How my comrades see the signal", after which the minister prayed in Gaelic. It was an evening I will long remember, with not so much as a breath of wind to drive the sound one way more than another. There we all stood under the cloudless canopy of heaven, singing "All People that in Earth", etc. Few as we are on this remote island. it is comforting to think we can, in unison, with the rest of the world, "Sing to the Lord with cheerful voice".'

The tourists frequently joined in acts of worship with · the islanders. Mrs Ann McLachlan, the missionary's wife, remembers in her diary of an occasion in 1906 when the SS *Hebrides* made its final call of the year to St Kilda. 'We went out just as the first boatload of passengers came ashore,' she wrote. 'There were some nice people among them and we had a nice time. I took some of them into the church and they sang "Oh for a closer walk with God" to the tune "St Kilda". It sounded so pretty. I am so glad the church was cleaned out, on Tuesday, by the girls.'

The St Kildans, however, did not take kindly to tourists arriving on the Sabbath, although they could not resist the opportunity of making some money. 'There was one occasion,' recalls Willie Clelland, 'when we couldn't do St Kilda through the week and we had to go out on a Sunday. That was very bad. When we got there they wouldn't show us anything, they wouldn't give us anything. They wouldn't speak to you hardly. What they did, they left the stuff outside, with the prices on it, so you could put the money down and go away. They weren't hurting themselves in that way, weren't sinning I suppose. They got the money, but they didn't have to ask for it.'

Many friendships were struck up between the islanders and their visitors. Letters were frequently exchanged and small gifts from the mainland occasionally arrived for the benefit of the people of St Kilda. Most of the gifts sent to the people were, if possible, shared out among everyone. For the islanders it was the first time in their history they had had the opportunity of making acquaintances outside their own community. It was a new experience which the St Kildans found it difficult to do without in those years when the mail service to and from the island was far from regular.

If the *Dunara Castle* and the *Hebrides* brought people of modest means to St Kilda, many other visitors who arrived privately showed the islanders a degree of wealth and luxury they could hardly have dreamed of. One Wednesday in September, as the islanders were attending their monthly church service, a boy came to the door of the church and brought the news that a big boat had just dropped anchor in the bay. 'It was a lovely large steam yacht, the *Vandura*, owned by Mr Mann Thompson,' wrote Ann MacLachlan. 'His sister, Mrs Heneage of Underwood, Kilmarnock, was there, also Mrs Robinson of Dunvegan Castle, another lady whose name we don't know, and two more gentlemen. The men went out in a boat to the yacht and were out a good while. They brought in word that the yacht's folk were coming to see us – which they did.'

'They were so kind to the people,' wrote the missionary's wife, 'and bought up nearly every available bit of cloth in the place, also socks and stockings. We were taken aboard to tea on the *Vandura* and had an awfully good time. We got papers, flowers, etc., and Mr Mann Thompson took us all through the yacht. It was quite luxurious. The bedrooms lovely, and fitted up with every convenience – lovely bathroom, bedrooms with double beds, etc. The dining room was lovely with oil paintings all round – and the drawing room opened off it. There was there a pianola and everything in the way of luxury. All were very kind and we had a lovely time.'

In May 1923, the *Sarpendon* of the Blue Funnel Line of Liverpool visited the island on her maiden voyage round the Western Isles. The owners of the Line, the Holt Brothers, were on board with a large number of business and other friends. Piloted by Captain MacArthur, the huge ship slowly drifted into the bay. The ship's motor tenders brought the visitors ashore, together with a large supply of provisions donated to the islanders by the Holts. The St Kildans looked with amazement when they caught a glimpse of some of the passengers. Included in the passenger list were a party from Japan and China. The islanders had never before seen a Japanese or Chinese person, and were amazed by the fact that they were so small and had strange faces.

St Kilda became a favourite attraction for ships making their maiden voyages. In June 1878 the steamship *Mastiff* of the Burns Laird Line made her maiden voyage to Iceland from the Clyde. Her owner, James Burns, who later became Lord Inverclyde, decided his new ship would call at St Kilda on the way. A select list of passengers, including the young novelist Anthony Trollope, landed on the island. 'The first care', wrote Trollope, 'was to land certain stores – tea, sugar, and such like – which Mr Burns had brought as a present to the people. It is the necessity of their position that such aid should be essential almost to their existence. Then we walked up among the cottages, buying woollen stockings and sea-birds' eggs, such being the commodities they had for sale. Some coarse cloth we found there also, made on the island from the wool grown

there, of which some among us bought sufficient for a coat, waistcoat, or petticoat, as the case may be . . . After wandering among
the cottages for an hour or two, and making acquaintance with
the people, we swarmed down upon the beach, all the inhabitants
accompanying us . . . Many of them went on board, not unnaturally
desiring to satisfy some little want, and to see the last of their
strange visitors.'

But not all the tourists possessed such a sympathetic interest in
the St Kildans. Although people attracted to the island were for
the most part professionals – doctors, sociologists, naturalists, ornithologists – some were less respectable. Dressed in Highland attire,
so that they might feel more at home among a people who never
wore a kilt, such tourists answered the call of the advertising hand-
bills, which declared that St Kilda was 'the land that wants to be
visited'. For them, a visit to St Kilda was a chance to view the only
human menagerie in the British Isles.

The St Kildans as often as not came to despise their generous
visitors. The hated Sassenachs were blamed for everything. 'I do not
wonder', wrote Heathcote in 1900, 'that they dislike foreigners, so
many tourists treat them as if they were wild animals at the
Zoo . . . I have seen them standing at the church door during service
laughing and talking, and staring in as if at an entertainment got up
for their amusement.' It is little wonder that the islanders, especially
the women, were shy and hated having their photographs taken.
They were aware of what was happening to them but could do
little about it. They were forever a generous people, and felt they
could do little but extend that kindness to those who came upon
their island by design rather than by chance.

Even to the last, the typical tourist could not bring himself to
regard the people with the equality that was due to them, and with
a charitable nature rather than with charity. 'She takes me for a
native,' wrote Alasdair Alpin MacGregor of one of the passengers
from the *Dunara Castle* on her last visit to the island before the
evacuation. 'She tells me such tall stories of Glasgow,' continued
MacGregor, 'and the more I plead ignorance of what goes on in
Scotland, so to speak, the taller grow the stories of Glasgow.'
Several visitors at times grudged paying the shilling expected of each
passenger by the men of St Kilda who rowed them ashore. 'And
although', wrote Alpin MacGregor, 'each tripper has paid £10 for
the trip, the more officious of them have kicked up hell with
Ferguson at the post-office when he has run out of penny stamps,

and have flatly refused to pay the extra halfpenny on the plea that the post office is a government institution and ought to be conducted as such.'

On one occasion in 1890, several kind-hearted inhabitants of the town of Sunderland, encouraged by Mr I. G. Campbell, decided to visit St Kilda for the marriage of John Gillies, then the only man of marriageable age on St Kilda. His bride-to-be, Ann, was about twenty-three years of age. John was but a year older and a widower, his first wife having died in labour. Mr Campbell worked hard at the arrangements. With the help of John Ross, the former schoolmaster, he went about organizing an expedition to St Kilda such as the islanders had never before witnessed.

A steamship, the *Clydesdale*, was chartered for the trip, which was scheduled for May, and an advertisement placed in the local English papers calling upon tradesmen and others to donate wedding presents for the young couple. As a result, Ann was to be dressed in the height of fashion. 'I really hope', wrote John Ross enthusiastically, 'the dress may be a good fit. She will not know how to walk in it. I suppose no sooner than that day is over, it will be laid carefully past in one of the many boxes, to be preserved as an heirloom.' Amongst the varied gifts got together for the young couple and the other islanders, were a pair of spectacles for an islander with failing eyesight, an American organ (not that anyone on the island could play it), numerous bottles of digestive syrup, the first jars of Bovril to be taken to St Kilda, a case of pork pies, a set of silver teaspoons, and, of course, a wedding cake.

The people of Sunderland had decided to attend Ann's wedding because, it was claimed, she was the Queen of St Kilda. In the 1830s the islanders had elected Betty Scott, a young girl from the mainland who was employed as housekeeper to the Reverend Neil Mackenzie, as honorary Queen of St Kilda. When she died tragically in a boating accident, the title passed first to her daughter and then to the most beautiful woman on the island. The Queen, however, in a society so founded in socialist principles, had little power. She was normally 'in charge' of the other females during the harvesting of puffins and eggs on the island, and organized the waulking of the tweed.

The unsuspecting St Kildans met the people of Sunderland at the shore. The men dragged a boat out to sea to go and meet what they assumed was yet another party of tourists, and the women got out their knitted goods and eggshells. When the islanders realized why the men and women of Sunderland had come to St Kilda they refused to allow them to stay. The presents, worth over £100, were never unloaded from the steamer. Only the books which had been meticulously got together by Mr Campbell, and which formed the foundation of the St Kilda Free Library, were accepted by the St Kildans. The pork pies that were to be part of their wedding feast were left to rot on a Glasgow wharf. Even the kind, the thoughtful, had a harmful effect upon the St Kildans.

Before the wedding party set out for the island, John Ross had written to Mr Campbell: 'You have done, sir, what they cannot sufficiently appreciate. You have led the way, and that way well, in bringing St Kilda true civilisation and making it part of Great Britain.' The couple, quietly, and according to the true traditions of the island, were later married by the minister. The islanders' attitude towards charity was understandable: it was in the main conditioned by the usefulness of the gifts bestowed upon them. They could and would accept gifts that in their eyes were useful – food, clothing, coal, paraffin – they could not however accept gifts that had no place in their way of life. They were a people who for centuries had suffered obscurity: they were conditioned to that state of affairs. When suddenly they were faced with having gifts lavished upon them by a society which had discovered its conscience, they found it hard to accept.

There was also an element of conceit: many tourists flattered themselves by being able to be generous to others less well-off. Along with charity, the St Kildans had to suffer the criticism and the intolerance of a society which thought itself civilized in comparison to them – a society generous rather than helpful, condescending rather than conscious.

The influx of tourists undermined the economy of the island. Their money led to a decline in productivity and in the people's interest in the traditional way of life on Hirta. With money obtained from tourists the islanders could purchase all the grain and foodstuffs required to maintain a dwindling population. But an economy based upon tourism placed too great an emphasis upon wind and sea, the two elements upon which the St Kildans had never relied. Within forty years of tourism, life on St Kilda became impossible.

The aim of society on the mainland was at all times to bring St Kilda into the fold. 'Though the life of a Robinson Crusoe or a few Robinson Crusoes may be very picturesque,' noted Anthony

Trollope in 1878, 'humanity will always desire to restore a Robinson Crusoe back to the community of the world.' Unfortunately neither St Kilda nor its people could adapt or be adapted to fit in with the aspirations and standards of modern society. At least, to those in the world outside, St Kilda was unable to change at a rate sufficient to secure a future for the St Kildans. The islanders themselves, dwindling in number, had lost heart in their struggle for survival, and preferred with hesitation and sadness to leave their home to the sea birds and the Atlantic waves.

9
A cause of death

A son was born to Neil Mackinnon's wife a little after midnight on 14 December 1886. The child was big and looked sturdy. No one, however, on St Kilda was surprised when, unchristened, the baby died within a fortnight.

'Last night at 10.30', wrote George Murray, the schoolmaster, in his diary on 27 December, 'after six days intense suffering the child departed this life. Every one expressed great wonder how it lived so long after being seized with illness, as they generally succumb at the end of a week after they are born. This one was thirteen days except one and a half hours. It had a frequent cry since it was born; but the first sign of its being dangerously ill was at the end of a week, when it ceased to suck the breast, but still sucked the bottle. The following day, *thuit na gialan* (the jaws fell), when all hope of its recovery was given up. From that time till its death it occasionally took a little milk in a spoon or out of the bottle. The last two days a little wine in water was given once or twice. It very often yawned and sometimes looked hard at you. It was pitiful to see the poor little thing in the pangs of death. May God prepare us all for the same end.'

Within twenty-four hours, the child was buried in the little cemetery. Murray followed the funeral procession. 'In the grave which was opened', he wrote, 'I saw the coffins of its two little brothers that died the same way. The one coffin was still quite whole, there being only about sixteen months since it was interred; the other was in pieces. I sympathize with the parents in their bereavement.'

The saddest sight Hirta has to offer, even to this day, is the small oval-shaped churchyard set a few yards behind Main Street. Surrounded by a sturdy stone dyke to keep out wandering live-stock, and with a rough, wooden gate for an entrance, the church-yard was always overgrown with nettles, irises, and grasses. Beneath the stony, awkward turf, was the last resting-place of the St Kildan.

When an islander died, a dirge in blank verse was composed.

The hymn would praise the virtues and good deeds of the departed. 'When anybody died,' remembers Neil Ferguson, 'all work stopped, nobody worked for a week, and they used to have a wake there every night until he got buried . . . They killed a sheep so they had some food for the folk that was at the wake all night. That's how it was.' Even the little school would close and remain so until a proper time of mourning had passed.

The remains of the body were dressed by the women. One of the red kerchiefs, so popular on St Kilda, was twisted round and round the face. Over the body itself was placed a coarse red sack of blanket material which was tied above the head. The corpse remained in the house of the departed during the wake, which usually lasted no more than two days.

One of the most difficult tasks was the making of the coffin. There were no trees on Hirta and so the St Kildans kept a stock of planks brought over from the mainland in one of the cleits not far from the manse. The coffin was made by the men down by the storehouse and out of sight of the village. They did their best to shape it in proper style at the shoulders. As the minister was the only person on the island who had a proper range to cook on, his was the only house that could provide adequate quantities of hot water. 'We knew', recalls Mary Cameron, 'when one of the men came to the door from time to time for a kettle of boiling water, that the making of the coffin was in progress.' The boiling water was poured over the wood to make it more flexible and easier to shape. The coffin was never painted and no handles of brass or any other metal were added.

The St Kildans waited until the sun's shadow had reached a certain place before beginning the funeral service. While in the house, 'Part of a psalm is sung, a chapter read, another psalm sung and someone engages in prayer,' wrote John Ross. 'Then', he added, 'the funeral procession starts for the churchyard, attended by all the islanders able to turn out.' Everyone took his turn to carry the coffin to the graveyard. It was supported on poles and the journey could take anything up to half an hour. 'Everyone would go to the funeral,' recalls Lachlan Macdonald. 'The minister would come and do the service, but we dug the grave ourselves. There was no man set aside for digging, you see, and they had to do the coffin themselves too. You had to be a good hand at both.'

Ross described the typical St Kildan grave: 'A rough stone at each end marks the resting-place and to all appearances the place is well nigh full. While the grave is being filled in, a number of women can be heard from amongst the nettles wailing over the grave of some departed friend.' As the coffin was lowered into the grave and the men began to shovel earth upon it, the women would begin 'keening' – wailing in honour of the dead. They would stay at the graveside long after the burial had finished, lamenting over the dead while the men returned to their homes.

There was never a church service for the dead. The funeral service was always carried out at the graveside, whatever the weather. A psalm was sung, then there was a reading from the Bible, then another psalm, and then the congregation engaged in prayer. Mourning on Hirta could last up to a week and was intensely emotional, reflecting not only the islanders' deep religious feeling, but also the seriousness of loss of life in a community so small and close. 'Their weeping at the grave', wrote George Murray, 'reminds me of "Rachel weeping for her children and will not be comforted for they are not".'

In recorded history, the St Kildans were always buried in the same little churchyard. The high wall that surrounded it served a double purpose – it kept the animals from digging up the bones and allowed the islanders to build up the level of earth within the enclosure to a height which made a proper burial possible. When the bodies had disintegrated, the bones of those long since deceased were transferred to an area of land to the west of the village which was fenced off like the graveyard.

The St Kildans never put up proper headstones. They did not know the art of monumental masonry and were never able to afford to import memorials from the mainland. A few older islanders remembered who was buried where, and such knowledge was passed down from one generation to the next.

The most important problem arising from isolation is that the community has to be able to maintain a critical level of population. For the most part, the people of St Kilda had to rely upon their own offspring to provide a future for the community. Immigration is possible when the would-be incomers are acquainted with, or can readily adapt themselves to, their new way of life; but on an island like Hirta, so remote from the rest of society, where life bore little resemblance to that experienced on the other islands let alone the mainland, the possibility of immigrants being assimilated was less likely. The St Kildans themselves had to maintain the strong, healthy descendants that would make habitation of the archipelago continuous.

The critical level of population for St Kilda was probably no less than one hundred. With that number of people living on the island – roughly half of whom would have to be male – life could be successful. Less than that number, or an unnatural imbalance between men and women, particularly if women heavily outnumbered men, meant that life would be a struggle.

When Martin Martin visited the island in 1697, he generously estimated that the population of Hirta was 180. He failed to give the proportion of men to women, but there was obviously enough men at that time to make for a thriving community. By 1758, Kenneth Macaulay gave the total number of inhabitants on St Kilda as eighty-eight. Thirty-eight of the people on the island were men. The big drop in population in little over sixty years was due to a smallpox epidemic. But by that time, and of major importance to the future of the community, there were more women than men. In fact women dominated St Kildan society numerically from that time until the evacuation – for practically two hundred years.

MacLeod of MacLeod naturally enough encouraged some of his other tenants to take up crofts on Hirta. By the end of the eighteenth century, the population had risen to nearly a hundred. It was to remain roughly at that level until 1851. In the following year, however, thirty-six St Kildans chose to make their fortunes elsewhere in the world and emigrated to Australia, and the population, reduced to about seventy souls, remained so until the beginning of the twentieth century. During the 1920s in particular the number of people living on St Kilda dropped rapidly, until by 1930 there were only thirty-six left.

The sexual imbalance that existed on St Kilda throughout most of the island's history was not in itself a problem. After all, it was the women who bore the children. The major difficulty was the number of men of marriageable age on the island. From the nineteenth century onwards, there were always considerably fewer men of an age to marry than there were women. In 1877, McDiarmid noted that only two St Kildan men were of a fit age, but so too were twelve women. The reverse of that situation would have proved less of a problem. The men could always find a wife while on a visit to the mainland, and frequently did so. For the women

on St Kilda, life was little different from that led by their sex on
other islands. But it was no easy task for St Kildan girls to entice
the man of their choice, if he were an outsider, to take up the
hazardous tasks that living on Hirta involved. Usually the excess
women on the island found it easier to follow to the mainland
visitors with whom they fell in love.

On Hirta, for 150 years, the population was never far above, and
usually below, its critical level. Likewise, there were always fewer
men than women on the island – a factor which may account
for the strenuous role that women had on St Kilda. McDiarmid
prophetically remarked, however, 'It must tell on the prosperity
of the island, such a large majority being females; they have to be
supported, and though able and willing workers still are unfitted
for the arduous and dangerous pursuit from which the St Kildan
derives his principal support.'

The St Kildan way of life depended upon the capture of sea birds.
That was a task for men. Women, of course, did more than their
fair share of work. It was the women, both young and adult, who
were the great carriers on the island; but in this respect they
performed a function with which their sisters in the Hebrides or
the crofting mainland of Scotland were equally burdened. The
women helped with the fulmar and gannet harvests, but were not
capable of taking out the boats to go to Boreray and the great
stacs. Throughout the last hundred years of the community, as the
availability of teams of men was reduced, the number of birds
slaughtered decreased. The wealth of the island suffered from a
shortage of men and the community was drawn closer to its death.

According to Macaulay in 1756, the St Kildans married at an
early age. He saw fit to remark, in terms of the community's
obvious prosperity, that St Kilda 'if under proper regulations . . .
might easily support three hundred souls'. In 1799, Lord Brougham
wrote with aristocratic self-assurance and gross exaggeration,
'St Kilda is capable of supporting a population of one thousand
five hundred souls with ease.' So comfortable was life on Hirta
that Colonel MacLeod of MacLeod wrote in 1774 of the inhabitants,
'The young fellows, even before their beards are well grown, if
they are possessed of a crooked spade, think themselves enabled to
marry; if the relations of the young pair can give them a cow, and
a couple of sheep, they are amply provided for; and upon this
fortune they build themselves a house and take to getting children
as fast as possible, who again go through the same scene.'

Marriage on Hirta was a solemn if festive occasion. 'Of marriage,' wrote Ross, 'the St Kildan takes a view too solemn to admit of anything of the nature of music and dancing as is customary in other parts of the Highlands, not even a song being indulged in.'

Three Sabbaths before the wedding, the banns were proclaimed by one of the elders and the parents then set about preparing a great feast. Sheep were slaughtered to feed the guests, the number varying according to the wealth of the parties concerned. The *reitich*, or contract, was celebrated a week before the wedding was due to take place, in the house of the bridegroom. To this celebration all the near friends and relatives of the couple were invited, and everyone would eat and drink. The men would sit down at the expense of the women if there was a shortage of chairs. It was one of the rare occasions when whisky was served on Hirta. The party would go on well into the night, and afterwards those concerned would rest until the day of the wedding. In earlier days the bride and groom would have no special clothes to wear on their wedding day, but would wear the best they had. However, white wedding dresses, complete with veils, found their way to Hirta before the evacuation in 1930.

On the wedding day itself, a smaller number of friends than attended the *reitich* accompanied the couple to the church. The order of procession from house to church was strict. 'The minister told us', wrote Atkinson in 1831, 'that from their method of climbing among the cliffs, each one following in the rear of the other, their marriage ceremonies present the same singular arrangement; the bridegroom walking first, followed by the bride, and they in a similar manner by the inferior performers.'

All the St Kildans got married in the little church. Frequently, however, couples would have to wait until there was a minister on the island. The catechists and the missionaries who were sent to St Kilda were not ordained and could not, therefore, perform the marriage rites. In those instances, the couple would have to wait until the annual visit of a minister in the summer. Even when there was a resident clergyman on Hirta, the marriage licence had to be applied for well in advance. Everyone would then have to wait until the mail arrived, either by steamer in the summer or by way of a passing trawler in the winter. The church service was the usual one, but instead of a wedding ring made of gold, a piece of woollen thread was traditionally used. There was only one metal ring, made of silver, on St Kilda. It had once been the property of

'California' Gillies's second wife, and she handed it over to an ageing spinster when she left the island for good.

After the wedding, all went quietly home. The bride, groom, best maid and best man, however, would almost immediately retire to the manse, with an offering for the minister. The offering was usually an ample share of the wedding feast – joints of fresh mutton and newly-baked scones and oatcakes. While the bridal party took tea and made pleasantries at the manse, the other St Kildans would do justice to what was left of the wedding feast. Before nightfall, the newly-weds would retire either to their own house, if a vacant cottage was available on the island, or to that of the groom's parents, where they would live until a croft became vacant. There was no such thing as a honeymoon. 'There is only the choice', wrote the journalist Robert Connell, 'of going to a friend's house ten yards off or one twice the distance.'

As food supplies became a matter of increasing concern to the St Kildans, the age at which they married went up. The men of Hirta, like many Highlanders to this day, remained single until they reached their late thirties or even forties, at which age they married women of equal years. Despite the fact that islanders married later in life, however, the birth rate on St Kilda remained relatively high. In 1877, George Seton calculated that of the fourteen married couples on Hirta, the average age of the wives was forty-three and a half years, yet the average number of children born to them was nine.

Emigration, forced and voluntary, could also have accounted for the sharp fall in the population. There is only one instance on record, however, of St Kildans in any considerable number leaving their island home up to the end of the nineteenth century. In 1852, thirty-six St Kildans decided to follow the example of many of the inhabitants of the Hebrides and less remote parts of the mainland, and emigrate to Australia. The thirty-six islanders made their way from Hirta to Liverpool, where on 13 October 1852 they boarded the barque *Priscilla*, bound for Melbourne.

Out of a total of 261 passengers, forty-two died of fever on the voyage. Twenty of the dead were St Kildans. When the barque was allowed to dock on 19 January 1853, there were only sixteen islanders still alive. There they settled and struggled to farm land near the city of Melbourne.

The effects of this emigration were drastic. The population of St Kilda was reduced to little over seventy. From that time a few young men occasionally left to settle on the mainland, but immigrants from the Hebrides helped counteract the drift.

Curiously, there was never any large-scale immigration to St Kilda during the nineteenth and twentieth centuries. It had been effected once before in the island's history. In 1724 St Kilda was sadly depopulated by smallpox, and the proprietor successfully persuaded and cajoled families from Harris to take up the crofts on Hirta. The Ferguson family was one such newcomer to Hirta. In the Minutes of the Directors of the SSPCK for 1731, members of the society were asked to note 'That regard might be had to the people of Hirta, which Island, by the yearly transporting of people to it, will soon be populous again'. In less than forty years immigration had increased the population to eighty-eight, and by 1815 there were 130 people living on St Kilda.

It is almost certain, however, that by the middle of the nineteenth century there were signs that it was not worth the proprietor's effort to encourage a similar exercise. MacLeod of MacLeod even then probably believed that sheep, which needed few people to tend them, were increasingly more worthwhile than the feathers and flesh of sea birds. At any rate, a repopulation on any scale was never suggested, let alone attempted.

The precipitous cliffs of St Kilda rarely claimed the lives of the islanders. The men were skilled in the art of climbing, being trained to the work almost from birth. Moreover, because the survival of the community depended upon fowling, those who practised it took extra care. Very few St Kildans 'went over the rocks', as they called it. From 1830 to 1846, only two islanders died as a result of fowling accidents, and in the subsequent forty years there were only five premature deaths.

During the last decades there were more accidents, perhaps the result of fewer men being involved in the work than of old. 'In the olden days,' remembers Neil Ferguson, 'everybody went together, but a few years before we left, maybe two families would go off and do their own.' He recalls one instance when two young men died because they did not take the care that their forefathers would have taken. They had decided to go to the cliffs on their own, but it happened to be a day when the boat bringing mail was due to arrive. They were in a hurry, therefore, to complete the work at hand and return to the village. 'This fellow must have slipped,' says Neil, 'and the other one didn't notice it until he himself was dragged over the rocks. The last one that went over must have swung in and there was a crack in the rock and he got jammed in there. The rope snapped and the other one went right over the rocks into the water. It was at the time of the war, and one of the watchmen with his spy glass noticed this body lying in a crack in the rock. They had an awful job lowering men down from the top to get to the place. They had a boat at the bottom of the cliff and they lowered the body right down to the boat. One of them was just married a few months – the one that they didn't get.'

Occasionally accidents happened to the men landed on Boreray during the bird harvest, or in the summer months when they stayed on the island to tend the sheep. Flora Gillies's father, in fact, died of appendicitis while on Boreray. A signal cut in the turf of the island meant that there had been an accident, or that someone was ill. 'So the rowing boat used to be sent out to see,' recalls Flora, 'and then when the boat came back the womenfolk used to go down to the pier, wondering who it was, you know. It happened that it was my father. He died at thirty-six and my mother was left with four of us. But the menfolk and that all helped, they were very good to her.' 'He died over there, I mind that,' says Lachlan Macdonald. 'In them days there wasn't a doctor on the island, so the habit was on the island that you put on a poultice and things like that, or give him a dose of salts. So seemingly they poulticed him and tried to kill the pain. But the guy didn't survive. His side was black as ink, so they make out it was appendicitis.'

Drowning accidents were also rare. Although the St Kildans lacked the finesse of the trained seamen of the mainland fishing communities, they were fearless without being careless sailors. They respected the Atlantic Ocean that surrounded them and took few chances. Like many who go to sea, however, the St Kildans could not swim, and were never to learn to swim until after the evacuation. Few, they argued, would benefit from the skill should they find themselves tossed into the cold and heavy swell of the ocean. The small island boats, moreover, were rarely used to make a voyage to the mainland. They were thought too precious to risk upon the rough waters that divide St Kilda from the Hebrides and Scotland. They were used primarily to make calculated and necessary excursions to the neighbouring islands and stacs. Even on those occasions, though, accidents could happen.

Lachlan Macdonald, who left St Kilda at the evacuation, lived twenty-one of his twenty-four years on the island without a father.

'I wasn't three and my father was drowned on Dun,' he recalls. They were over there with the hogs, they put them over there for the winter. The boat just turned upside down. There was my father and another chap drowned, but the rest were saved. They make out that my father had clogs on. He was, right enough, floating for a good while; but just at the time they got to him, he went and turned his head down and his feet up, so they made out that it was the clogs that caused his death.'

Intermarriage, often thought to be the curse of small, isolated communities, could possibly have resulted in death on St Kilda apart from the breeding of an enfeebled race. The island, however, is remarkable in that there are no ill-effects recorded as the result of consanguineous marriages. In 1878, John Sands remarked, 'Although they have intermarried possibly for a thousand years, and at all events for several centuries, none of the pernicious effects that one has been taught to expect seem to have resulted.' In an article written by Dr Mitchell in the *Edinburgh Medical Journal* for April 1865, he states that of the fourteen married couples on St Kilda at that time, in not one case was the relationship that of even full cousins. In five couples the relationship was that of second cousins to whom a total of fifty-four children had been born. Thirty-seven of them had died in infancy, as a result of disease. Of the surviving seventeen, not one was in any way abnormal, either physically or mentally.

It seems certain that on St Kilda, as is the case with most primitive societies, a strict observance of marriages was kept. The results of inbreeding were known and feared, if only through knowledge of the Good Book. The minister who was responsible for keeping the records of marriages on the island must also have made sure what the relationship of the couple was before agreeing to the match. 'You would know yourself if you were grown up anyway,' says Lachlan Macdonald. 'You would go to school and you were told who was your cousin or second cousin, who were your relations and so forth. It wasn't any different from being on the mainland.' On several occasions, St Kildans took to the mainland in search of a wife, and a little fresh blood injected now and then into the community went a long way towards separating close blood relations. By the last years, however, the nurse on the island and the naval doctor who was in attendance at the evacuation agreed that relationships by then, with a population so small, were becoming too close for comfort.

The St Kildans of the last century on the island do not seem to have been physically as strong as their ancestors. There was an increase in rheumatism, headaches and colds on Hirta. On 3 March 1887 the schoolmaster, having visited those islanders who were confined to their beds that day, drew up a list.

At the manse, the housekeeper, Mrs McKinlay, was laid up with swollen feet. Ewen Gillies, who was staying in the manse, had sore feet as well. In house number one, Christina McKinnon had a pain in her breast and was constipated. Next door, Finlay McQueen and the Macdonalds were in bed with headaches. Neil Ferguson had a pain in his side, and two doors along, Mrs Angus Gillies was suffering, she claimed, from insomnia. Rory Gillies, who lived in house number seven, had rheumatism in his legs, and John Macdonald, his blind neighbour, had a pain in his head that day. So too did Norman Gillies and old Rachel MacCrimmon, the last on Hirta to bear that name. At the end of the street, Mrs Macdonald, Lachlan's mother, was laid up with rheumatism. Few on Hirta were really ill that day, but no one felt particularly healthy either.

Other ailments were common. 'The ailment par excellence', reported Staff-Surgeon Scott of HMS *Flirt* in 1877, 'is rheumatism, as might be expected from the exposed nature of their island home. This disease is common to both sexes, and in a number is attended with pain in the cardiac region . . . Dyspepsia is also common . . . There were several cases of ear disease, and there is a tendency to scrofula. One boy had disease of the bones of the leg. Colds and coughs are common enough, but no case of phthisis presented itself. We saw only two cases of skin disease and these were trifling.' In addition, gastric troubles were as common to the St Kildans as to most people.

The proprietor made it his duty to send out annually a supply of medicine to the islanders. Always included were large bottles of castor oil, senna pods, salts and various tonics, as well as a supply of bandages and the like for the treatment of small wounds.

Both while tracking down sheep and while hunting sea birds, the St Kildans frequently got grazed and cut. 'There is a great deal of bandaging to be done,' recalled Ann MacLachlan, the missionary's wife. 'The men got terribly cut limbs on the steep rocky hillsides while chasing down sheep, a system of catching the sheep which is very bad both for man and sheep. The poor people did not understand the need for keeping wounds clean and consequently suffered much more than they might otherwise have done.'

The medicines and the bandages were normally kept at the manse until the time came when a nurse was sent to St Kilda. In 1886 George Murray, the schoolmaster, was shown how to set sprains by two doctors visiting the island, and was given a box of medicines that he was charged with dispensing. The St Kildans, who soon developed a weakness for medicines, however inadequate they proved themselves to be, were keen to call upon his services.

The islanders themselves had little of their own in the way of medical aids, let alone knowledge. 'One of the men', wrote George Atkinson in 1831, 'has a lancet and bleeds them occasionally, and in cases of fracture and dislocation, splices and replaces to the best of his ability.' Even as late as 1907, in fact, bleeding was still used to cure disease. Every house on Hirta also had a bottle of whisky or port, which was reserved exclusively for medicinal purposes, as well as an ample supply of mustard and a container of both fulmar and castor oil.

Against the most dangerous diseases the St Kildans were vaccinated at the proprietor's expense. Dr Webster of Dunvegan was sent to Hirta in June 1873, and immunized seventeen children and adults against smallpox. The remainder of the population was vaccinated three months later by Dr Murchison of North Harris. From that time on, the St Kildans were periodically vaccinated against smallpox by the numerous doctors sent out over the years to conduct examinations of the islanders. There was never, however, anyone on Hirta able to perform even minor surgery, and appendicitis frequently led to death.

The destroyer of life on St Kilda was in fact to be disease. In 1684, according to Martin Martin, leprosy struck at the community. When he visited the island thirteen years later, there were still families suffering from the affliction. In 1724 a 'contagious distemper', thought by Macaulay to have been smallpox, ravaged the population, and only four adults, who had left Hirta to collect sea birds from the stacs, survived out of twenty-four families. 'At last', wrote the Reverend Neil Mackenzie in 1829, 'there were scarcely sufficient left to bury the dead.' As they had then no spades, one man is said to have dug eleven graves with the back board of a wool card about eighteen inches by nine in size. Despite the fact that the epidemic killed seventeen heads of twenty-one families and left twenty-six orphans, the St Kildans survived. This was the first and last recorded instance of smallpox on the island, and St Kilda was repopulated. The St Kildans survived a cholera epidemic in 1832–3, and there are no records of any other diseases, either contagious or infectious, that were capable of bringing the entire community to its knees, until 1913, when an epidemic of influenza and pneumonia paralysed island life.

The St Kildans were afraid of disease. Tuberculosis, rife in less remote parts of the mainland, was an illness that few on St Kilda appear to have suffered from, although inadequate diagnosis probably disguised many cases. The last missionary's wife, Mrs Munro, however, remembers how scared the islanders were of TB. 'When one of the Gillies boys had TB,' she recalls, 'one of the other sons and his wife were in the same house. They left the house immediately and the mother was left to look after the boy alone until he died. And then, of course, when Mary Gillies died she had TB and the nurse was going back and forth tending to her. I know that the whole time she was ill, Nurse Barclay had to take all her food to her and even the nightdress and the stockings she was buried in.'

Their fear of infection was justified. The St Kildans had little natural resistance to diseases common on the mainland. They isolated any of their number who contracted an illness, and were sensibly wary of visitors who might unwittingly bring disease. A band of shipwrecked sailors or a party of innocent tourists could carry common diseases which could be fatal to the islanders.

On Hirta, the people were particularly prone to catching the 'boat-cold'. So called because it was invariably contracted after a visit had been paid them by mainlanders, the boat-cold normally sent every man, woman, and child on the island to bed. The symptoms began with a cold sensation and pain and stiffness in the muscles of the jaw, accompanied by a sore head and a feeling of acute depression. The pulse rate would increase, and after a time a severe cough developed. The common cold could and did kill. According to the records kept by the Reverend Neil Mackenzie, between the years 1830 and 1839 four islanders died from it. Between the years 1839 and 1846 a further two succumbed.

The most important result, however, was that the 'boat-cold' could incapacitate the entire community. The routine of island work was interrupted, sometimes for weeks. If caught during the fowling season, or when the crops were ripe for harvest, the cold could and did cause almost certain deprivation. The population of St Kilda, however, was to be decimated for over a century by a disease that struck the newborn.

That which strangled children was the *Mundklemme* of the Dane, the *Ginklofie* of the Icelander, the 'sickness of eight days' of the St Kildan, known to medical science as Tetanus Infantum. Although the disease was common on the mainland of Scotland at one time, and a more serious death toll was found in Iceland between the years 1827 and 1837 (when 4,478 people died of the disease), its presence on St Kilda was ultimately to make life on the island impossible. No one knows how tetanus first came to St Kilda or why it continued to ravage the community for so great a period of time. The toll it claimed of the poor people, however, is undeniable.

In the sixty-one years between 1830 and 1891, seventy-seven babies died of tetanus on Hirta. When the Reverend Neil Mackenzie became the resident minister in St Kilda, he assiduously kept the parochial register from July 1830 until he took his leave of the island in October 1846. During those years, there was a total of 68 deaths on St Kilda – 39 male and 29 female. Of the total, some 37 deaths were infant mortalities, 26 male children and 11 female. 32 out of the total 68 deaths were caused by tetanus. 23 male babies died before they could even focus on the cliffs and stacs that would have been the objects of their labours in life. The rest of the infant deaths were caused by still-births and other diseases more commonly expected at birth. According to statistics published in the *British and Foreign Medico-Chirurgical Review* in 1838, eight out of every ten babies born on Hirta died of 'the sickness of eight days'.

In 1856, St Kilda formally became a registration district as a result of an application made by the proprietor. Mr Duncan Kennedy, the Free Church catechist on the island, was appointed registrar. From that date, more accurate records of births and deaths on Hirta were kept. In the period 1855 to 1876, there were 56 births on the island, 32 of them males. There were 64 deaths during the same period. 37 females died and 27 males. The total infant mortality was 41, of which 26 were males. The staggering fact that emerges from the records, however, is that of all the deaths that occurred on Hirta during that period, all but one male death and a few female deaths were the result of tetanus infantum.

Although the disease normally struck at birth, sometimes older children contracted it. Annie Ferguson, just ten years old and one of the brightest pupils at school, was suddenly taken with the disease. The schoolmaster, George Murray, noted her symptoms in his diary. 'On Thursday last,' he wrote, 'she was unable to read as usual in School in the forenoon. I thought it was merely her throat was sore, for so I was told. She returned not in the afternoon and now her life is quite despaired of. What she suffered since Friday is terrible to think upon. She is affected exactly the same as the infants who are seized with it. The muscles of the body appear to be in a state of lasting rigidity, while at the end of every three or four minutes, paroxysms of spasm occur, followed by intervals of comparative ease and a desire to sleep, till she is suddenly aroused by the excruciating pain which attends the paroxysm. She cannot rest in the same position five minutes, but must be turned from side to side or kept sitting or standing. She takes a little gruel occasionally. The mind is quite entire.'

Five days later the child was still suffering. 'Every limb and part of her body is affected,' wrote Murray on 5 March 1887. 'Her very toes are bent downwards. To add to her affliction there is a stoppage in her bowels for more than a week and medicine she cannot take, her throat being so much closed. Offered to give her an injection, but the people are so very curious that they will have their own way, do what you will. I remonstrated but to no purpose.'

Annie Ferguson finally died at three o'clock in the afternoon of 10 March. 'It was to us nothing less than a great wonder how she stood it so long', wrote the schoolmaster, 'under pain that is indescribable. So great had been the pain that the body was entirely out of shape. What a warning to all of us! This day fortnight she was in school with us and tonight the body and soul are separated.' Amid a heavy fall of snow, she was buried in the little graveyard in a plot close to the gate.

Tetanus hit several families hard. When Emily MacLeod visited the island in 1877, she was distressed to learn that one woman had given birth to twelve children and had succeeded in rearing but one. Tetanus had, by that time, been with the community for over a hundred years and had unceasingly snatched away half the newborn babies. 'On looking through the churchyard,' wrote the schoolmaster in 1886, 'I felt sad at the sight of so many infant graves. One man, not yet fifty years, I should say, pointed the place to me where he buried nine children. He is left with four of a family. Another buried no less than a dozen infants and is left with two, now grown up. Sad to think of the like.' The disease became part of the St Kildan tradition. It was part of the islanders' way of life, like fowling. 'To show the uncertainty with which a woman regarded the life of her child,' wrote Nicol, 'she rarely provided any clothing until the eight days had passed.' The St Kildans grew to accept to the best of their ability the blatant fact that the funerals of their children followed so closely and so often upon their births.

According to the St Kildans nothing could be done. 'If it's God's will that babies should die,' they told Emily MacLeod when she suggested that a trained nurse might help avoid so many deaths, 'nothing you can do will save them.' Robert Connel, who visited St Kilda in 1885 as a special correspondent for the *Glasgow Herald*, discovered on his return to Glasgow that the simple-minded minister of Hirta was not alone in his view of the situation. He met up with 'a great gun of the Free Church, who was not ashamed to say that this lock-jaw was a wise device of the Almighty for keeping the population within the resources of the island'.

Emily MacLeod, having failed to persuade one of the St Kildan women to leave the island to be trained as a nurse, sent to Hirta in 1884 at her own expense 'a fully trained and proficient nurse, who had spent the greater part of her life in the capital of Scotland'. The St Kildans, however, were wary of accepting her new-fangled ideas about midwifery, and deaths from tetanus continued. It is likely that she was never allowed to be present at the birth of a child, or near the baby in those vital days during which the disease was contracted. The St Kildan women would not allow it, and they were supported in their decision by the Reverend John Mackay and his dominant housekeeper, who exercised their own brand of opposition. So life and death were allowed to go hand in hand on Hirta, decade after decade, until 1890, when the incumbent minister, the Reverend Angus Fiddes, decided to go to Glasgow during his summer leave and seek help.

Fiddes was convinced that tetanus was the result of a situation created by man. Those who had observed the plague from afar before him had attempted to put forward reasons for the prevalence of the disease. Some believed the islanders' oily and unvaried diet to be responsible; others, the St Kildan habit of weaning children on a mixture of wine or spirits with milk. Many had come to the conclusion that the abject squalor in which the people lived was the answer — the atrocious condition of their hovels in which home, byre, and refuse heap were inseparable was the cause. The construction of the new cottages by 1862, however, put paid to that theory. The damply warm, airless condition of the interior of their homes could well have played a part in bringing about so sudden and painful a death, but St Kildans' homes were not unique. Angus Fiddes had another theory.

In many of the more remote islands of Scotland, certain traditional customs were associated with birth. Few communities enjoyed the services of a trained nurse or midwife, and so one of their number, a *bean-ghluine*, or 'knee-woman' as she was called, was present at every birth and would perform several time-honoured rites upon the severed umbilical cord. In some parts of the country, the custom was for the knee-woman to take a rag, held to the fire by tongs, and then dress the cord of the newborn. In some parts of the Outer Hebrides, notably in Barvas on the isle of Lewis, the rag was frequently smeared with salt butter before the ceremony. Perhaps, it was argued, in St Kilda the custom was also practised, except instead of using butter which was scarce on Hirta, the knee-women used the ruby-red oil of the fulmar. As Dr George Gibson was to write in the *Caledonian Medical Journal* in 1926, 'The Bible would furnish plenty of precedent for anointing with oil, which in a devout community was bound to have its effect upon the semi-religious, semi-superstitious ministrations of the midwife.' The fulmar oil, of course, would have to be stored in a convenient vessel, and on Hirta the oil was normally stored in the dried stomachs of solan geese. The tetanus bug was thought to originate from such a container. 'Such a jar,' wrote Gibson, 'frequently refilled, never properly cleaned out would be a suitable nidus for the tetanus bacillus.'

No one knows for sure whether such practices ever took place on Hirta. No outsider, not even the minister or the schoolmaster, knew what went on when a baby was born. Such rites as were supposedly carried out were performed in secret, away from the prying eyes of all who were not St Kildan by birth.

In 1890, disturbed, anxious and concerned, the Reverend Angus Fiddes went to Glasgow and sought the services of a nurse. Nurse Chishall agreed to help and went to St Kilda. During the ten months she was on the island, three babies were born. Two of them died and one lived beyond the eight days. The fortunate mother was the then 'Queen of St Kilda', and Nurse Chishall believed that the baby survived 'because it had all new things at birth'. What is certain about the nurse's time on Hirta, is that superstition and a determined fear of new ways made sure that she had little chance of taking the place of the island's traditional midwife.

Before they returned to St Kilda in July 1891, Nurse Chishall and the Reverend Fiddes called on Professor Reid of Glasgow University. The professor diagnosed the cause of the disease as best he could, given their descriptions of the symptoms, and sketched out a method of treatment of the umbilicus which, he believed, would give any future baby born on Hirta the best chance of surviving the plague. The treatment, however, though satisfactory on paper and medically sound, proved of little benefit in practice. During the ten months up to May 1892, five children were born on St Kilda and only two of them lived. The nurse, it seemed, had failed in her duty, despite much encouragement from the occupant of the manse. The opposition of ignorance and custom proved too strong for her modern antiseptic ways.

For many years after Nurse Chishall took her leave of Hirta, the Scottish Board of Health was unable to find a nurse who was willing to submit herself to a period of virtual exile on St Kilda. Angus Fiddes soldiered on. He returned to the mainland to consult various experts in the world of medicine as to the best ways of treating the umbilical cord. He was still of the opinion, as were the doctors he consulted, that it was at the very instant of birth that tetanus was contracted.

Under Dr Turner of Glasgow, Fiddes took a course in midwifery. Armed with knowledge and tins of antiseptic powders, he returned to St Kilda to join battle with the 'knee-woman'. For hours and days he patiently attempted to convince a stubborn people that his way was best. On 18 August 1891, the last baby to suffer death from tetanus passed away, amid much wailing and weeping on the part of the women. On Christmas Day 1912, Miss Maclean, the daughter of the then minister, was able to claim in a letter to Thomas Nicol that not a single child during her three-year stay on Hirta had died of tetanus infantum. The opposition had been overcome.

The reason given at the time and held to this day by many medical authorities for the presence of the tetanus bug on St Kilda, was that the container in which the fulmar oil was kept was the culprit. Inseparable as were dirt and the St Kildan way of life, the germ normally associated with the earth could easily have entered the stomach of the gannet where it would have been allowed to breed at will.

The antiseptic methods introduced by Fiddes and continued after he departed from Hirta undoubtedly cleared up the disease. No one, however, can say for certain that his methods conquered the problem. Perhaps tetanus had by then run its course, and the rites that doctors assumed were carried out on the island never in fact took place at all. Whatever the reason for the disease, its consequences were undeniable.

Throughout the thirty years of the twentieth century that were left to the St Kildans, the mainland saw to it that they were provided with adequate medical facilities. The Department of Health for Scotland sent a nurse to look after their needs whenever they could find one prepared to fill the post. A room in the factor's house was made available for her, and she was amply supplied with medicines. Once a year a qualified doctor was sent by the Board to examine the population and vaccinate the children. But medical aid was forever limited : surgery was always impossible, and from September to May those who took seriously ill on St Kilda were in danger of their lives.

Because of the high mortality rate among infants, the seventy islanders left were for the most part adults. Tetanus had robbed the community of not one, but many, generations. The population was never to increase, in part, perhaps because few St Kildans even then thought there was much of a future in their way of life. St Kilda was never an attractive place to live, and by the end of the nineteenth century it was questionable whether economically it was still worth the struggle. The morale of the few that remained had been broken by a plague upon their children.

St Kilda was not to be repopulated by inhabitants from the other islands of Scotland and beyond. Although at one time life on Hirta had been better than that on many other islands, St Kilda had stood still whilst all around was changing. The island was to die and only the passage of time made death the easier to accept. The rest of society was growing away from St Kilda, and only charity and a dogged spirit kept the island populated until 1930.

10

A need to make contact

On 5 March 1877 a meeting was held in Edinburgh at which participants urged the government of the day to provide a postal service for the St Kildans. The meeting was hopeful that the authorities would agree. Earlier in the year the General Post Office had established postal communications on a fortnightly basis with the people of Fair Isle, off Shetland, and those at the meeting assumed the government would consider constructing a proper landing-place on Hirta, so that mails, provisions, and people could be more easily put ashore. The authorities turned the proposal down on the grounds of cost, but did at least agree to formalize the mail service which up till then was a fairly disorganized business. From the summer of 1879, John Mackenzie, the island's factor, based at Dunvegan, received a small subsidy for carrying mail to St Kilda.

Certain factors worked to make the St Kildans desire more contact with the mainland. Illness and the high mortality rate made life more difficult on Hirta, and improved communication was thought to be essential if people were to survive on the island. Thanks to the educating influence of the Church, more St Kildans were able to read and write, and could therefore keep in touch with those who had emigrated to Australia in 1852. What was wanted was a postal service.

In 1877, Emily MacLeod, the sister of the island's proprietor, independently suggested that HMS *Jackal*, which was based at Stornoway, be used to deliver mails to Hirta. *Jackal* had made the emergency trip to the island in February of that year to deliver supplies of food, but the men of the Admiralty refused. 'As St Kilda is the property of a private individual and within the jurisdiction of the Parochial Board of Harris,' wrote a civil servant, 'it is not considered that the services of HM ships should be called into requisition to supply the needs of a civil population.'

But the delivery and the collection of mail was sporadic. In March 1878, the surveyor in charge of the Scottish district of the GPO reported to his superior in London that letters often lay for months at Dunvegan before they were forwarded to St Kilda. He suggested that the Post Office should make arrangements for mail to be delivered in the spring and autumn so that, together with the factor's annual visit in the summer, the islanders should at least get mail three times a year. His idea was acted upon, and that summer a representative of the GPO visited Hirta to find that there were only three letters to deliver to the St Kildans, and that the islanders had written only ten to be collected. He estimated, therefore, that the total number of letters annually was 120, and that the provision of a proper postal service would be a waste of the taxpayers' money. To his way of thinking, quantity mattered more than the principle.

The mail continued to be put in the hands of ships' captains who for one reason or another included St Kilda on their itinerary. The problem appeared to be solved when two steamers, the *Dunara Castle* and the *Hebridean*, took in Hirta as part of their summer cruising programme. The two steamship companies involved, John McCallum and Martin Orme, received an annual payment of £500 between them from the Post Office for the fortnightly delivery of mail to St Kilda as well as providing an all-year-round service to the islands of Colonsay and Soay. By 1895, the two ships provided the people of Village Bay with six deliveries of mail a year. But for nine months of the year, the islanders were still without any means of communicating with their friends and relatives on the mainland and beyond.

The development of steam-driven trawlers provided a solution to the problem. They had a greater range than the old sailing vessels, and the rich waters of the north-west Atlantic were henceforth within reach of the fishermen of Aberdeen and Fleetwood. In the 1890s the trawlermen, eager for the rich catches of cod and halibut that were to be found around St Kilda, frequently called into Village Bay to mend their fishing gear or escape the discomfort of a storm. The GPO were happy to rely on the goodwill of the fisherfolk of Aberdeen and other ports, who could provide the St Kildans with a postal service during the months when no other shipping would dare to chance the North Atlantic. During the winter of 1897-8, the trawler *Evening Star* made no less than twenty-five trips to Hirta and delivered mail on each occasion.

In May 1898, it was announced in the *Post Office Circular* that 'all correspondence for the island of St Kilda should for the future be sent to Aberdeen'. Despite official recognition of the service rendered by the trawlermen, there was still no mention made of payment by the Post Office. The St Kildans had to rely on goodwill. They handed over money to the skippers, who took the letters and parcels along to the post office in Aberdeen to be stamped when they reached their home port, some thirty-six hours after they left Hirta. After a time, however, the postmaster of Aberdeen made the trawlermen a small *ex gratia* payment of ten shillings every time they brought mail from St Kilda or were prepared to take some out. It was a makeshift method of providing the inhabitants of Village Bay with a service that most on the mainland regarded as their right.

In the autumn of 1899, the factor, John Mackenzie, asked the GPO if they would consider setting up a proper post office on Hirta. He estimated that nearly 250 letters had been delivered to St Kilda during the previous twelve months, and that some 500 had left the island. The GPO took heed of his suggestion. They were worried that the bags containing mail were being delivered to a community in which no one was officially responsible for them. Administratively, they agreed, it was a bad situation.

At first the GPO said they would allow a post office to be set up on St Kilda provided it remained open in the summer months only. There would be a sub-postmaster appointed, who would be responsible for door-to-door delivery of the mail, and they would pay him £2 a year for his trouble. The factor, however, finally persuaded the authorities to allow the post office to stay open all the year round. With the proprietor's blessing, a room on the ground floor of the manse became the sub-post office of St Kilda, sanctioned by an official GPO Minute on 20 September 1899.

Up until then, the minister on Hirta had acted as self-appointed organizer of the mail. He had made himself responsible for sorting out the incoming letters and parcels and making arrangements for the collection of outgoing post. It was logical, therefore, that the Reverend Angus Fiddes be appointed sub-postmaster at an annual salary of £5 plus bonuses. The first steamer to visit Hirta in May 1900 brought the brass mailbag seal, and by July of that year the St Kilda Post Office, complete with its own date-stamping equipment, was fully operational. When Fiddes was succeeded by missionaries as spiritual leader of the community, they in turn acted as postmasters.

In December 1906, the first and last St Kildan ever to become postmaster was appointed. Neil Ferguson, the factor's representative on St Kilda, took over the work and the salary from the missionary. Four years after his appointment he was being paid £10 a year and a bonus of £2 15s. A rural post and delivery service was introduced in Hirta on 14 November 1910. Neil Ferguson was henceforth to be paid a shilling every time he transported the mailbags to and from the steamers and trawlers, and sixpence for delivering the incoming mail from door to door. By 1926, Neil was receiving three shillings and sixpence for ferrying the mail, and elevenpence each time he had occasion to walk up the little street and hand the post out to his fellow islanders. At the evacuation, in fact, Neil Ferguson was the richest man on St Kilda and the islander who had the most to lose by abandoning the island.

There still remained the problem of delivering mail in winter. The trawlermen proved to be reliable carriers only as long as it suited them to fish around St Kilda. Peter MacLachlan, while missionary on the island, wrote to John Weir, MP for the Western Isles, suggesting that perhaps the Northern Lighthouse Commissioners' ship *Hesperus* might be employed to service St Kilda. The ship already paid monthly visits to the lighthouses on the Monach and Flannan isles, both of which lay about forty miles away from St Kilda, and it seemed sensible to MacLachlan that the *Hesperus* call in at Hirta. The GPO had sounded out the Commissioners frequently since 1903, but in March 1907 the Post Office officials were bluntly told that there was no possibility whatsoever of co-operation.

The situation became more acute when the fishermen of Aberdeen decided to give up fishing round St Kilda. Cod and halibut deserted the waters, so the trawlers went elsewhere. Dogfish, however, were to be found in increasing numbers and, although thought too coarse to eat by Scots, were the foundation of the northern Englishman's fish and chip supper. From 1906, the Fleetwood trawlers took over the fishing grounds of the north-western Atlantic.

The informal arrangements for transporting mails to St Kilda were transferred from the postmaster at Aberdeen to the postmaster at Fleetwood. The St Kildans, however, were to suffer from the frequent arguments that broke out between the GPO and the trawler owners. Although individual skippers were happy with the *ex gratia* ten shillings they received at both ports, their masters believed that if their boats were to be used to deliver the Royal Mail they should be paid the going rate by the Post Office. The trawling companies of both Aberdeen and Fleetwood demanded that they be paid £10 a trip. The Post Office refused: after all, their total revenue from the postage involved during the winter months never exceeded four shillings. Besides, the GPO claimed that they had never officially commissioned the trawlers to carry the St Kilda mail, but had agreed they could do so only if it was convenient.

In 1909, the Head Postmaster at Aberdeen negotiated with the trawling company of Bookless Brothers with a view to formalizing the St Kilda mail service. In the previous two winters, their trawlers had been to Hirta eleven times, and it seemed the time had come to make some arrangement with them. Bookless demanded £10 a trip. The GPO, wishing only to make formal the payment they were already making of ten shillings a trip, thought his demand preposterous. The trawler owner reduced his demand to £2, and the Post Office upped their offer to £1 for a round trip in which mail was not only delivered but collected. Bookless agreed, and it looked for a while as though the problem of providing the people of St Kilda with a postal service during the winter had been solved.

By the winter of 1910 Bookless Brothers were managing to provide a fortnightly service, and when a rival company (Don Fishing) decided to contribute, the St Kildans received deliveries of mail four times in one month. But the trawlers were controlled not only by the fishing but by the weather. The four trawlers that visited Hirta in January 1911 were the last the islanders were to see for three months.

Bad weather, illness, poor harvests, and the consequent lack of food were to frustrate the St Kildans at regular intervals throughout the twentieth century. The lack of reliable communication made such occurrences even more troublesome in the period up to the outbreak of the First World War.

Shortage of food was something that the St Kildans had always had to live with. 'The people are suffering very much from want of food,' wrote the Reverend Neil Mackenzie when, as resident minister, he was forced to live among the St Kildans between the years 1829 and 1843. 'During Spring, ere the birds came, they literally cleared the shore not only of shell-fish, but even of a species of seaweed that grows abundantly on the rocks within the sea-mark. For a time they were better off, particularly as long as fresh eggs could be got. Now the weather is coarse, birds cannot be found, at least in such abundance as their needs require. Sorrel boiled in water is the principal part of the food and even that grass is getting scarce. All that was near is exhausted.' But in earlier times the islanders usually managed to survive, if only because they were prepared to scour their homeland and consume all that was edible. In later years they put their faith more in an increasing contact with the mainland to help them in moments of need.

The financial resources required to provide for the St Kildans in time of need existed from 1859. In that year a benevolent gentleman called Kelsall had died in the West Indies and, aware of the existence of the people of Hirta, he made allowances in his will that a sum of £600 be given to the Highland and Agricultural Society for the express purpose of helping the islanders. The only condition that Kelsall had made in giving the money was that the society should not spend it in a way that might be of benefit to the proprietor of the island. By the 1880s much of the money had been spent (£254 in fact) in supplying the St Kildans with such items as a new boat, seed corn, and a bull. It was forever a problem, however, for the society to decide when the Kelsall Fund was applicable, for as Mr Fletcher Menzies, the Treasurer to the society, remarked in 1877, 'It is not very easy to benefit the inhabitants without in some way benefiting the proprietor.' Moreover, the society considered it wise to keep from the people of Hirta knowledge that such a fund existed, lest they might come to depend upon it and be spoiled. The important problem, however, was summed up by John Sands when he wrote, 'The Kelsall Fund was left by the benevolent donor to assist the people of St Kilda in seasons of emergency. But when distress occurs, how are the beneficiaries to let the treasurer know of it, or if a messenger, by rare chance, happens to get from St Kilda to Edinburgh, how is he to make Mr Menzies believe that he is speaking the truth?' Sands suggested that perhaps the money could be put to better use. A store of emergency supplies on Hirta and an annual handout of basic foodstuffs to the poor on the island would, he argued, be of more help. The Highland and Agricultural Society, however, always aware of spending money that was not theirs, continued their policy of deliberating for months before committing a penny of Kelsall's bequest.

In 1911, having experienced the luxury of four mails in January, the islanders were cut off totally from the mainland for three months. Severe gales made fishing impossible. The islanders were not relieved until April, when a fishery cruiser, HMS *Pathfinder*, was sent from Greenock with mail and foodstuffs. The following winter was equally disastrous. For four months in the spring of 1912 the St Kildans were without mail, and for part of the time their food stocks were depleted. By May the community of Hirta faced starvation.

James Rennie, captain of the trawler *Strathmore*, brought news of the islanders' plight when he docked at Aberdeen on 18 May. Severe gales had kept the trawlers away since Christmas, and a ship with stores had tried twice unsuccessfully to land them. When the news of the famine broke, the *Daily Mirror* newspaper decided to organize a relief expedition. Although it was difficult to obtain provisions on a Saturday, Sir Thomas Lipton and Sir Joseph Lyons agreed to contribute generously. Within three hours of first hearing the news, the *Mirror*'s relief expedition was on its way from London to Glasgow, where one of the fastest tugs on the Clyde, the *Victor*, had been chartered.

On Monday 20 May, the *Victor* reached St Kilda. Meanwhile Winston Churchill, then First Lord of the Admiralty, had decided to send HMS *Achilles* with an emergency supply of foodstuffs. The people of St Kilda were saved from starvation. 'Dear Editor,' wrote the missionary on behalf of the St Kildans on 21 May, 'A thousand thanks for your great kindness to the lonely St Kildans in their distress for the want of provisions. Your help reached us un-expectedly and left us the more thankful for it. Could you see those lonely people at this moment dividing the "spoil", I am sure you would not consider your kind efforts thrown away.' The *Mirror* was certainly delighted with its efforts, and gave the story every prominence in the paper for several days complete with banner headlines and pages of photographs. The newspaper decided that they would campaign for a wireless transmitter to be put on Hirta and opened up a fund.

H. Gordon Selfridge, owner of one of the largest department stores in Britain, was so moved by the situation that he immediately donated £100, and the newspaper had high hopes that the station might be operational within a few weeks. 'That the inhabitants of St Kilda', said the *Mirror*, 'may never again be faced with the terrible spectre of famine without being able to appeal for help is the reason that *The Daily Mirror*, with Mr Selfridge's help, has determined to make communication between the island and the mainland possible at all times.' Permission to erect the station was readily given by the proprietor, and an application to the Postmaster-General was made in June by Mr J. H. Webb on behalf of the newspaper.

Several government agencies were quick to raise objections and impose conditions upon the scheme. The newspaper had hoped that they would be able to call upon the transmitter managed by the Northern Lighthouse Commissioners to relay messages sent from Hirta. Although from the start it was intended that the wireless on Hirta would be of the simplest type possible for use solely in emergencies, the Commissioners flatly refused permission. It was agreed, therefore, that communication would have to be made via Lochboisdale. The Post Office were immediately suspicious of the scheme, fearing that they would very quickly become responsible for maintaining the station, should the *Mirror* decide to abandon its creation. After much debate and discussion as to the rates that would be charged for telegrams from St Kilda, the Post Office finally granted a licence in January 1913, seven months after the initial application had been made.

At 10.35 in the morning of 20 June 1913, Captain William Rilatt of the trawler *Mercury* sent a telegram. He had just returned to Harris from St Kilda which he had visited on 15 June, and had been shocked by what he saw. The telegram was addressed to the editor of the *Daily Mirror*. 'Sir,' wrote Rilatt, 'Would you kindly insert this in your newspaper – that every man, woman and child on the island of St Kilda is stricken down with influenza or pneumonia, and they are in need of assistance, having no one to attend them or cook their food.' Three days prior to the trawler skipper's visit to St Kilda, the *Dunara Castle* had paid her first visit of the year and had brought influenza with her passengers. The islanders had always lacked resistance to the common cold, and within a week the entire population was laid up. About twenty children were seriously ill, the women were equally stricken, and there was little food left after the hard winter.

The newspaper immediately contacted the Admiralty, and was informed by a secretary : 'We would like to make further enquiries before doing anything. It is an interesting item of news, but I cannot possibly say whether we shall do anything or not.'

The newspaper immediately chartered the *Flying Serpent*, one of the fastest steamers on the Clyde, and a reporter and photographer were put on the two o'clock train to Glasgow. Fortunately, the Scottish Board officially asked that a cruiser be sent to relieve

St Kilda. HMS *Active* was sent from Lamlash in Arran on 21 June with a medical officer on board.

The following month, the wireless station was finally installed on St Kilda. A firm of London building contractors was sent by the *Mirror* to install the two seventy-five-foot masts. The transmitter, which had a range of seventy-five-miles, was installed in the factor's house, and a corrugated iron shack was built by house Number 5 to accommodate the Post Office. A representative of the British Telegraph Instruments Co. Ltd. tested the machinery, and the missionary, Mr MacArthur, was shown how to use it. On 29 July the first messages were sent – one to the King, another to the newspaper which had been responsible for installing the station. The ceremony was completed when a metal plate was fixed to one of the masts, inscribed: 'This wireless station was installed by the *Daily Mirror* for the use of the inhabitants of St Kilda in time of acute distress.'

On 6 October the station broke down. The *Mirror* made some improvements to it, and sent a German called Gustaf Flick to operate the set throughout the coming winter. Contact with the mainland was maintained and a few telegrams were sent.

On 5 April the newspaper announced that it wished the GPO to take over the station. It was what the Post Office had feared would happen, and estimating that the cost of operating the wireless on St Kilda to be in the region of £400 a year, said they would have nothing to do with it. They later agreed they would buy the station from the Marconi Company who actually owned it for £350, if some £200 could be provided annually by a guarantor. The guarantor would also have to bear the cost of training an islander to operate the wireless. No one could be found to put up the money. The station was closed down and the *Daily Mirror* began dismantling the wireless. The St Kildans were forced to return to their state of isolation. Only when war came to Britain in 1914 was the government to think a wireless station on Hirta something worth paying for. The station was not made operational for the benefit of the islanders – mainland society needed to defend itself and Hirta was admirably suited to the task of maintaining a watch on north Atlantic shipping.

When Martin Martin, the island's first historian, had visited St Kilda in the seventeenth century, he commented on the virtues of the community's isolation. 'The inhabitants of St Kilda', he wrote, 'are much happier than the generality of mankind as being the only people in the world who feel the sweetness of true liberty.' His only proviso was that the St Kildans themselves were not in a position to discover how lucky and how much happier they were. By the end of the nineteenth century, they were perhaps increasingly aware of how lucky their forefathers had been. For the latter-day islanders, the sweetness of true liberty was turning sour.

11
The beginning of the end

A German submarine surfaced at the head of Village Bay at precisely 10.40 in the morning on 15 May 1918. 'We had a phone down to the wireless,' recalls Neil Gillies, then a young man, more enthusiastic about being at war than were his elders, 'and we phoned down that the submarine was making for the bay. He came quite close, to the point where you could have flung a stone right into the conning tower.' The captain, in the best English he could muster, warned the St Kildans over a loud-hailer that he was about to shell the island in order to destroy the Navy's wireless station. The islanders took rapid cover in the Dry Burn, a deep gully that lay behind the village street. The captain fired seventy-two shells: the St Kildans were literally bombarded into the twentieth century.

Shortly after the outbreak of the First World War, the Admiralty decided to send a naval detachment to St Kilda. If nature had designed a place suited to the observation of shipping in the North Atlantic, it was Hirta. The island became a War Signal Station, and on 12 January 1915 the first naval personnel under the command of Captain Frank Athow, RMLI(Retd), landed there. The little party comprised two Petty Officers, twelve ratings, and a Marine batman. Their first concern was to put right the old wireless donated by the *Daily Mirror*. Although Captain Athow had been on the retired list since the Boer War, somehow he and his men managed to get the old Marconi set operational, and regular daily communication was kept up with the Naval Centre at Aultbea in Wester Ross.

They were good days for the St Kildans. Apart from being in constant radio contact with the mainland, the islanders were able to buy supplies from the tiny garrison which was regularly supplied with food by HMS *Cyclops* based at Scapa Flow, and later by His Majesty's Depot Ship *Manco*, which worked out of Stornoway. The personnel was changed every four months by the navy in case the men should find the isolation of St Kilda too much for them. Mail was delivered from the mainland every week, and the islanders were able to make use of the service. Armed trawlers and whalers based at Stornoway provided the people with that luxury throughout the entire period of the war, in winter as well as summer.

The St Kildans became prosperous during the first war they had ever been involved in. Money circulated freely, not only among the men of the navy but also among the islanders. Most of the St Kildan men were employed round the village area – digging trenches, erecting the wooden prefabricated huts sent over from the mainland to accommodate the detachment, and laying telegraphic cables from the look-out posts in the hills to the wireless station. Some were employed by the navy to act as watchmen, at a pay of two shillings a day. The look-out posts were set up on Conachair, Oiseval, and Mullach Mor, and from the three of them, depending on weather, only the far horizon put a limit on what could be seen. 'Four of them,' recalls Neil Ferguson, 'were watchmen in the hills. They took it in turn to watch.' The navy normally gave the islanders the worst shifts. 'You were given fifteen bob a week,' says Neil, 'including Sunday and all, for doing your back shift – eight to twelve, twelve to four, four to six, and six to eight.' The islanders reported back to the wireless station any shipping seen, and the information was radioed to Aultbea. When stores had to be landed the St Kildans were again employed. 'The other civilians,' remembers the Reverend Donald Gillies, 'were also trained. At certain hours during the week, one would attend the lectures that would let you know just exactly how to act in an emergency.'

The bombardment of the island in May 1918 was the first experience the St Kildans had ever had of the reality of war. Fortunately, the shelling did not bring about any loss of human life. 'It wasn't what you'd call a bad submarine,' says Neil Gillies, 'because it could have blowed every house down because they were all in a row there. He only wanted Admiralty property. One lamb was killed,' remembers Neil. 'We had the sheep down at the shore at the time, they were lambing. All the cattle ran from one side of the island to the other when they heard the shots.' Apart from destroying the wireless station, the shelling did considerable damage to the church and the manse. The storehouse by the jetty was also hit, as were two cottages, and two boats were ruined.

No compensation was ever paid to the St Kildans or the proprietor of the island. Because the islanders were not party to the government's Insurance Scheme the authorities claimed that they were not liable, despite the fact that St Kilda would never have been shelled in the first place had there not been a Navy wireless station on the island. Even as late as April 1919, the Navy firmly claimed that they were 'not concerned in the matter'.

Instead they decided that the St Kildans needed the real machinery of war. A 4in. Mark III QF Gun, which had been cast in 1896, was sent over to the island in August 1918, and was installed on a raised promontory that gave a commanding view of the bay. The St Kildans were paid to lay the foundations of stone and concrete upon which was set the gun that would defend them. By the time the work had been completed, the war was virtually over. The gun was never fired.

The authorities, however, were much concerned with the maintenance of the gun they had gone to such great lengths to put on St Kilda. Neil Ferguson was made its custodian: for an annual payment of £25 he was made responsible to clean and grease it regularly so that, should war break out again, the money spent could still be justified. The Navy removed the breach block at the end of the war. Neil continued to be paid for several years, then the money stopped coming. 'So father,' says Neil Ferguson, his son, 'stopped greasing the gun.'

On 6 February 1919 the men of the Royal Navy were removed from Hirta. With them went some of the hearts of the island girls. A few of the young women left St Kilda to settle elsewhere in Scotland, and some of the younger men thought in terms of finding employment on the mainland. In two years, 1919 and 1920, the population of St Kilda fell by 25 per cent.

'Due to the First War, we had navy men there from various parts of Britain,' recalls the Reverend Gillies. 'They were friendly with the population and I think that the younger generation came to learn quite a bit regarding the other parts of the world like London and Glasgow. They pictured this, and I think that this was a contributing factor for so many of the young people leaving. The information that was given to them by those individuals; they knew of a life which was entirely different from the life that they were living on the island. There was no comparison.'

The war was the first time the St Kildans realized that they could have a good life without having to endure the hardship associated with their traditional existence upon Hirta. The stories that they had previously heard from tourists were perhaps true after all. People, it seemed, were prepared to pay the St Kildans money for the performance of simple tasks. The experience of wartime showed that, with enough money, the St Kildans could buy all the things they needed to exist.

Smitten with the thought of an easier life, William Macdonald was the first St Kildan to decide to evacuate his entire family. The departure of the Macdonald family was a blow to the morale of those left upon Hirta. 'After we left,' recalls Malcolm Macdonald, William's son, 'they used to write, the rest of the islanders, and they were saying it looked very sad when they passed through the village to find our door closed. We were the first family who ever departed as a whole family from the island and to find the door was now closed was very depressing for them. We all lived as one big family and this was the first final break in the community. I'm sure they felt just the same as we were feeling departing from them; but it was the beginning of a new life for us.'

Other islanders followed the Macdonald example. Among the young who chose to seek a life elsewhere was Donald John Gillies. 'I saw myself alone there,' he says. 'As far as my age was concerned there was no one. The time had arrived that I would have to do something myself.' Donald John left Hirta in the summer of 1925. 'The boat was in,' he recalls, 'and I said, "Well, I'm going today." I just packed a few things that didn't take too long and was aboard the *Hebrides*. I had an uncle in Glasgow and an aunt and cousins and I was with them for a week until I made up my mind as to what I was actually going to do.'

Donald John Gillies worked on a dredger owned by the Clyde Trust Company for a month or two. But he decided that perhaps his calling was the ministry, and he applied to the Bible Training Institute in Glasgow. At the same time, he was working at the Argyle Mission on the south side of Glasgow. One Sunday in church, he listened to a preacher who was to make him change his plans. 'There was a stranger that preached the sermon,' remembers Donald John, 'and he said he was a graduate of Knox College, Toronto, and that his mission to this country was that he was recruiting for the ministry of the Presbyterian Church in Canada.' Gillies grasped the opportunity presented to him and applied there and then.

On Sunday, 7 May 1927, he arrived at Quebec on board the *Old Americana*. He studied hard and once ordained he went to British Columbia, where he has preached ever since. For some time after he retired from the Church, he acted as minister to presbyterian prisoners in a local state penitentiary. Donald John has proved to be the most successful of all the St Kildans.

For the few young men left on Hirta life was hard. Lachlan Macdonald stayed to look after his mother. His father had died in a drowning accident when Lachlan was young and his mother had been left to bring up the family. By the 1920s, only Lachlan was prepared to carry on living on St Kilda. 'My brother went away to Glasgow and my mother was bad with rheumatics,' he recalls. 'She was all crippled up and she was on sticks at the end. So I was doing most of the work myself and I was only young. I used to do the spinning, do everything just to help my mother.' Not yet twenty years old, Lachlan was also having to manage the croft, go with the men to hunt sea birds, and in the winter, of course, weave the cloth that would pay the rent. 'When the winter came,' he says, 'you think you are going to have a rest, but it was as hard in the winter as it was in the summer. You were out through the day looking after your sheep and cattle, then when it come night you were sitting there in the house and you had a pair of cards to comb up the wool and then spinning it and weaving it and so forth. It was maybe two or three o'clock in the morning before you would get to your bed. Then you were up again in the morning, away back to work again. There was nothing, just work, work, all the time.' Lachlan felt himself trapped. Like the rest of the young men left, he saw his task as staying on St Kilda to look after the older islanders who could not be persuaded to leave. 'A few young ones,' he says, 'would stay for the sake of the old folk and the work was getting that heavy that they weren't able to cope with it. And the young ones were not only helping their parents, they were helping everyone, according to tradition. If there was a lady there and she hadn't got a son,' says Lachlan, 'you would try to help her, or any old man, you would try to do a turn for him too.'

Ewen Macdonald, working in Glasgow, tried hard to persuade Lachlan to join him. Occasionally Lachlan agreed to spend a few weeks on the mainland in the summer months. He saw for himself that life need not be so hard. 'When I went back,' he says, 'I couldn't settle myself right on the island after that. There was nothing there – no enjoyment, or whatever you call it, just working from one day to another, even nights.'

After the war, the community became more dependent upon supplies of food coming from the mainland. The weather, it seems, was considerably more severe during the post-war winters. There were frequent disastrous harvests, similar to those that had brought the community to its knees in 1912 and 1913. Moreover, the war years had given the St Kildans a taste for imported foods. Although to the passing stranger their traditional diet of sea birds appeared substantial, it was monotonous, and the islanders lost little opportunity to incorporate items of food such as jams, sweets, tea, sugar, cocoa, and bread. Neil Ferguson remembers that in his day, the first meal of the day had altered from that of his forefathers. 'In our day,' he says, 'it was a cup of tea and an egg in the morning, that was the diet, and maybe butter or cheese or something like that; but in the older days they'd a plate of porridge. That was done away with in our day.' The main meal of the day was normally fulmar, puffin or gannet, but the St Kildans turned more to mutton. When they were away from the village for the day, they would take a picnic. 'When you went up the hill to cut peat or anything,' recalls Neil Ferguson, 'you had to carry your lunch. Maybe you'd boil two or three dozen eggs (taken from the nests of sea birds) and a flask of tea and bread and oatcakes. You had plenty of food with you.' Fewer fulmars and gannets were killed, in part because there were fewer men to hunt them. Instead, the community relied upon the trawlers that frequented the area during the winter months to bring out essential supplies of food. 'You depended on the boat more so in my day than they did in olden days,' says Lachlan Macdonald. 'In the olden days they had their own grinding stones to make meal and all that, and milked the sheep and cattle and made their own cheese and butter. In my days that was all done away with. Most of it was coming from the mainland and we were depending on the Fleetwood trawlers that used to come there fishing.'

It was only twenty-five years since the schoolmaster had noted in his diary how amazed the St Kildans were at the sight of a trawler in the bay. 'The landing of the men off any of these strange vessels', wrote John Ross in 1889, 'is the cause of the greatest consternation in the island even in these enlightened times. The women tending the flocks in the Glen hurry home with the dreadful news. *"Tha Goill air a Ghleann"* ["Foreigners are in the Glen"].' The St Kildans of the post-war period were to long for the arrival of the 'foreigner'.

The skipper of one such trawler was Donald Craig. Today he remembers vividly his early voyages to Hirta. He was remembered most by the St Kildans as one of the few skippers who could find his way into Village Bay even in misty weather, by following the flight of the sea birds. As captain of the *Brilliant Star*, he paid his first visit to St Kilda in 1903. 'When I went ashore,' says Donald, 'I fell in love with the St Kildan people and they fell for me.'

Craig and his fellow trawlermen did much to make life not only bearable but possible in the last years. Not only did they take essential supplies of flour, fresh fish, meat, sugar, and tea to Hirta, but they also supplied the islanders with ship's coal and paraffin to light and warm the homes of the few that were left. Rarely would they accept money. They were charitable because, as men who sailed in cramped trawlers through fair weather and foul, they more than most knew what deprivation was all about.

Donald Craig claims he was the first to introduce the game of football in St Kilda. He discovered on a visit that the children had never seen a proper ball before and resolved to correct such ignorance when he paid his next visit to the island. He had to return, in the meantime, to Aberdeen to land his catch. 'I went to see Aberdeen beat Rangers 2–1,' he recalls, 'and I followed the secretary round the pitch. I said, "I want that ball to take to St Kilda." He said, "You'll get a ball for two shillings and sixpence anywhere," and I said, "I want *that* ball for St Kilda – it beat the Rangers 2–1. Come on, I'll give you ten shillings for it." So I got the ball and when I went back to St Kilda the four boys and the four girls were down at the water's edge shouting, "Have you got the ball, Donald, have you got the ball?" So I got the ball ashore and the minister and his wife and daughter were in goal and the other people watched. We showed them how to play. When we went back one month later, however, they showed us.'

Captain Craig took the first mirror to Hirta. 'I gave it to a man called Norman MacQueen,' he says, 'and he used to keep it in his pocket. One day when I was in the bay I blew the horn and in a hurry he took it out of his pocket and put it below his pillow in his bed. His wife thought, "Now I'll have a look at her" – she thought it was a picture of a woman he was looking at. And when she looked into the mirror, she said, "Huh, she's not a beauty anyway!" '

The White Man's League of Friendship was also founded by Craig. On shore leave in Aberdeen, he purchased some eighty wooden daggers resembling crosses, and with much ceremony he presented them to the St Kildans. Each islander put the dagger round his neck. 'They wore them on their breasts,' says Craig, 'and they used to hold them in their hand and say, "By the help of God, may the day that I betray my fellow man or woman, may this dagger pierce my heart. Fear God, fear no man." ' The hierarchy of the White Man's League was simple, Craig informed the islanders: 'God's the President, Jesus Vice-President, and Donald McBain Craig, DSC, RD, the Recruiting Officer.'

As long as the waters round St Kilda abounded with fish, the islanders were well served by the trawlers. On one occasion, Mary Cameron, the daughter of the missionary, counted forty-seven trawlers in the bay, all of which were willing to help the islanders in some way or another. 'Our parents', she recalls, 'used to hang a lamp as a guiding light in the window of the house which directly faced the mouth of the bay,' as there were no navigation aids to help small boats find safe anchorage. Most of the young men on Hirta had learnt semaphore signalling from the Navy during the war, and the skill proved useful in communicating with trawlers that otherwise might have passed the island by.

The inhabitants of St Kilda got to know the trawlermen well. Captain Donald Craig was of course a regular visitor from Aberdeen. From the port of Fleetwood, the islanders looked forward to visits from the Wright brothers, the Brewster family and the Sandhams. Many of the ling fishermen from the east coast of Scotland were strong Sabbatarians, and the strains of Moody and Sankey tunes frequently wafted across the becalmed waters of Village Bay.

In the summer months, apart from the steamers that regularly visited Hirta, the St Kildans could rely upon the whaling ships. Manned mostly by Norwegians, these ships worked out of the station at Bunavoneddar in Harris. The captains of the vessels felt a sense of obligation to the islanders, as they frequently had to leave their inflated whales in the bay, thereby polluting the air, until they had caught enough to tow back to their base.

Throughout the early 1920s, the GPO managed to maintain a fairly regular mail service during the winter months. Up until September 1924, the St Kilda mails were carried almost exclusively by the trawler *Erna*, operating out of Fleetwood. Throughout the two following winters six trawlers were regularly employed by the Postmaster of Fleetwood to carry mail to Hirta. For a time it looked as though, at long last, a solution had been found to a problem that had beset the Post Office for nearly half a century.

In the autumn of 1926, however, the GPO was lucky to find one trawler, the *Robert Murray*, skippered by Sidney Tonner, to take the mail to Hirta. The trawler owners were again calling into question the paltry sum the authorities were prepared to pay them to carry out such an essential service. Tonner managed on his own to deliver and collect mails from St Kilda once a month, for two winters. To the St Kildans left on Hirta, such a service was becoming vital, if only because letters to and from those who had left the island were regarded as important. Often they contained money as well as news from sons and daughters who had emigrated to the mainland. In January 1928, Tonner himself wrote to the Postmaster at Fleetwood demanding £5 for each round trip to St Kilda, instead of the £1 which he thought derisory. The skipper of the *Robert Murray* said in his letter that his previous trip on 6 December 1927 had cost him £50 more than it should have done because he had had to go to St Kilda. Bad weather had delayed his landing on Hirta, and he had had to burn fuel and waste time while he waited for a favourable tide. The GPO stubbornly refused to up the money, so Tonner refused to take the mail to St Kilda.

The St Kildans went without mail for eleven weeks. When the trawler *Loughrig* finally agreed to take the letters and packages to the most westerly inhabited part of Britain, there were nearly a dozen sackfuls waiting. The GPO had tried to persuade the trawlermen of Aberdeen to take mail, but were unsuccessful. The trawler owners stood firm in their claim for better payment. Even Captain Craig was forbidden by his employer to take mail aboard his trawler. The government and the trawler owners had reached an *impasse*. While they argued, the inhabitants of St Kilda were left to suffer.

Whenever a post managed to get through to St Kilda, the mailbags were rowed ashore by the postmaster, Neil Ferguson Senior. In an ex-navy hut adjoining the manse, Ferguson broke the seals and began sorting the letters and parcels. 'Everybody gathered expectantly at the door.' recalls Mary Cameron, 'and, as the name and address of each item was called out, the recipient stepped forward and claimed it as it was passed from hand to hand over the heads of the little crowd.' Much of the mail was for the missionary and his family; occasionally he was entitled to a small red sack of his own. Many people on the mainland sent him quantities of newspapers and magazines for his personal enlightenment, as well as that of the flock he dutifully tried to serve.

When the mails were infrequent, the missionary did his best to complain and draw attention to inadequate service being provided.

'Once I remember we were eleven weeks without mails,' says Mary Cameron, 'and were opening our Christmas cards in March . . . In a newspaper which arrived by that mail, there was a sensational report of the hardship inflicted upon the people of London who had, owing to a printing dispute, been obliged to go without their morning papers for (I think) three days. My father was so struck by the humour of it that he wrote to the paper concerned, telling of the length of time which His Majesty's subjects on St Kilda had had to wait for their Christmas mail.' The letter was published and resulted in huge sackfuls of mail arriving on the island. 'People from all over the country (some of whom had probably never even heard of St Kilda before) sent reading matter,' recalls Mary Cameron, 'and one gentleman sent my father the *Manchester Guardian* regularly from then on for quite a long time.'

The last ten years the St Kildans lived on Hirta consistently illustrated the fragile nature of their existence. In February 1923, the Chief Constable of the Inverness-shire Police Station at Tarbert in Harris paid a visit to St Kilda and reported that despite the fact that the seventy-five inhabitants were in good health, 'some families were completely out of flour, meal and sugar. Those who had supplies shared them as far as they would go among their neighbours.' The islanders, said the Chief Constable, had been saved from starvation by a trawler from Fleetwood and by the arrival of the ship *Sarpendon* of the Blue Funnel Line. The directors of the shipping company, on a maiden voyage in their new passenger liner, had been generous enough to land sufficient stores of food to keep the St Kildans alive until the *Hebrides* arrived in late May. The lack of foodstuffs had been brought about by a bad harvest the previous year. 'Last year's potato crop', wrote Chief Constable Ross, 'was a failure and the potato crop this year is very uncertain. The corn and hay is well advanced and promises well . . . Last year's fulmar season was also very successful but the natives are very uncertain of this year.'

In the year 1926, when Britain was in the grip of a General Strike, the people of St Kilda caught 'flu. The strike was to make little difference, in the long run, to the survival of the United Kingdom, but the influenza epidemic that took a hold on St Kilda killed four islanders and made sure that the island would have to be evacuated.

'I went into the bay one day,' remembers Donald Craig, 'and I said, that's funny – there wasn't a movement, there wasn't a dog barking, there wasn't any smoke or anything . . . I said surely they must all be dead.' Every St Kildan – man, woman, and child – was laid up with 'flu. Neil Ferguson Junior remembers how the epidemic happened in May 1926. 'We went out to this trawler,' he says, 'and they said don't come aboard, a load of the crew is laid up with the 'flu. The men wouldn't stop and they went aboard to get newspapers. Two or three days after the whole crowd were laid up with the 'flu.' There was a resident nurse on Hirta at the time – Nurse Littlejohn from Banchory in Aberdeenshire, but she too fell ill, and besides, her supply of medicines was almost exhausted.

Owing to the General Strike there was little chance of help in the form of a trawler arriving. 'One night,' remembers Mary Cameron, 'Nurse and a few of the young men dragged themselves to a hilltop with materials for a bonfire, hoping to attract the attention of passing shipping.' No ship passed : four islanders died. Lachlan Macdonald, who had just finished his schooling, was one of the few able-bodied men on the island. It was up to him and one or two others to make coffins for the dead. 'We had to make a coffin for this old lady,' he recalls, 'and there wasn't any wood. We had to use the wood from her own ceiling.' The old woman's cottage was ransacked to find planks big enough to make a box in which she could be buried. Lachlan had never made a coffin before, but had to do the best he could; the plank was half cut where the shoulder was to be, and then boiling water poured over the wood so that it could be bent into shape.

In the evening of the day the fourth St Kildan was laid to rest in the graveyard, the *Hebrides* paid her first visit of the summer. Only then was the world informed of the disaster that had struck Hirta. 'I can still remember the horror at that time,' says Mary Cameron who, with her younger sister, was also struck down. 'We were delirious, with soaring temperatures, and our biscuits were all finished, so there was nothing light with which to tempt our capricious appetites. I think my mother made fruit drinks for us with spoonfuls of jam, and she had a few table jellies left.' The St Kildans recovered medically from the epidemic, but influenza had dealt a mortal blow to their morale.

When Police Constable McKay from Harris made his report in May 1928, he wrote of a community in the throes of death. There were only thirty-seven St Kildans left on Hirta, but, noted McKay, 'There is talk of some more of the natives leaving the island because the living obtained is so poor.' The only article of wealth they

Above 17. The adult men of Hirta were responsible for the hazardous task of harvesting the seabirds which bred annually on the cliffs of the archipelago

Left 18. The puffin was the staple diet of the islanders during the summer months. The birds were skilfully lassoed with a fowling rod, then boiled and eaten with potatoes

Above 19. On Conachair, the fowlers, working in pairs, lowered themselves down from the cliff-top. The men worked in their bare feet in order to get a better grip on the treacherous grass ledges of the cliffs

Right 20. Everyone had a part to play in the fulmar harvest which took place every August. Women and children carried the heavy birds down from the top of the cliffs of Conachair to the village

21. At the end of each day's killing, the seabirds were shared out equally. Even the old and infirm, who played no part in their slaughter, received a portion. The same night, the birds would be plucked, and then preserved for eating during the long, winter months

22. Rent day, St Kilda. The factor, representing the owner of the island, visited Hirta once a year to claim the rent. As the years wore on the native produce became less and less valuable

Left 24. The St Kildan way of life would not have been possible withou the cleits. Not only were they essential for the preservation of the islanders' staple food, the seabirds, but they were also storehouses of fishing tackle, ropes, and other belongings which would otherwise have rotted in the damp heat of their homes

Below 23. It took eight men to pull th island's boats clear of the water. Without boats and the men to act as crew, St Kilda could not have survived

Above 25. St Kildan
sheep were never sheared. The
islanders plucked the wool
with the help of a penknife in
order to obtain only the softest
fleece

Right 26. Every household
owned at least one spinning
wheel. Once plucked, the wool
was carded and then spun by
the women. Most of the yarn
went to make tweed

Left 27. The St Kildan women were rarely seen without their knitting. Thousands of socks and hundreds of scarves were made annually from the soft, warm wool of the domesticated and Soay sheep

Above right 28. In winter the simple handlooms which were stored in the loft of each home were brought out and assembled in the living-room

Centre right 29. The St Kildans paid rent to their landlord in kind. Every year, thousands of yards of homespun tweed, together with stones of feathers, were handed over to MacLeod of Macleod's representative

Below right 30. Normally the women ground the scant crop of oats in the quern, but the men enjoyed giving a demonstration for a visiting photographer

Right 31. The summer months were busy ones. The children, like Rachel Gillies, had to do their share of the work

Below 32. The St Kildans took little interest in raising cattle. Sadly, at the evacuation in 1930 the few cows on Hirta were the islanders' only possessions of value

possessed was their tweed, the product of long and hard winter hours of work. 'Regarding the dipping of their sheep,' continued the police constable, 'I learned they were doing their best under the different circumstances in which they were placed, there being only seven able-bodied men to engage in this work. The rest are either old or too young.' The St Kildans had managed to reap a generous harvest of fulmars the previous summer, but the crops had not fared well. 'Last autumn the weather was very stormy and consequently the potato crop suffered to a great extent,' wrote McKay. 'They had a fairly liberal supply of provisions during the winter, and any family that happened to run short were fortunate in obtaining a supply from the trawlers operating in the waters round St Kilda. On the whole, their winter's supply met their needs and there was no actual want.' The St Kildans, according to the policeman, were pleased to inform him that they had managed to get all their crops into the ground for the coming winter's supply of food, and McKay concluded that 'generally speaking the prospects for the coming winter are good'. Unknown to everyone, the winter of 1929 was to be the last the St Kildans would spend upon their inhospitable isle.

The last tourist steamer of the season left Village Bay on 15 August 1929. It was the last contact the islanders had with the mainland for over two months. When skipper Tonner, now in charge of the trawler *Merisia*, called in in mid-October he discovered there had been an outbreak of wet eczema on the island and that medical supplies were urgently required by Nurse Barclay. As soon as he could, Tonner passed the information on to the GPO, who informed the Board of Health for Scotland. The Board did nothing. As they had not heard from their nurse on the island on the matter, they could not confirm Tonner's message and would therefore wait. The fact that it had been impossible for Nurse Barclay to send a letter from Hirta for two months did not seem to occur to them.

The newspapers were already sensing an impending death. They began to hound the trawlermen with enquiries as to how the people of St Kilda were faring. In doing so they put an end to any possibility of concerned skippers looking in on Hirta. The skippers had always exercised a degree of independence while at sea, and had frequently gone against their owners' instructions not to go to St Kilda. The owners, however, had installed radios in their trawlers and skippers could no longer 'lose' themselves at sea while making a dash to St Kilda with mail or provisions. The head postmaster at Fleetwood wrote an embittered memorandum to his superiors. 'In the past,' he wrote, 'despatches have been secured mainly by the good offices of trawler skippers who have frequently acted in this matter in opposition to the wish of the owners but this source of help has been lost by newspaper publicity. There are so many free-lance journalists in this town who subsist on such scraps that a sailing to St Kilda is as important as a Government defeat and is usually broadcast at once.'

The missionary on Hirta had tried since the summer to get the Scottish Office to do something to help solve the mail problem. He had written in August to Tom Johnston, the Under-Secretary of State for Scotland, suggesting that the two lighthouse steamers, *Pharos* and *Pole Star*, be employed to keep the St Kildans in contact with the outside world during the winter. Again, however, the Northern Lighthouse Commissioners had proved intractable. On 25 October, Dugald Munro again wrote to Johnston, telling of the grave situation that was developing on Hirta, and adding, 'They, the St Kildans, are like many of us expecting equity and considera-tion from a Labour Government, that was denied them by previous administrations.' Munro's letter was the last to leave the island that year.

The Lighthouse Commissioners grudgingly agreed that one of their ships would make a trip to Hirta before Christmas to take out mails. On 16 December the *Hesperus* left Oban with twenty Post Office bags on board. Bad weather forced the ship to make for shelter before the captain had had the opportunity of landing the mail.

The first contact the St Kildans were to have with the mainland was not until the end of January 1930. The trawler *Caldew* decided to look in on Village Bay on her way back to Fleetwood. The skipper found a community depressed by lack of news. One islander, Mary Gillies, was ill with acute appendicitis. On 30 January the captain of the *Caldew* contacted the GPO in Edinburgh and told officials of the situation. It took two weeks before the various government departments involved agreed to send help. On 15 Febru-ary 1930 the fishery cruiser *Norna* sailed from Tarbert in Harris to take Mary Gillies off the island and deliver mails and food supplies to the comunity. The help was too late in coming. Mary was carefully taken aboard the *Norna*, only to die in Stobhill Hospital, Glasgow, two days later.

Despite the visit of the *Norna*, Nurse Barclay decided to send a letter to the Department of Health, that she had penned before the cruiser arrived. 'The St Kildans', she wrote, 'have plenty of flour, meal, salted mutton and fulmar, but there is a shortage of cream of tartar and a few articles of diet and at no distant date they will all be short of tea. They have not grumbled much over the food shortage but they do weary for news of their friends. I have an ample supply of stores to keep me going till May, my only want is potatoes and these I can do without as I have plenty beans, rice, macaroni, etc. I am afraid the manse folks will be badly off if stores and mails don't arrive soon. I warned them to get all stores in the summer, but they thought they would get all they wanted by trawler.' Nurse Barclay was later to discover that she had greatly overestimated the amount of food that was available to the St Kildans. The nurse, however, had made it clear to the Department that a potentially dangerous situation existed on Hirta.

The St Kildans had no further contact with the outside world until April. The trawler *Henry Malling* left Fleetwood on 15 April 1930, and arrived at Hirta round midnight the following day. 'A few strident blasts on the trawler's whistle', read *The Scotsman*, 'announced to the islanders that the relief ship had arrived. Immediately lights appeared in every home, and within a short time the islanders had launched their small boat and come alongside the trawler. A large stock of provisions, comprising potatoes, onions, cabbages, butter and bacon, together with eight bags of mails were transferred to the boat.' The crew of the *Henry Malling* found the St Kildans totally despondent. 'The islanders were greatly relieved when we arrived,' said Skipper Quirk, 'as they had been living on meal and water and salted fulmar. Though they were food-hungry, they were also news-hungry and when the bags of mails were opened at the house of the islanders' postmaster there was a scramble for letters. For several hours everybody was reading letters or opening parcels. Fires were lit and the cooking of provisions was started. There was no school for the children next day. Some had been without footwear for weeks, and as soon as the parcels were opened children put on laced boots received from the mainland.'

Everyone living on St Kilda had had enough. Only one islander had bothered that spring to turn over his croft and sow some crops for the following winter. Already the talk was of evacuation. 'They have gone through such privations this winter,' concluded Skipper Quirk, 'that they don't want to face another.'

12
The changeless and the changed

John Sands of Ormiston visited St Kilda twice. He had spent longer on St Kilda than any other outsider when he came to write his book *Out of the World*. An aspiring politician, Sands felt he had a mission 'to liberate the poor serfs, who had been so long incarcerated and cruelly used, and to bring them into communication with the rest of the world'. He was a true product of the age of liberalism and, as he said in the preface to his book, 'I felt as if I had had a Divine call to perform the work.'

By the end of the nineteenth century the community of St Kilda had become an embarrassment to many people on the mainland who were enjoying the material benefits increasingly bestowed upon them by an advancing society. Although in many respects life on St Kilda was no more nor less primitive than that found on many other remote islands, the people of Hirta attracted most of the attention of amateur sociologists and do-gooders who saw the assimilation of the St Kildan community into their society as their duty. Every aspect of native life on the island was investigated and seen as a reason why the St Kildans had remained apart from the rest of society for so long. The way in which the island was owned and managed, the religion practised by its inhabitants, the lack of educational opportunity, were all seen as aspects of the St Kildan existence demanding enlightenment. Only then, argued the critics, would life on Hirta be viable. But they wrote and spoke in vain. As the mainland moved closer and closer towards adopting an economic yardstick as the measure by which survival should be gauged, so the St Kildans were forced nearer and nearer the inevitable.

The islanders were trying to understand the implications of a way of life based upon money. They were still finding it difficult because never in their history had they had to consider that to survive on Hirta involved finance. Their dilemma was simple enough. If their forefathers had been able to exist by slaughtering sea birds on the cliffs, what had happened to make that no longer possible? That was still the great imponderable when they boarded the *Harebell* in August 1930.

One fact was apparent to them: life was difficult because there were too few of them on the island. They were unaware, however, of the other forces which had contributed to their abandoning some of their more dangerous and demanding pursuits, and which were instrumental in persuading the young to forsake their birth-place for the mainland. But if the St Kildans failed to realize that their way of life had to change if they were to survive as a community, there was also a failure on the part of those on the mainland to recognize what the islanders needed at a time when something could have been done about it. A link had been made with society at large, and instead of satisfying the islanders' wish to strengthen that contact, the mainlanders decided that it was better for the St Kildans to join them in the larger amorphous society of Scotland.

The destiny of the people of Hirta depended to a large extent upon the attitude of the owner of the island. 'The inhabitants', remarked the Reverend Kenneth Macaulay in 1865, 'must, I am afraid, to the end of time be wholly at the mercy of some one person, who may swallow up all the small commodities this island can afford and rule the whole community with a rod, unless restrained by honour, conscience or an uncommon share of humanity.' Extortion not only took place, but to some extent was expected by the St Kildans. During the seventeenth century, so the story goes, the islanders were on one occasion forced to eat sea-weed gathered from the shores of Hirta because the tacksman and his retinue were eating them out of house and home. In 1794, Robert Heron remarked that the tacksman received as his due all the milk from the islanders' cattle from May to Michaelmas, every second ram born on the island, every seventh fleece, and every tenth ewe lamb, in addition to eighty bolls of barley and potatoes. The tales concerning the treatment of the islanders by their landlord naturally grew more wicked as they spread farther from the island itself. During their Highland jaunt in 1773, James Boswell informed Dr Johnson that he was considering buying the island of St Kilda. 'Pray do, sir,' was the learned doctor's reply. 'Consider, sir, by buying St Kilda you may keep the people from falling into worse hands.'

The islanders, it is true, may have been victims of occasional hardship, but they were never so oppressed as to make them want to leave the island. For as long as their survival depended upon the barter system, no matter how unfairly it worked against them, they were safe. They did not have to consider anything beyond their natural experience on the island – beyond their traditional simple way of living and paying their rent. The prices fetched by the tacksman on the mainland for their produce were his responsibility, not theirs.

For most of the island's inhabited history, the problem of how it should be managed was immaterial. St Kilda was a source of profit and the people were happy. By the end of the nineteenth century, however, the problem of ownership became a real one. MacLeod of MacLeod himself faced economic hardship, and the authors of the St Kilda story were quick to point out that his lonely island people were suffering.

Many writers, like John Sands, wrote of the despotism of the laird of Dunvegan Castle. They informed the public that the St Kildans were by nature a go-ahead people who were being thwarted from making a success of their island existence by the 'ogres of Dunvegan'. The author of an article in the London *Standard* published in 1885, remarked sarcastically, 'The owner of this lonely spot is a gentleman, who by one of those curious contrasts in which civilization delights was until recently Secretary of the Science and Art Department. Perhaps – who knows? – amid the perusal of the dreary Minutes of "My Lords", and the calculation of "payment by results" he may have sometimes heard the waves dashing on distant Dunvegan, or the scream of the sea mews as they circled his far-off lordship of St Kilda.' It was a time when it was fashionable to be critical of absentee Scottish lairds, who preferred to dabble in the political and social life of the great capitals of Edinburgh and London rather than live among the people who occupied their estates. As a result of Sands's campaign against MacLeod, dozens of letters were sent offering to supply sugar and soap at twopence less than the island's proprietor to the St Kildans. One correspondent suggested that a pair of rabbits be sent to Hirta to supplement the fulmar diet which MacLeod forced his tenants to eat.

Such sentiments, however, were those of commentators who failed to understand the implications of a feudal system which was naturally-enough alien to their experience. The lairds had always lived away from their lands for some time of the year, and their children had invariably been educated in the South of Scotland and beyond. Such writers, products of an age of liberalism, believed that the condemnation of benevolent paternalism was more important than trying to find a competent substitute. After all, if St Kilda be taken away from MacLeod of MacLeod, who was there to accept the responsibility for the island's people? Who would foot the bill for the maintenance of their homes? Who would guarantee them a sale for their meagre produce? The answer could only be society as a whole represented by government. The St Kildans were incapable of managing on their own the consequences of increased dependence upon the mainland. Their affairs had always been managed by their hereditary owner. The proprietor, moreover, had a vested interest in their well-being. Both shared a mutual love of St Kilda. Those who attempted to sow the seeds of liberalism did so among a people who geographically and practically were among the freest people in Britain. Within their own small community the St Kildans enjoyed a liberty that they knew to be real, and were perplexed by attempts to arouse their discontent.

'My view is that they lead a very happy life,' remarked Norman Heathcote when he wrote of his visit to St Kilda in 1900. 'They are better housed and better fed than any other people in their rank of life. It would be a misfortune to them to be removed from their present home. I do not mean that I would discourage emigration. If any of them wish to push their fortune in other parts, let them do so, and let them have every encouragement and assistance. Probably as they become more educated, many of them will become discontented with their primitive life and wish to take a more active part in the progress of the world. All I say is that emigration will not add to their happiness. They have plenty of work, but can do everything at their own time. Theirs is indeed a happy life without solicitude.'

The majority on the mainland thought that St Kilda should be considered purely in economic terms. If profit for the owner in time became loss, then the islanders should be freed from the yoke of MacLeod and evacuated as soon as possible. Writers like Robert Connell, a journalist from the *Glasgow Herald*, dismissed schemes to develop St Kilda as a fishing station. 'Undoubtedly', he wrote, 'the island could be made a good fishing station, possibly the best on the west coast, providing they built a good harbour. Three schemes for a place of shelter to accommodate fishing boats have been put before the public. The factor of the proprietor of St Kilda estimates the entire cost of his scheme at less than £1000. With such a harbour the people would be able to add largely to their wealth, for unquestionably the waters around their island abound with fish. Moreover, if the island became a fishing station it would be more regularly visited by steamers. But when all has been said in favour of making the island a fishing station, the fact remains; the most effectual way of benefiting the St Kildans is to enable them to settle in one or other of our colonies.'

Throughout its long history, St Kilda was never sensibly thought of as part of the area governed by Westminster. It was a republic within a democracy. The people paid little heed to what went on in Edinburgh, let alone London, and there was no reason why affairs of state should interest them. What the politicians talked of and made decisions about were irrelevancies. The geographical position of St Kilda made it an anomaly even in the system of local government. The island was attached to the mainland county of Inverness, as were Rhum and most of the smaller islands of the Hebrides. In the latter part of St Kilda's history, when the island became a registration district for births, deaths, and marriages, duplicates of the records were returned to Register House in Edinburgh only once every ten years and not, as was the case with the remote islands of Foula and Fair Isle, once every five years. When education came to the children of Hirta, the responsibility of providing schoolmasters was passed from the SSPCK, to the Gaelic Schools Society, then to the Ladies' Association, and finally to the School Board of Harris.

Curiously, a nation that could administer the largest Empire the world had ever seen failed to provide adequately for a people who lived but a hundred miles out into the Atlantic. The governing of St Kilda was more of an embarrassment to Westminster than the whole of India. Departments of state saw the community as a unique problem, and as such preferred to ignore rather than help.

St Kilda was a distant cousin who could only be supported by her age-old caretaker. 'He has it upon his shoulders,' wrote Anthony Trollope in 1878 of MacLeod of MacLeod, 'and on those of his sister, the onerous task of sustaining by his private means the existence of the community and of relieving their wants . . . It is good to find a man who will do this, but it is not good to have a state of things in which such doing is necessary.'

The MacLeods of MacLeod did all within their power and pocket to help their distant tenants. Sir John MacLeod was responsible during the years 1860 and 1862 for building on Hirta the most advanced houses of their type in the entire Hebrides. Maintenance of the village, including a share of the manse, the schoolhouse, the church, and the store, was an additional responsibility from which the family never shirked. Of the nine ministers to serve on St Kilda between the years 1710 and 1843, five were MacLeods. The chief and his family also took an active interest in the health and education of the islanders.

The rents payable by the islanders were usually moderate. By 1814 the proprietor, Lieutenant-Colonel MacLeod, was receiving 140 stones of feathers, the product of 46,000 sea birds, as rent. Five years later MacCulloch noted, 'The rent of the island is £40, which according to the present average of Highland farms and including the value of the sea fowl is a very low rate.' By 1841, the total rent of the island was £60. The rent due from each family was calculated in terms of the house and land as well as the cattle and cows kept on St Kilda. By the middle of the nineteenth century, the head of every family was paying one pound a year for his house and land, seven shillings a year for each cow, and ten shillings for every ten sheep. The produce required to meet the rent was approximately seven old stones of feathers, worth five shillings a stone. An old stone comprised twenty-four pounds, and represented the plumage of approximately 200 fulmars or 800 puffins.

In those days, the St Kildans had little difficulty in paying their rent to the factor. In 1860, Captain Thomas noted that the St Kildans were able to pay half a year's rent in advance, and when Alexander Grigor arrived a year later to take the official census of the island, he noted in his report that the St Kildans were better off than many had supposed, and that the catechist on the island at the time had told him that every St Kildan had some money put away.

By the late nineteenth century, the annual rent was fixed at two pounds for a croft and seven shillings for a cow. A dual rate applied to the sheep owned by the islanders: those grazing on Hirta were rated at ninepence a head a year, while those on the other islands were charged sixpence. By this time the St Kildans were much in debt to the proprietor, but there is no instance on record of them being penalized. 'They are never pressed for arrears,' wrote McDiarmid in 1877, 'and so far as could be made out they are contented with their lot and consider that they are fairly dealt with . . . They speak of their landlord, MacLeod, in the very best of terms, and consider themselves very fortunate in being under his guardianship.' In 1900, Norman Heathcote added, 'If the people get in arrears with their rent, which the St Kildans are quite prone to do as other tenants . . . they are not evicted.' From the turn of the century and until the evacuation of the island in 1930, the rent on the croft was reduced to thirty shillings a year, while the grazing rents for their livestock remained the same.

The proprietor was generally agreeable to making alterations in the way in which rent was calculated. At one time, the St Kildans used to pay rent each year on a fixed number of sheep. They protested to MacLeod on the grounds that under this system some families who owned fewer animals were paying too much, while others who owned more than the set number were paying too little. The owner readily agreed to amend the method of payment : thereafter the people paid rent on the actual number of sheep each family owned.

Above all, the islanders' supplies of food and seed were guaranteed, whether or not they had enough money to pay for them. In his report accompanying the 1851 Census, Roderick Macdonald noted, 'They would often be in want were it not for the benevolence of their kind-hearted Proprietor who sends a yearly supply of meal to the island.' Apart from the cost of the supplies, there was also the cost of transporting them and himself to Hirta. The factor paid at least one visit to the island each year, frequently more. In 1875, the proprietor's smack, the *Robert Hadden*, visited St Kilda three times, at a cost of nearly £15 a visit. As one old island woman said in 1870, 'It would be a *black* day for us, the day we severed ourselves from MacLeod's interest.'

The traditional wealth of the community depended in large part upon the valuable oils extracted from the fulmar, the puffin, and the gannet. The oils of the solan goose and fulmar were also thought highly of as a medicine. According to John Sands in 1875, the islanders exported 906 pints of fulmar oil (the equivalent of 4,530 English pints) every year. The factor gave the islanders a shilling for each St Kildan pint. The oils, some of which were extracted from the sea birds by boiling up the carcass and then skimming the oil from the top of the pot, were not only used for medicine, but also for lighting and greasing purposes.

The value of such oils greatly diminished towards the end of the nineteenth century. On the mainland paraffin was discovered and was a cheaper, more efficient fuel for lamps. Mineral oils proved themselves superior for greasing axles, and advances in medicine demoted the using of gannet and fulmar oil as a remedy prescribed by old wives. By 1902, only 640 English pints were exported, and were worth only sixpence a pint to the factor. Within a few years the price had fallen to a mere fourpence halfpenny a pint.

There was a time when the St Kildans could even find a market for salted sea birds, especially the young gannet. But those on the mainland no longer had to rely on dried and pickled produce. Improvements in methods of transportation and the introduction of refrigeration enabled fresh foods to be marketed in the cities of Britain. People soon lost whatever little taste they once had for the oily flesh of young sea birds. *Gugas* even began to disappear from the menus of some of the steamships that plied the Western Isles.

The St Kildans had long since been unable to export any agricultural produce to the mainland. In 1799 they could get sixteen shillings per boll for their barley and three shillings for every barrel of potatoes. By the middle of the nineteenth century, however, they were finding it difficult enough to provide for their own needs. Certain products associated with their livestock found markets late into the same century. In 1875, over seventeen St Kildan stones of sheep tallow were sent to the mainland, for which they received the equivalent of six shillings and sixpence per stone. The St Kildans were also famous for their cheese. 'The cheese,' wrote MacCulloch, 'which is made of a mixture of these milks (cows' and ewes'), is much esteemed, forming one of the prevailing articles of export to the Long Island.' In 1875, the islanders exported over thirty-nine St Kildan stones of cheese for six shillings a stone. Within two years, however, only four stones of cheese were taken off the island by the factor, as the islanders required most of the milk for their own consumption.

The greatest blow to the St Kildan economy, however, was the decline in the market for feathers. Feathers taken by the factor in lieu of rent had been sold in the mainland markets for centuries and had always fetched a good price. In 1794, Robert Heron claimed that the proprietor's annual profits from the sale of feathers sent to Liverpool were very considerable. The St Kildans at that time were given three shillings a stone by the factor, who was selling them for ten shillings a stone. By 1842, he was able to pay the islanders five shillings a stone and received fifteen shillings for the same in the southern markets.

By the end of the nineteenth century, the market began to collapse. The St Kildan feathers were forced out of the competitive

markets by the development of substitute materials in the manufacture of mattresses. Moreover, a rapid rise in transportation costs
stimulated the decline: feathers imported from Hirta became too
expensive. The mainland was a place where men had to be paid a
wage to do a job of work, and the new means of transportation
such as steamships cost a lot of money to build, fuel, and man.
The cost of going to St Kilda had to be reckoned with.

Sheep and cattle were about the only exports that found a ready
market. In 1799, the factor was prepared to pay the St Kildans
three shillings and sixpence per head of sheep and thirty shillings
for a cow. Half a century later, the islanders could still reckon on
the factor paying them twenty-five shillings a head for their cattle.
Sheep had changed little in value. The factor could still afford to
pay the islanders anything from ninepence to a shilling for every
lamb he took off St Kilda and still make a reasonable profit. In
1875, John Mackenzie, MacLeod's factor, paid the islanders two
pounds fifteen shillings to three pounds for each cow, which he
estimated would fetch between three pounds and three pounds
fifteen in the market. At the time of the evacuation, in fact, sheep
and cattle were all that the St Kildans possessed that was of value.

The St Kildans also developed a market for their fish. In 1875
over 1,080 fish were taken by the factor. The islanders were given
sevenpence for ling, threepence for cod, and a penny for each
bream. The fishing industry, however, was not developed by the
St Kildans because of the dangers involved. In addition, as Mac-
Culloch remarked, 'their distance from a market and the absence
of commercial habits prevent them from undertaking a fishery for
the purpose of foreign sale'. During the twentieth century the
people themselves consumed more fish, and their interest was
confined primarily to supplying their own wants. Even in the years
immediately prior to the evacuation, however, a quantity of fish,
particularly ling which were split down the middle and salted, were
still accepted by the factor.

Cloth was the main article exported from St Kilda from the
middle of the nineteenth century. In Stornoway, where the factor
found a market for much of the St Kildan tweed, the cloth was
held in great esteem and thought very suitable for tailoring. In
1885 the factor paid the islanders about three shillings per yell of
tweed and two shillings and sixpence per yell of blanketing. The
yell was the old Scots measure reckoned to be equal to 'forty-seven
inches and a thumb'. From the 1900s the factor gave them a fixed

price per yard, irrespective of the quality.

In 1892 a St Kildan, Alexander Gillies Ferguson, emigrated to Glasgow where he set himself up in business as a tweed merchant. As well as handling the tweeds woven in the Hebrides, he also bought direct from the St Kildans. At the time it was believed that this new outlet would be of great advantage to the community. 'I believe the factor will *not* get any more of the St Kilda webs,' wrote John Ross, the schoolmaster. 'They are beginning to see through things a little better and I should not wonder although *everything* would soon go and come direct from Glasgow. I suppose they find it goes further.' The St Kildans were to send much of their tweed in future to 'Uncle' Alexander Ferguson, but kept back a fair quantity to give to the factor and sell to the tourists. By 1911, the St Kildans were able to produce over three thousand yards of tweed every year, which was valued at about three shillings a yard. Even in the years immediately before the decision was taken to evacuate the island, over two thousand yards were woven on the islanders' simple looms.

On the mainland, however, cloth was being produced in small factories. On more modern looms it could be woven better and more cheaply than on the primitive looms of Hirta. The cost of transportation again made St Kildan cloth too highly-priced to be able to compete in the open market, and if the factor was to sell the cloth easily he was unable to give the islanders a price which made their effort profitable. As it was, he had to rely on a few well-developed contacts in order to dispose of it at a price fair to himself. The sale of St Kildan cloth increasingly depended upon the whims of a fickle, fashion-conscious public. The St Kildans could do little to improve upon the quality of their cloth or increase the quantity produced without acquiring not only new looms but new skills. No one believed such an exercise to be worth the capital involved. On the other islands of the Hebrides, notably Harris, the people were able to compete because a larger population could maintain a more organized domestic industry incorporating near-factory methods.

The community of Village Bay, it was claimed, lacked personal initiative. 'After thirteen days on St Kilda,' wrote Connell, 'I came to the deliberate conclusion that this nibbling at socialism is responsible for a good deal of the moral chaos which has so completely engulfed the islanders.' The four rowing boats that had been given to the islanders were, according to Connell, 'simply going to wreck in their hands, and one apparent reason is that they are common property'. 'I know for a fact', wrote Ross in 1889, 'that if each man worked for his own good, great changes would take place. The standard of living would be greatly elevated. As it is, if a native were to talk of making any improvements in his house or lands he would only be mocked out of it by his fellows. I myself heard one man expressing a desire to have one end of his house floored with wood, so as to make it more comfortable, but he had to give up the idea, some of the others coming down on him with most peculiar arguments leading him to understand the folly of his plan. This is a pity for the pushing man like this would go on from one thing to another and by time would induce most of his neighbours to follow his example. There are pushing men in St Kilda, if they had any inducements.'

Many writers believed that the barter system worked against the islanders, and demanded that they be allowed to trade freely. 'They would find themselves competing in the wider markets,' argued R. A. Smith who visited St Kilda in 1879, 'and would occasionally have to suffer; still they would feel themselves among men, and be relieved from the idea of isolation and helplessness, which latter feeling is painfully strong at present.' In 1913 MacLeod of MacLeod gave up his monopoly trading position and allowed the islanders to trade direct with the mainland.

The economy of St Kilda during the last century suffered through no fault of its own save its inflexibility. When the traditional markets for the community's exports waned, the island ceased to be an economically viable proposition. Charity was all that stood in the way of total evacuation. Even as early as 1878, Anthony Trollope prophetically remarked, 'I think it may be taken as a rule that no region can be of real value, the products of which must be eked out by charity from other regions. Many a rich and useful country will not provide itself all that it wants; but no country can be rich and useful unless it can provide itself by supplying its own wants or can purchase what it requires by the sale of its own products. That certainly is not the case with St Kilda.'

In latter years, St Kilda was classed as an object of charity, and with the concept of charity went the idea of a people too poor, too deprived to be able to cope with life. Those upon the mainland who felt sorry for the St Kildans, however, equally condemned them to a life of constant distress. Society became increasingly critical of those values that were the cornerstones of the traditional way of life on Hirta, and found itself oscillating between being charitable and wishing to deprive the St Kildans of their homes. 'The best way to overcome this difficulty', wrote John Ross, the schoolmaster, 'is to put the means of an honourable living within their reach in the shape of a good pier, or other improvement, and give them at least a quarterly steamer call in winter and monthly in summer and harvest, to enable them to send their labour to and bring goods direct from the market. This would leave them without excuse and if it is not done, the sooner St Kilda is cleared off the better for all concerned. For as they are, the inhabitants must come to grief sooner or later depending on public charity more than on anything else.'

The St Kildans understood that life on Hirta offered little in the way of material comfort. They rarely voiced a complaint because for them the independence and freedom associated with their way of life were the underlying forces governing their community. It was an independence, however, that those on the mainland wished to undermine. They believed their society superior, and the way to prove it to themselves was to entice or, if necessary, force the St Kildans to accept their values. Material progress had established itself as the prime motivating force of Western society. It was the supreme value, and those who failed to comprehend materialism, or were incapable of adapting their lives to accept it, were thought of as illiterate, ignorant peasants who were not able to realize what was good for them.

There emerged an ever-widening distinction between the level of expectation on the mainland and the traditional puritanical level of a community like St Kilda's. Those on the mainland could not understand how a people could continue to wish to live on an island that offered so little in terms of economic advancement. If the St Kildans themselves could do nothing to improve their material condition upon Hirta, then their existence upon that island was surely questionable. St Kilda was a barren rock, void of any promise and therefore uninhabitable. It could only be an act of great humanity, therefore, to remove the St Kildans from the lonely outpost that was their home.

Many external forces had a noticeable influence on the St Kildan community. The ministers, the schoolmasters, and the tourists were the vanguard: they were the first to bring word to Hirta of mainland society's attitudes towards such a primitive and remote people.

As long as the St Kildans found life on their island successful in their terms, they accepted without question the religion and the little education they were offered, and above all the charity occasionally shown by visitors from the mainland. But as soon as their way of life ceased to be valid, the St Kildans were seduced into thinking that perhaps their way of doing things was no longer the best.

Circumstance conspired to help the seduction. The effects of the dreadful infantile mortality showed themselves in the reduced numbers of young people left to carry on life on the island, and less visibly in a slackening in the tempo of life on Hirta. Those who actively sought to do away with the patriarchal system of ownership that existed on St Kilda had nothing to put in its place: those forces that made the barter system uneconomic and unworkable put a severe strain on the proprietor. MacLeod of MacLeod lacked sufficient funds to support the community, and although he allowed the islanders an independent sale for their cloth in the hope that it would help them adapt to a money economy, they lacked the ability to take up the challenge of free enterprise.

Increased contact with the mainland helped isolate the St Kildans perhaps even more than did geography. They were unique and inflexible. Neither they nor their way of life was capable of change, particularly the violent change in values and attitudes that would have been required to continue the struggle. There was but one solution. But 'Who shall say', wrote Trollope, 'that these people ought to be deported from their homes and placed recklessly upon some point of the mainland? I have not the courage to say. They themselves if they were consulted, would probably be averse to such deportation. Were they so deported each individually would suffer, at any rate for a time, by the change.' The attempts made by the few to stave off evacuation were noble and well-intentioned but bore marks of the pathos and futility of working against the inevitable. St Kilda stood in the Atlantic, the changeless amid the changed. All that could be done was to wait and allow the men and women of Village Bay the courtesy and privilege of making for themselves the decision that would make Nature's defeat of man a reality.

13
God will help us

By April 1930, Nurse Williamina Barclay had spent three years ministering to the needs of the people of St Kilda. She was without doubt the best trained nurse the Scottish Department of Health had ever managed to send to the island. She had studied at Glasgow Royal Infirmary and had taken a course in maternity at Dundee. At the age of forty-six, and despite her qualifications and experience, Nurse Barclay had agreed to go to St Kilda. She looked forward to being her own boss. 'I was cock of the walk,' she says of her stay on Hirta. 'There was nobody there but me.'

Nurse Barclay, however, saw it her duty not only to tend the community in sickness but also to take an active interest in the people when they were well. Frequently she invited the women and children of the island to take tea with her at the factor's house, where she would listen to their problems and their hopes and do her best to advise. One day in April 1930, she decided to extend the invitation to tea to the men. She spent several days baking sufficient scones and cakes to feed over thirty St Kildans. When the day of the great tea party came, 'It was a bit of a crush in my sitting-room,' remembers Nurse Barclay, 'but we all fitted in.'

After everyone had eaten heartily, the nurse raised the question of evacuation. 'We had a chat about it,' she recalls, 'and we discussed conditions on the island. They asked me what I thought about it and I said, "Well, between you and me and the deep sea I think you're on your last legs." I said, "Just you all have your tea and enjoy it and think over the fact that I could evacuate you quite easily and get you homes and see that you got jobs. I can do that but talk it over yourselves." ' The St Kildans retired to their cottages. The talk that evening was of evacuation.

It was not the first time they had talked about abandoning their home. In 1875 a plan was put forward to transport the entire population to Canada, but the people had decided against it. Ten years later, when the St Kildans appealed to the mainland for food supplies to prevent them from starving, the matter was again raised.

On 20 October 1885, Mr Malcolm McNeill, Inspecting Officer of the Board of Supervision, was instructed by the Scottish Office to go to St Kilda. He spoke at length with the minister and the schoolmaster and not least with the St Kildans themselves. In April the following year his report was made public. McNeill had found that the islanders 'were amply, indeed luxuriously, supplied' for the winter, and that on the whole they were well-off. It would help them immensely, McNeill thought, if a proper landing-place were constructed; but, he concluded, it might also be worthwhile investigating the possibility of assisting the St Kildans to emigrate, as nearly all of them had told him they would like to.

John Ross, the schoolmaster, confirmed McNeill's opinion when he spent a year on Hirta. He found that all the young men were eager to leave the island, but that 'it is either aged parents who are unable to provide for themselves, or weak families that have kept them there so long'. But bad harvests which raised doubts were normally followed by good ones reinforcing the bond between the people and their island home. Some of those younger islanders had indeed drifted to the mainland in search of the better life; but the community as a whole rejected the thought of evacuating Hirta.

In 1928, a son and daughter of one of the St Kildans who had gone to live in Australia returned to Hirta. The Reverend Finlay MacQueen and his sister made the long journey from East Rew in Victoria, in the company of a party of some six hundred Australians of Scots extraction who wished to see for themselves the land of their ancestors. Seventy years old, and a man made wise by his experiences, the Reverend MacQueen was shocked by what he saw. Never for a moment had he imagined people could live in such squalor. He attempted to persuade the younger St Kildans to return to Australia with him; but the bird harvest, the islanders claimed, had been a good one that year and the crops were sufficient for another long winter. One old woman declared that she would not move from her island home unless forced physically to do so. So many arguments were brought forward against MacQueen's suggestion that not one St Kildan left aboard the steamer that summer, bound for Australia. Only an Australian flag, presented by the minister on behalf of the Mayor of St Kilda, Melbourne, showed as it fluttered over the village that he had ever been there at all.

The disastrous winter of 1929, however, brought matters to a head and the plight of the St Kildans was again brought to the attention of the government. T. B. W. Ramsay, MP, informed William Adamson, Secretary of State for Scotland, in April 1930, 'I have written to the Highlands and Islands Distress Committee, 18 Duke Street, Edinburgh, asking them to do something to help the people on the island who are in such dire straits as regards food supplies.' The Committee had decided, according to Ramsay, to take no action, so he wrote to the Secretary of State in the earnest hope that he would do something 'to relieve these people in their terrible plight'.

The Scottish Office realized that the end was in sight for the St Kildans. William Murrie at the Department of Health was asked by Tom Johnston, the Under-Secretary of State for Scotland, to solicit a report 'on the possibility of bringing the inhabitants of St Kilda off the island'. Moreover, Murrie concluded in a memorandum to the Department of Agriculture that Tom Johnston 'regards this matter as peculiarly urgent since he thinks that the question of St Kilda will probably be raised in the House at an early date'. Meanwhile the civil servants played for time by telling Ramsay that the Scottish Office had received no confirmation that there was a shortage of food among the islanders, but that they were investigating. Ramsay soon after received a letter from Dugald Munro, and again wrote to Tom Johnston to say that according to the missionary, many St Kildans 'hoped to be assisted to leave the island this year as the unsatisfactory conditions which prevailed throughout last winter have left them very unsatisfied'.

The St Kildans themselves knew there was no alternative but to give up the struggle. They were, however, totally ignorant of how they should go about evacuating their island home. Nurse Williamina Barclay had therefore taken it into her own hands to help the community reach a decision, and in return she promised to do her best to ensure that the Department of Health would look sympathetically on a request from the islanders to be removed from Hirta. The nurse's major concern was for the children. 'I just suddenly thought, what of the young people,' she says. 'There were eight of them still of school age, some of them were under it, and I thought these little things wouldn't have a chance in life.'

The villagers met again at the factor's house. 'We sat down at the table for hours,' recalls the nurse, 'and one old man with the tears trickling down his face came and put his arm around my shoulder. He said to me. "We all think God sent you here. We were at the end of things. We didn't know how we were going to carry on any longer." ' It was only at the second meeting that Nurse Barclay realized the extent of the community's deprivation in the months previous. She had always given the children sweets once or twice a week, for instance, and had thought little of it. She realized that afternoon that the children had taken them straight home where they were shared with everyone in the family. A handful of sweets had been the main source of sugar for most of the islanders that winter.

The Mackinnon family, the largest on the island, had long since run out of margarine, sugar, and flour. Six of Norman's eight children had gone without boots and shoes for months. John Macdonald, who lived next door, was also finding it difficult to make ends meet. The tweed he had made the previous year had been claimed by the factor in payment of the stores supplied by him. Macdonald could only manage to purchase the minimum of foodstuffs. Soon he, Widow Gillies, and her daughter Mary would be in dire need. From what the islanders told her, Nurse Barclay estimated that the average annual income of each household on Hirta was less than £26 a year. Some families were obviously better off than others – but the poor forced the issue that day.

Dugald Munro was asked to compose a petition. The letter was short and written in meticulous copperplate on ruled foolscap paper issued for the use of the children of Hirta by the School Board of Harris. 'We the undersigned, the natives of St Kilda,' wrote the missionary, 'hereby respectfully pray and petition HM Government to assist us all to leave the island this year and find homes and occupations for us on the mainland. For some years the manpower has been decreasing, now the total population of the island is reduced to thirty-six. Several men out of this number have definitely made up our minds to seek employment on the mainland; this will really cause a crisis as the present number are hardly sufficient to carry on the necessary work of the place. These men are the mainstay of the island at present as they tend the sheep, do the weaving and look after the general welfare of the widows. Should they leave the conditions of the rest of the community would be such that it would be impossible for us to remain on the island another winter.

'The reason why assistance is necessary is that for many years St Kilda has not been self-supporting and with no facilities to better our position, we are therefore without the means to pay for the costs of removing ourselves and furniture elsewhere.

We do not ask', concluded the missionary, 'to be settled as a separate community, but in the meantime we would collectively be very grateful of assistance and transference elsewhere where there would be a better opportunity of securing our livelihood.' The plea, simple and dignified, was signed by all the adults – twelve men and eight women. Finlay Gillies and Finlay MacQueen, who had never learnt to write, appended marks. Dugald Munro and Williamina Barclay witnessed the signing and testified that the petition was valid. The letter, addressed to 'William Adamson, the Secretary of State for Scotland, Westminster', was handed over to the skipper of the first trawler to appear in the bay.

The British government was thus faced with a problem it had never been up against before, namely the evacuation of part of the British Empire. St Kilda was not, of course, the first island in Scotland to be evacuated. In 1911, the last five islanders on Mingulay had chosen to live elsewhere, but the government had not been involved. Plans had once been drawn up by the Colonial Office to evacuate the island of Tristan da Cunha in the South Atlantic, but fortunately they had never been implemented. In the case of St Kilda there seemed little choice in the matter – a formal petition, dated 10 May 1930, had been received.

The civil servants were naturally cautious. An evacuation was going to involve the spending of taxpayers' money, and it was realized that if St Kilda could not be thought of as a special case, other communities might request similar assistance. Memoranda between departments at the Scottish Office pointed out the factors that would have to be considered before the government could commit itself. 'The decline in cultivation', wrote one official, 'may be partly due to lack of manpower and partly to indolence, the islanders having been encouraged by tourists, trawlers, etc., to expect sympathy in the practical forms of money, coal, fish, etc., for the asking.' The civil servants, however, were not unaware of the problems of settling the St Kildans upon the mainland of Scotland, nor ignorant of the fact that some islanders wished to desert their island home. 'It is regarded as doubtful,' commented an official at the Department of Health, 'if the St Kildans as a body would desire to be removed from the island. So far as the able-bodied males are concerned and so far as information can be obtained without a special visit and report, only one has expressed a wish for settlement on a holding, one is at present employed at

Glasgow, two or three others desire settlement in Edinburgh or Glasgow, while the remaining two (the postmaster and his son, probably the most prosperous family on the island) have given no indication of a desire to migrate. Even if the whole of the able-bodied males and their families were removed and settled either in guaranteed urban or agricultural occupation – and it is not probable that the islanders would remove voluntarily except under guarantee of maintenance – the fringe of older and unfit males and of widows and dependants – perhaps fifteen to twenty persons – would also require to be removed and supported either by means of parochial or similar relief.'

Some senior civil servants were of the opinion that it might be better to try to help the St Kildans remain on Hirta. 'It has to be kept in mind', wrote one official, 'that the St Kildans have been and are to a great extent "out of touch" with the conditions of life elsewhere. It would appear that the most urgent need of the islanders is the provision of guaranteed periodical communication (at least during the autumn, winter, and spring months of, say, September to May inclusive) either by subsidized trawlers, naval vessels or Departmental vessels such as Fisheries Cruisers. It was thought that while it is often impossible to take off from or to effect a landing on the island, that means of delivery or supplies and mails could be devised.'

Two officials were despatched by way of the first available trawler to see for themselves how things were on St Kilda. 'They came into the cottage,' recalls Nurse Barclay, 'and one turned to me and said, "My God, we've been trying to do this for years, evacuate the place."'

On 20 May, George Henderson, the General Inspector of the Department of Health, submitted a full report of his visit to St Kilda. He advocated that swift action should be taken to remove the St Kildans. 'Some months ago,' wrote the Inspector, 'Norman Mackinnon, who has found it particularly difficult to make ends meet because of his large family, expressed a strong desire to the nurse to get away from the island, but thought that certain difficulties – in regard to clothing, furniture, etc. – were insuperable. The nurse showed him how these difficulties could be overcome and he has since then apparently been quite determined to leave. His family totals ten and contains four of the workers of the island. It can be appreciated that if that family leaves the position of the remainder becomes almost hopeless – there would not, for example, be enough able-bodied men left to man a boat. Mackinnon's decision made all the difference between the former spasmodic murmurings of discontent and the united action that has resulted in a petition to the Secretary of State.'

The Inspector, like many visitors before him, was shocked by the condition in which he found the people of Hirta living. 'Personally,' he concluded, 'I have no hesitation in expressing the opinion that from the point of view of the State, the Local Authorities, and the St Kildan himself, the removal of the whole population is very desirable.' Henderson, moreover, discovered the reason why the St Kildans had allowed the situation to deteriorate so greatly before applying for help. 'In the past,' he wrote, 'the influence of Neil Ferguson Senior has always prevented any definite action being taken. He is comparatively well off and would be quite content to remain on the island if he could be assured of a continuance of the profit the presence of the others brings him. Recently there have been distinct signs of a revolt against his domination.' Even Neil's son was now openly declaring his intention to leave the island with his wife and his decision forced his father to sign the letter along with everyone else. 'The fact that he has signed the petition', concluded Henderson, 'is substantial proof of his realization that matters have reached a climax.'

Careful account had to be made of how much an inhabited St Kilda was costing the British taxpayer. The total bill for the five years up to 1930 was reckoned to be £2,388. The Department of Health was carrying by far the greatest share of the bill – £1,642. In the year 1925, over £237 had been spent by the Department in providing the people of Hirta with the services of a trained nurse and an annual visit by a medical officer. By 1930 it was costing £325 to give the islanders the same unsatisfactory service.

The Department of Education reckoned they had spent only £453 in five years. It was a smaller sum than had been imagined – less than £120 a year, two-thirds of which was being paid for out of government grants. The remainder, in order to provide the little children of Hirta with a basic education, was met from Inverness County Council rates. But, 'So far as rates are concerned,' wrote an official of the Scottish Education Department, 'it is doubtful whether it would make any difference to the cost if the children were educated on St Kilda or in one of the other schools on the mainland.' Some slight saving, it was thought, might be made if the children were educated in a school already serving a community elsewhere. The cost of supplying the St Kildans with an education, in fact, was small because no qualified schoolmaster was being sent to Hirta. The missionaries took it upon themselves to teach the children to read and write.

The Department of Agriculture had spent least of all government agencies in the period 1925–30 – a mere £82. Most of the agricultural requirements of the community had been met from the Kelsall Fund. The fund had been used to purchase a winch for the island to help the St Kildans drag their boats ashore, and every year flour and meal had been sent out by the first steamer, also debited to the fund. The Department's accounts were simple. At a cost of £40 a bull had been sent to Hirta in 1926. Three years later another beast was sent at a cost of £39. The only other expenditure they had incurred was £3 which had been spent repairing the small crane on the pier.

The Post Office, however, were quick to point out that they had paid a high price for the little revenue they received. Some £211 had been spent in the previous five years in the attempt to provide the St Kildans with a mail service, and a hefty proportion of the £800 that was paid annually to the steamship company, McCallum Orme, for the provision of a mail service for some of the more outlandish Hebridean islands, also had to be debited to St Kilda. During the winter months the payments made to trawlermen had averaged £9 a year, and the maintenance of the sub-post office on Hirta itself cost over £34 a year – a sum that included Neil Ferguson's annual salary of £25.

It was decided that evacuation was the only solution, and on 10 June 1930, Tom Johnston visited St Kilda. He saw and heard enough to convince him absolutely of the need to take the people off the island as soon as could be arranged. Swift government action, moreover, would have to be taken. In two months' time the weather would deteriorate and condemn the St Kildans to another winter on Hirta. It was agreed that the last weekend in August was the date to aim for.

Two considerations were uppermost in Tom Johnston's mind. Some St Kildans, he realized, would require poor relief, but he was adamant that no St Kildan should be committed to an institution. Instead, every effort would be made to include them with other families or make accommodation available to them near those islanders who could work. The Under-Secretary of State was equally determined that the government should make its position clear to the islanders. Jobs would be provided, but if any other assistance was required by the able-bodied on the mainland, 'it should be by way of providing furniture and not by a continuing exemption from rent which might induce them to look upon themselves as a specially and permanently subsidized class'.

In the newspapers the correspondence was about avoiding the inevitable. The journalists and commentators, who so often in the past had drawn the public's attention to the remote Atlantic archipelago, now encouraged their readers to help them rescue their distant cousins. The *Oban Times* had run a campaign since the world first heard of the St Kildan petition demanding an improvement in the shipping services available to Scotland's outer isles. 'Government assistance or interference', remarked the editor in reply to a letter published in the newspaper, 'need not have gone to the extent of complete clearance of an island which has nurtured people in bad times and good times for centuries. A Government's duty would have been fulfilled by establishing and maintaining some kind of reasonable communication between the island and the mainland.' The author of a letter published in the same newspaper was aware not only of the problems facing the St Kildans but also of the economic depression that hung low over Britain in 1930, when nearly two million people were unemployed. 'What is to become of the St Kildan people', he asked, 'when they are removed from the island? There is plenty of unemployment in the mainland already in skilled industries and in ordinary labour, so there is not much chance of occupation being found for the able-bodied men from the island. Are the people being removed to fall upon what I think is now called Public Assistance, *viz* Poor Relief, or are they going to be settled as a community in crofting and fishing with necessary housing, etc.? I gather that there has been a petition from the St Kildan people asking for their removal, but do these people in that remote island really understand what their removal means, and how and where they are to be settled? They probably imagine they are coming to a sort of paradise on the mainland, where all is "milk and honey" . . . I suppose the epidemic of expecting something for nothing and a wonderful bounty from the air, has spread even to this isolated spot in the Atlantic.'

One government department, however, still saw fit to negotiate in case the St Kildans should ultimately choose to stay on Hirta. While others planned evacuation, the officials at the Post Office were trying to make a deal with the Fleetwood Fishing Vessel

Owners' Association. At long last, it seemed, the Post Office agreed that the provision of a winter service for St Kilda could not be determined by the postal revenue that could possibly accrue. The officials suggested that the sum of £15 per trip per month should be paid to the trawlermen – a cost that would be jointly borne by the GPO and the Scottish Department of Health. The Iago Steam Trawler Company Ltd. of Fleetwood agreed to the proposal. Too late, the problem that had plagued the community for nearly half a century seemed to be resolved.

John Mathieson, the geographer, suggested that the government should more fully investigate whether it would be viable to quarry stone on Hirta or else develop St Kilda as a base to serve the fishing fleets in the area. *The Scotsman* took Mathieson's suggestions seriously. 'It is not one of the rich or indispensable outposts of our island kingdom,' admitted the leader writer, 'but St Kilda has an established place in the romance of our history, and if for many years it has been a rather tarnished romance, with the sadness of the Atlantic rollers in its song, and a monotone around its shores of humanity in distress, it is possible although not perhaps very probable, that Mr Mathieson's hope of a revived and happier St Kilda is not altogether visionary.'

The civil servants swiftly put paid to Mathieson's ideas. 'Although I did not mention it in my report,' wrote George Henderson to Tom Johnston, 'I have not overlooked the possibility of the economic development of the island, but I regarded it for various reasons as unpracticable. The appeal for the retention of the population on the island is wholly a sentimental one – I do not think it could be seriously contended that even the greatest possible development of its natural resources could give it any real economic value to the nation.'

The debate about the future of St Kilda, short as it was, was not confined to the Scottish newspapers. In the House of Commons on 28 June, William Ramsay asked the Secretary of State for Scotland whether the Scottish Office had any plans to re-settle the island with people from other parts of Scotland. Tom Johnston replied: 'The arrangements for carrying out the evacuation and for placing the inhabitants are now receiving attention. There is not in view any scheme for the re-settlement of the island.' Sir Bertram Falle for the Conservatives pressed the Under-Secretary of State for Scotland on the question of finance. Who, he asked, was to pay for the evacuation? 'I would be greatly obliged,' replied a cautious Johnston, 'if the Honourable Member would not press me for details at the moment. It is obvious that every endeavour will be made to sell the sheep and apply the proceeds to the cost of the evacuation and the balance to the future subsistence of the islanders.' The St Kildans listened to the BBC news reports of the parliamentary debate that evening on two wireless sets. Even the great British Parliament, it seemed to the perplexed islanders, was concerned with their lot now that they had made the fateful decision.

The island's proprietor, Sir Reginald MacLeod of MacLeod, decided that the less he said the better. He estimated that the lone outpost of his estate was worth only about £37 a year to him in rent, and when he came to make up his accounts he discovered that the St Kildans owed him £537 17s 4d in arrears. Few on the island had been in a position to offer him his dues for nearly thirteen years; but MacLeod of MacLeod decided he would not make any claim on his tenants. 'My father,' recalls Dame Flora MacLeod of MacLeod, 'felt that the evacuation was a thing he should thoroughly approve of and accept, but that he would not take any active part in it because he knew that there was so much prejudice in some circles against the lairds. He was afraid that people might say that the laird was anxious to evacuate the people from his land, so, though he co-operated, it was entirely in a negative way.'

MacLeod of MacLeod's only concern was that the government should get the islanders to formally give up their crofts. Since the Crofters Holding Act, 1886, all Scottish crofters had not only enjoyed fair rents but also fixity of tenure, 'Before evacuation is effected,' wrote MacLeod of MacLeod to Tom Johnston, 'the Scottish Office would need to ensure that each holder should formally renounce his tenancy. Without formal renunciation it is possible some may attempt to re-establish themselves and thus defeat the whole purpose of the serious enterprise you have undertaken. This is most important.'

Meanwhile, amidst the preparations being made by the St Kildans to evacuate their island, tragedy struck. Mary Gillies, only twenty-one years old, contracted tuberculosis and died on 21 June. The trawler *Chorley* from Fleetwood tried unsuccessfully to rush a doctor to the island in May. Nurse Barclay, who alone was left to tend her, wrote with relief to George Henderson, 'The problem of Mary Gillies has solved itself. She died this morning and I am truly thankful as I am about worn out.' Henderson paid another visit to Hirta shortly after Mary Gillies's funeral, and was greatly concerned about the health of the rest of widow Gillies's children. 'I think that as soon as the family get settled,' he noted, 'both Rachel and the younger daughter Flora should be medically examined in view of possible TB infection. Rachel especially looks thin and pale.' Fortunately both girls were to survive, but the death of their sister Mary helped reinforce the St Kildans' belief that they had made the right decision.

On Hirta the islanders were deciding their future, and their fears and aspirations were patiently noted by the nurse and the missionary and passed to the Scottish Office. First it was realized that they did not want to be settled upon crofts. They were not interested in crofting. Nor did they want to be settled on another island. If there was to be a break with the past, the St Kildans wished it to be complete.

The Scottish Office officials sought the advice of Alexander Ferguson of Glasgow, who in the past had placed a good many of the younger St Kildan men in work. 'He confirms the view', wrote Dr Shearer of the Department of Health, 'that at first the islanders will be out of their element on the mainland and will require a considerable amount of looking after.' Out of a total population of thirty-six, the authorities reckoned that only eight men were fit enough to take up paid employment.'

Homes and jobs were found for the islanders on government-owned land. All the able-bodied men were offered employment by the Forestry Commission, on condition that if they failed to work properly, their services could be dispensed with. The Commission agreed to provide houses for twenty-five islanders on their estate at Ardtornish, Argyll. The Department of Health agreed to provide the poorer St Kildans with furniture and bicycles to enable the men to travel to and from their work.

The Forestry Commission, however, were hesitant over settling the matter of wages. 'Mr Sutherland stated that the men would not at first receive full wages,' noted a Memorandum on a conference held on 21 July, at which the Commission stated their case, 'but that they would get payment commensurate with their work, though a liberal assessment would be placed on the value of their services. He stated that he preferred that, if possible, no definite sum should be mentioned as wages.' Tom Johnston, however, was determined that the wages issue be resolved before the St Kildans be asked formally to accept their new jobs. It was grudgingly decided by the Commission that reasonable wages would be paid from the start, and that 'any criticism might be answered by regarding the initial wages as payments to persons in training'. Tom Johnston also pointed out that the impoverished islanders would have little money of their own during those first weeks, so it was agreed that the first wage packets would be paid at the end of the first full week's work and thereafter fortnightly.

Alexander Ferguson of Glasgow had gone to great lengths to stress to the Department the need to make clear to the St Kildans that they were going to have to work for a living. 'Mr Ferguson who knows intimately all the inhabitants,' wrote Dr Shearer, 'warned me that he was afraid they had an idea that when they were taken off the island "they were to occupy an Eden provided by the Government", and that it would be necessary to impress on those who could work for themselves that they would be expected to do so.' On 27 July 1930, George Henderson once again visited St Kilda to explain more fully to the inhabitants the offers of housing and employment. 'I explained the situation to them,' he wrote, 'and they expressed their gratitude at the action taken on their behalf.'

George Henderson had already suggested in his Report how those St Kildans too old or too feeble to work might best be cared for. Finlay MacQueen did not wish to live with any of his family. 'The Poor Law Authorities', he therefore suggested, 'should provide a room for him with attendance when necessary. He should be placed near either Neil Ferguson or widow Annie Gillies.' The oldest St Kildan, Finlay Gillies, would likewise have to be supported.

The five widows of Village Bay were also a cause for concern. Mrs Macdonald could rely on her two sons, Ewen and Lachlan, both of whom would be offered work; but the other widows would have to be kept by the poor law authority. Henderson suggested that Widow MacQueen, who lived in house Number 11, be housed in 'a small cottage somewhere near the Mackinnons. She may be able to maintain herself partially by knitting and spinning,' and Widow Annie Gillies would be happiest if she were housed near Neil Ferguson, as her daughter Rachel was to be engaged by Alexander Ferguson as a maid. The other Widow Gillies, concluded Henderson, might be 'maintained by one or other of her three sons or relatives. No action necessary.'

By the end of July, most of the arrangements for the resettlement of the St Kildans had been made. Some islanders, however, had still to make up their minds as to where they wanted to go and what they wanted to do. Talk of the future, however, divided the community. The younger the men, the more eager were they to try their hand on the mainland, and in the Ferguson household, father and son agreed to go their own separate ways. 'One can't help feeling just a bit sorry for the man but he has brought it on himself and to be frank it is evident that he is work shy. I have assured young Neil and his wife that you will do your best for them and I think to ease matters you could write them a short note telling them so.'

The islanders did not find it easy to understand the offers being made to them. Even the young men, like Lachlan Macdonald who had spent some time on the mainland in previous summers, found it difficult to reach a decision. 'We got a choice, right enough,' he recalls, 'but we weren't sure what to take so we left it to them that was taking us off. I got a job in the Forestry Commission which was quite good, but I wasn't any the wiser. I wasn't sure what kind of work I would be given to go and do.'

Neil Ferguson Senior, however, was still to be catered for. The officials were as patient as he was cussed. From the start he had expressed the view that he did not want to go with the others and work for the Forestry Commission in Argyll. The Department had therefore offered him a smallholding at Ullinish in the Isle of Skye.

By July, Ferguson had changed his mind. 'Neil Ferguson', wrote Henderson, 'threatens to remain on the island unless a suitable dwelling house and employment is found for him. He is fit only for light work. I persuaded him to make an application to the Post Office for transfer to any vacant sub-postmastership and promised to see the GPO in Edinburgh in support of his application.' The Post Office found a vacant post at Manish in Harris. It was not a full-time job, but the authorities believed Ferguson 'ought to be able to supplement it by opening a small shop, especially as he is in a particularly good position to market Harris tweed through his brother in Glasgow.' Ferguson turned the sub-postmastership down. He would, after all, work like the others for the Commission. The Department officials found a house for him at West Green, Culross, in Fife, and the Commission offered him light work on the Tulliallan estate. Neil promised Henderson he would consider the offer.

Men from the Department of Agriculture also went to Hirta in July. Two shepherds accompanied by their dogs were sent over from Uist to help Macaulay of the Department organize the rounding-up of the sheep. The St Kildans, however, proved reluctant to tell the officials exactly how many sheep they owned. 'When a question appears to suggest an enquiry into means,' noted an official of the Department of Health, 'the number is obviously minimized and on the other hand an enquiry that suggests compensation brings out a much higher number.'

It had been agreed from the beginning that the sheep would be sold and the proceeds would go towards meeting the cost of the evacuation. It was thought that the beasts would sell for anything up to £1 a head, but doubts had been raised by the West Highland Auction Mart as to their true value. In a letter to the Department the auctioneers stated that in their opinion the sheep of St Kilda were so wild that 'their legs might have to be tied', and that they thought the islanders would be lucky to receive fifteen shillings per head for them. 'After taking everything into consideration,' concluded the auctioneers, 'we candidly consider the removal of the sheep will not be an economic success.' The sheep of St Kilda, moreover, had not been dipped for some years, and the Chief Constable of Inverness had issued an order that no sheep from the island were to be shipped or offered for sale. The policeman agreed to rescind the order on a guarantee by the government officials that the sheep would be dipped immediately they arrived at Oban. The cost of the exercise, of course, would be borne by the sale. On 6 August, 667 sheep, almost half the total on the island, were transported aboard the *Dunara Castle*.

The patience of the Scottish Office officials was sorely tried in the weeks leading up to evacuation day. The men on the island, angered by Neil Ferguson's distinct lack of interest in the events of the moment, refused to help round up his sheep. Macaulay, helped by the missionary, managed with money to persuade them otherwise. The stubbornness of the people of Hirta, however, was matched by the intransigence of others more wise.

When evacuation was first mooted, Inverness County Council, within whose authority lay the remote Atlantic isle, took fright. The County Clerk was instructed to write to the Department of Health, as the councillors feared that 'certain of the islanders, self-supporting at present, might, by reason of their transfer to the mainland, become a burden on the county'. Since the government was evacuating the St Kildans, argued the Clerk, the government should be responsible for financially maintaining those who could not support themselves. Tom Johnston demanded that the Council be prepared to pay poor relief, and instructed 'that a strong letter should be sent to the County Council expressing surprise at their attitude and pointing out that the Government could not relieve them of a statutory liability'. The Council were forced to agree to pay relief to the older islanders, but proved so slow in handing over the money that the Department of Health was obliged to make several interim payments to the St Kildans in the weeks following the evacuation.

If charity had been available to the St Kildans while they lived on Hirta, it was noticeably absent at the time of the evacuation. Very few offers were made to house or employ the islanders on the mainland. The Scottish Office received only five offers worthy of consideration. The Duchess of Montrose, a Mr Wood of Newark, Mrs Wallar of Pitlochry, and Nurse Mackenzie who had served time on Hirta offered to assist individual islanders. The Countess of Warwick wrote to the Department and asked if she might employ Donald Gillies as a shepherd on her Essex estate. The Countess thought that the sheep of St Kilda were of the four-horned variety. When she discovered that they were not, she swiftly withdrew her offer. A society which had occasionally been criticized for over-indulging did not stir. The St Kildans, in return, agreed to ignore all help save that of the Scottish Office in whom they felt trust.

Even the charitable societies could not bring themselves to be generous. The Clerk of the Highlands and Islands Fund, even as late in the day as 30 July, still questioned the advisability of coming to the aid of the St Kildans. 'The application made by the Under-Secretary of State for Scotland for a grant of approximately £500 to be applied for the behoof of the inhabitants of St Kilda has now been respectfully considered,' wrote Archibald Campbell. 'The Trustees, after most careful consideration of the whole circumstances, decided against making the block grant desired by the Under-Secretary. I was instructed to inform you, however, that my Trustees would most sympathetically consider any individual cases of distress arising out of the evacuation upon receiving the usual forms of application.' The Clerk dutifully enclosed a number of application forms. If the islanders hoped for charity, they were going to have to justify the need for it on paper.

33, 34. The St Kilda mailboat was a romantic invention of visitors to the island. The little wooden vessels attached to an inflated sheep's stomach did, however, convey messages to the mainland. On more than one occasion this saved the islanders from starvation

Above 35. The 'Steamer Season' (in this case 1928) from June to the end of August brought tourists and prosperity to the islanders. In time the St Kildans came to rely on the visitors and their money. *Below* 36. The tourists invariably took an opportunity to pose before the camera. They wished to record for posterity the

fact that they had visited the most remote and primitive part of the British Isles.
Above 37. The St Kildans were quick to exploit the popularity the island achieved.
Socks, scarves, tweed, and the inevitable postcard brought much-needed money
to the people. A photograph taken in 1890

38, 39. Visitors to St Kilda
were struck by the lack of
children on the island. For
nearly a century Tetanus
Infantum took its heavy toll.
In the graveyard unperished
coffins were exhumed to make
room for new victims

Above 40. Three generations of Gillieses photographed in 1927. There were only five surnames on the island, and by the time of the evacuation the Gillieses, together with the MacKinnons, accounted for over two-thirds of the population.

Below 41. By the 1920s St Kilda had become a community of old people supported by a decreasing number of able men. The elderly were reluctant to leave, but there was no alternative

Above 42. At the time of the evacuation the MacKinnon family was the largest on the island. During the winter of 1929 they went without sugar and margarine, and the eight children had no shoes

Below 43. Evacuation. Everyone helped pack and carry the little they had

Left 44. The able-bodied men were employed by the Forestry Commission. A people who had never seen vegetation taller than a cabbage were employed planting trees which would outlive their memories. For the first time the women were separated from their husbands all day

Below 45. The new life in Morvern, Argyll, was difficult for the older St Kildans to accept. Even the younger islanders, for whom it was thought evacuation would bring happiness and prosperity, suffered by the change

Right 46. For the few St Kildans able to go back in the summer months after the evacuation, memories of a past life were all that remained

Below 47. After the evacuation the village street soon crumbled before wind and storm

The Highland and Agricultural Society of Scotland felt similarly inclined. Tom Johnston asked if they might consider using the money that was still left in the old St Kilda Fund to make the new homes a little more welcoming. 'The view taken by my Directors', wrote John Stirton at the beginning of August in reply to the Under-Secretary's enquiry, 'was that it would not be proper for this Society to use the money from its St Kilda Fund to pay for necessary furniture in connection with the re-housing of the St Kildans. The cost of evacuation and of re-housing, etc., it was understood, was a charge which should be met from the public funds.' The Society, however, agreed to consider any request for money that 'might be spent in purchasing for the St Kildans things which were over and above the bare necessities of life'. If, said the Secretary to the Society, any St Kildans were settled on crofts, help might be given in the purchase of livestock. None of the islanders, however, were to take up crofts, and as 29 August drew near, Tom Johnston was still trying to provide them with the basic essentials.

It was left totally to the Scottish Office to furnish those homes lacking sufficient furniture. Seven beds and mattresses complete with linen and blankets, seventeen wooden chairs and a deal kitchen table had to be ordered and arrangements made to deliver them to the appropriate houses in Morvern.

The Treasury, the most conservative Department of State, was quick to make clear to the Scottish Office that the evacuation should cost the Exchequer as little as possible. Tom Johnston had written estimating the entire operation would cost some £500. 'We have been prepared from the start to deal with the situation as sympathetically as possible,' came the swift reply from the Treasury, 'in the confidence that while everything necessary would be done to secure finality in resettlement of the inhabitants on the mainland you would not incur expenditure other than on a reasonable scale.' £500, commented the anxious author, 'is somewhat higher than we expected'. The accountants of Whitehall, most of whom had never heard of St Kilda before May 1930, requested that the Scottish Office refer back to them if it was found necessary to incur any extraordinary expense, such as the building of new homes for any of the St Kildans. Further correspondence that summer from London continued to remind the Departments of Agriculture and Health 'to keep the amount to be borne on public funds to a minimum and to meet the requirements as far as practicable from other sources'.

On 2 August a final conference, attended by all the departments of state concerned with the evacuation, was held at the Admiralty. It was agreed the HMS *Harebell* would be available at a cost of less than £100 to transport the thirty-six St Kildans and their few belongings to the mainland. Twenty-seven islanders would disembark at Lochaline, and the remainder, bound for other parts of Scotland, would remain on board until the ship reached Oban. Four days before the evacuation, the St Kildans formally accepted the offers of employment that had been made to them. Even Neil Ferguson, the postmaster, was finally forced to succumb. He would, after all, go to the Tulliallan Forestry estate, provided the Commission agreed to a trial period.

A former St Kildan, Christine MacQueen, claimed a fortnight before the evacuation that the whole operation had been 'the work of despairing Sassenachs'. It was an ignorant accusation. The officials at the Scottish Office had, in less than four months, found what was thought even by the St Kildans to be an acceptable alternative to living on Hirta. By that fateful day in August, the dead hand of bureaucracy ensured that the one problem to be resolved was who should foot the bill. The civil servants, however, had otherwise worked hard and with sympathy. Only events would now show whether the St Kildans could cope with their new-found future.

14
Morvern and beyond

It was seven o'clock on Friday evening before twenty-seven exhausted St Kildans arrived at Lochaline in Argyll. It had been agreed that they would disembark from the *Harebell*, taking with them a few essentials that could be carried by hand. The *Princess Louise* had been chartered by the government to sail from Oban at a later date with the heavy luggage and the few pieces of furniture. The main concern of the authorities on 30 August was to allow the St Kildans to get into their new homes as quickly as possible and with the minimum of fuss. The *Harebell*, with the remaining nine islanders, the missionary and his wife, and Nurse Barclay, sailed on down the Sound of Mull to Oban from where, after a good night's rest, all would go their separate ways.

Most of the newspaper reporters were at Lochaline to meet the St Kildans. Excluded from covering the final moments of the evacuation, they sought to concentrate their efforts upon the little wooden pier. The shy people from Village Bay did not expect the throng that surrounded them. 'There was an awful lot of reporters and journalists there,' recalls Lachlan Macdonald, 'and most of us who had come from St Kilda were awfully annoyed with it. As far as I can make out, they were thinking when they were coming from St Kilda that they were odd folk who didn't know anything, they were more like wild beasts or something like that. Folk was coming to see them as a curiosity, just as if you were going to the zoo to see some wild beast or something like that.' The Government officials had made every effort to keep the whole operation free from publicity, but they could do little to stop a demanding press at the end of a long and arduous summer's day. Editors demanded that their reporters reap as much as they could from the occasion. They were there, after all, to do the job of work that everyone on the mainland expected of the Press.

'We couldn't get moving for reporters,' recalls Flora Gillies, then ten years old. 'I remember an instance my mother and my sister and I were walking off the pier and this young fellow was trying to get our photos and he fell over a pile of wood and we were trying to cover our faces. That didn't stop him, he came back again.' As the St Kildans tried to get into the cars that were to take them to their new homes scattered round the Ardtornish peninsula, reporters took to the running-boards in the hope of a picture or word that would capture the sadness of the moment. For Flora Gillies, her mother, and her sister, this was to be their first impression of the mainland, and they were disconcerted by the welcome given them by the gentlemen of the press. 'I think,' says Flora, 'they thought we had horns or something; it was all in the papers, you know, that we were queer looking and all that kind of thing.' By the end of the day, the children of the party were tired if excited by the day's events; the older St Kildans were annoyed and showed no emotion. It was agreed by the government departments that what was needed for all of the newcomers was a few days' rest to settle down.

Until the outbreak of war in 1939, Lochaline was one of the prettiest villages in Argyll. It was the principal township of the diamond-shaped peninsula of Morvern. Bounded by Loch Sunart to the north, Loch Linnhe to the east and the Sound of Mull to the west, the peninsula was as barren of vegetation as of people. The hill and moorland of Morvern had suffered heavily during the Highland Clearances, and by 1930 the total population was little over five hundred souls. Such a remote, sparsely populated peninsula, bounded on three sides by water, was the most suitable home the government could find for the St Kildans. No one claimed that Morvern was ideal, but at least they could be offered sheltered employment there, and in time, it was hoped, the people would come to accept their lot. 'I am agreeably surprised at the type of people, their intelligence, their desire to start work,' wrote William Whellans, the Forestry Commission's representative to the Department of Agriculture. 'I have, however, allowed them to have a few days at home, and some intend going to Oban to see their sheep sold and in the case of Donald Gillies to bring his cow home.'

Several St Kildans took the steamer from Lochaline to Oban on 3 September to watch the sheep sale. They stood in silence as their beasts were sold at prices which were a disappointment to them, but which were expected by all on the mainland who had seen their condition. In total, the sale of over 1,200 sheep fetched £799, plus a few shillings and pence. The former islanders returned to Lochaline uncertain as to whether they would ever see a penny of the money. It was still to be decided whether the sale of the sheep would go towards paying the cost of the evacuation. The only St Kildan who left Oban happy was Donald Gillies with his cow. All the islanders had been given the opportunity to hold on to their cattle, and all but Donald had decided to part with them, believing they would be of little use to them in their new life.

To the St Kildans, the early weeks were difficult times. Their new environment proved to be as cruel and implacable as the Atlantic Ocean that surrounded their former home and had helped determine their destiny for a thousand years. They knew and understood, however, the Atlantic and its fury; they were ignorant of society on the mainland and of the young trees they were to tend.

The inhabitants of Lochaline had been prepared to expect the worst. The stories in the newspapers made them wary of their new neighbours. 'There was a shepherd next door to myself and in them days they used to go away for two or three days from their house,' remembers Lachlan Macdonald, who took up residence, together with his brother and mother, in a house at Savary. 'The first thing he did,' recalls Lachlan of his neighbour, 'he put locks on all the doors – barred everything so that nobody could get in. Even when he would come round to see the St Kildans he would take his pipe out of his mouth, thinking that the St Kildans would steal it.'

The local doctor tried hard to correct the false impressions the people of Morvern had about their new neighbours. 'They all wondered what sort of folks they were going to get,' says Dr Miller. 'One man had a very strange idea about it and had no hesitation in expressing his opinion. A St Kildan family was going to be put into a house just next to him and he was very indignant about this. He said to me, "What are they sending a lot of these beggars down here for, a lot of lazy scroungers?"'

There was much that was new and unnerving for the St Kildans. Most of the five adults who had never been off Hirta before in their lives were old. Some like Finlay MacQueen could speak or write no English. In Morvern, few locals could speak Gaelic. The fact that the St Kildans had been given cottages miles apart from each other made Finlay's life even more unspeakable.

For all the St Kildans it was the first time they had lived in houses with running water, let alone dry or water closets. Some of the houses even had staircases with rooms upstairs. The older people, most of whom suffered badly from rheumatism, found going to bed a painful task. Mrs Macdonald, Lachlan's mother, who was crippled with rheumatism, found her new home less than convenient.

For the children, who would adapt more easily than their parents and grandparents, everything was new. Flora Gillies remembers that the first thing that struck her on the mainland was the sight of a horse in a field. 'The young boys,' recalls the wife of the postmaster at Lochaline at the time, 'thought that bicycles were wonderful, and thought they just had to be on them and they would go off. They weren't in the habit of seeing pictures of bicycles, just cars. It was a great novelty.' The St Kildans might have seen photographs of motor cars in the magazines and newspapers sent to Hirta, and had been told how they worked, but they were ignorant of how to contend with them when they met them on the open road. 'They weren't accustomed to motor cars,' says Dr Miller. 'Instead of stepping aside when a car came along, they would simply run in front of it.' Used to climbing the steep slopes of Conachair and Oiseval, they walked everywhere in Morvern and the local inhabitants were amazed at their speed.

The government authorities at the time of the evacuation knew that the St Kildans would be out of their element on the mainland and would require a considerable amount of looking after, no matter where they were settled. As none of the islanders had any money to set up a new home, they had not only to be provided with jobs but also with somewhere to live. It had not proved easy to find accommodation on Forestry Commission land at Morvern, and the St Kildans were offered little more space in which to live than they had had on Hirta. In a five-roomed house at Savary, Mrs Macdonald, her two sons Ewen and Lachlan, Mrs Neil Gillies and her two daughters Flora and Rachel, and old Finlay Gillies had to begin their new life. Donald Gillies and his family moved into one of a row of cottages built especially by the Forestry Commission to house its workers at Larachbeg. John Gillies, his mother and his five-year-old son Norman went to a cottage at Ardness. In a house at Achabeg, Norman Mackinnon, his wife and their eight children were settled, and two rooms in Lochaline village itself were made available to Widow MacQueen, who had turned down the Department of Health's offer to transport her to her mother's house in Harris.

The rents on the houses were fixed at the lowest economic rate the Department could arrange. For two-roomed dwellings, the former islanders had to pay four pounds a year, whereas a pound more was required for houses with three rooms or more. As the few pieces of furniture owned by the St Kildans had been of little value and not worth transporting to the mainland, the Department of Health, at a cost of £56 19s 10d, had commissioned Messrs J. & R. Allan, of South Bridge, Edinburgh, to provide the islanders with new beds, mattresses, blankets, pillows, tables, and chairs. The Department also provided each male adult St Kildan with a bicycle to get him to and from his work, which it was calculated would never be more than five miles away from his home.

The eight able-bodied men of Hirta had accepted jobs on the Forestry Commission's new estates in Morvern. It was hoped that a people used to turning their hands to anything would not find the work too boring. Under the Commission, the St Kildans would work at road-mending, build fences, and help with the planting and the care of young trees. For a 45-hour week they were to be paid 38 shillings, and the Commission guaranteed to employ them for a minimum of 105 days every year. In return, the men were expected to work until the age of retirement looking after forests that would outlive not only them but their memories of a former land upon which no tree ever grew.

The men took to the work with difficulty. When they agreed to do the job, they had done so ignorant of what was involved. Their decision had been taken on the advice of the nurse and the missionary on Hirta. Even some of the younger men, like Lachlan Macdonald, who had spent many months working on the mainland before the evacuation, now admit that they had no idea of what was in store for them. Apart from having to travel some three or more miles to work each day, they had to learn an alien discipline – that of working for a boss. On Hirta, the men had been their own masters; on the mainland the patience of the Commission's foresters was severely tried by their late or non arrival for work. 'I am having a considerable number of complaints from Fuinary regarding the St Kildans,' wrote an official of one of the forests in Morvern to the Department of Agriculture, 'and I am afraid that the matter may end in some of them being asked to find work elsewhere. However, we shall advise your Department before any steps of this sort are taken so that if possible you might find them other employment.' The readjustment was to take time, if only because the premise of work had changed.

The men of St Kilda were accustomed to performing tasks

immediately concerned with survival. Their lives had revolved around the provision of food, heating, and clothing for their families. It was difficult to accept doing work that did not directly relate to either themselves, their wives, or the physical security of their children. The St Kildans were now working for money, and money was an intermediate with which they had to purchase the life and happiness they believed was available to them on the mainland.

It was difficult to get used to a way of life totally dependent upon money. Apart from having to pay higher rents for their homes than they did on Hirta, the St Kildans had to pay money for every essential commodity of life. They had to purchase coal to heat their homes, for instance – something they had never had to do on Hirta where they burned indigenous turf. In such circumstances, thirty-eight shillings a week did not go far. 'I shall not take a home here at all,' wrote Donald Gillies of Achabeg. 'I haven't enough wages as to pay two shillings and sevenpence a hundredweight of coal. You shall see me soon in the poorhouse. Please I understand from Nurse Barclay that we would be better off, but I am situated in a worse place.' At Savary, Ewen Macdonald was making the same discovery. 'A working man', he wrote to the Department of Health, 'with thirty-seven and threepence have to look where he will put it and I have to pay twelve shillings for the ton of coal.' By the time he had paid for his coal to be transported from the pier at Lochaline, Ewen was having to pay nearer three pounds for a ton.

More important, the St Kildans realized they had to purchase every bit of food they required. They could no longer rely upon the charity of trawlermen, or the goodwill of the factor. There were no sea birds to catch and preserve for eating, and they no longer had any sheep to kill and cure. Most of their new homes had a plot of land attached which they worked, but none was sufficient to provide the St Kildans with enough food to live on.

One of the few families to benefit immediately from the change were the Mackinnons. With three of them working for the Commission, they had never enjoyed such prosperity on Hirta. 'At first I did not know what to expect from them,' said a young forestry foreman to a reporter from the *People's Journal*, 'but they are obliging and eager to put their best into the work. I believe they are grateful for the interest taken in them. Naturally they are strong after their hard life on St Kilda and are capable of heavy work in the open. They start work at half past eight in the morning and finish at five o'clock at night with an hour for dinner. They are quite well off, and the Mackinnon family between them bring in a weekly wage of between six and seven pounds. Considering that they had a hard job to make £30 a year in St Kilda, their present condition compares very favourably with their former state.'

The younger, unmarried men also found the work easier and more worthwhile. In the latter years on Hirta they had worked to maintain the entire community. Now they had only themselves to think of. 'When I started working,' says Lachlan Macdonald, 'we were a few together and the job was brushing trees and things like that and I thought it was grand. We thought it was great to get a pay packet and all that. You could go home and could relax and if you felt like it you could go and enjoy yourself – go to a ceilidh, or a concert or something like that, or a dance if you were able to dance. There was nothing like that in St Kilda, so I thought it was great right enough.' For Lachlan, like many of the young men, fixed hours of work and a guaranteed wage meant a new life. Although he and his brother Ewen still had their mother to support, they could afford to buy what had previously been luxuries. One of Lachlan Macdonald's first purchases with money saved from a few weeks' work was a new suit with which he could grace the local dances, and impress what to him seemed like a surfeit of young unmarried ladies.

For the St Kildan women, life on the mainland proved difficult and lonely. They were not used to their men being away at work all day and every day. On Hirta man and wife had done much together, and when the husbands went away to the neighbouring islands and stacs the wives had always had plenty of work to do round the croft. On the mainland the wives, like the elderly, were isolated from each other by the distance separating their homes. Christina Gillies found it particularly difficult to cope.

The only traditional task left to the St Kildan women was knitting. 'When they went along the road,' recalls Mrs Gillies of Lochaline Post Office, 'they took their knitting with them,' just as they had done on Hirta. Every Christmas the women would donate to the church the product of their labours, or else would give the socks and scarves to neighbours who had shown kindness to them.

The evacuation of St Kilda had in large part been agreed to by the islanders for the sake of their children. It was believed that the mainland would afford them a better education and a reasonable chance in life. However, they found themselves split up for the purposes of education. Three went to the little school at Larachbeg, and three went to the school at Claggan several miles away. 'They are very clever,' commented one local child in 1930, 'and speak English quite well. If someone speaks to them in Gaelic, the boys reply in that language, but they are quite at home with English. They are taught English, arithmetic and writing, and managed well from the first day they came to school. They give the teacher no trouble. While the rest of us are taught rug-making, the St Kildan boys get knitting. When they were on the island they were good at knitting and this has been continued. After school hours they play with us. At first they could not play our games, but after a few days they became clever at them, and many a time they have beaten us at our own games. I like them,' concluded the schoolboy in his comments given to a reporter from the *People's Journal*, 'and they seem to enjoy playing with us.'

The St Kildan children were always spotlessly clean and tidy. 'They always looked as if they were just freshly out of a bath,' recalls the local doctor. 'Their faces were what Shakespeare described as "their shining morning face". They always seemed to have this fresh complexion.' They were not, however, accustomed to receiving medical attention when they injured themselves. Dr Miller remembers an instance that involved one of the Gillies children. 'The boy was about seven or eight at the time,' he says. 'He had been playing football and he was kicking goals. This was about dinner time. He hurt his arm and he didn't come to see me until about four o'clock. So I had a look at it and he had a broken arm, and he had been there until school closed before he thought of coming to see me.'

Although they attended school with great regularity, few of the St Kildan children fared better as a result of the parochial education they received in a remote Argyllshire village. They would probably have done equally well on Hirta had they remained in the care of the missionary. None of them advanced beyond a basic education, or were equipped at the end to take up occupations much different from those of their parents.

The St Kildans at Morvern were certainly not deprived of their former spiritual leaders. The United Free Church decided to give them the benefit of two of their former missionaries. Donald Cameron, now ordained, worked at Easdale near Lochaline, and

Dugald Munro had agreed to go with the St Kildans to Morvern at the evacuation. The older islanders kept up their church-going habits at the expense of little other socializing. 'They have not attended local dances,' remarked one inhabitant, 'and cannot be induced to come to meetings except at church.'

Nurse Williamina Barclay also kept a caring eye on the islanders. Her sister, Nan Barclay, had been responsible for helping prepare the new homes, and together they tried hard in the early months to make the St Kildans feel at ease. In those last days on Hirta, Nurse Williamina had tried to persuade the people to take with them anything that might prove of use to them on the mainland. The St Kildans, determined to abandon not only their island but the way of life associated with it, disappointed her. 'I did my very best', wrote Williamina Barclay in September 1930 to the Department of Health, 'to get each family to retain the looms, and it was not until I visited Lochaline that I found out that they had failed to keep their promise that they would take them to the mainland. I knew that Donald Gillies had sold his to a gentleman in Dumfries, he did this in spite of much discussion on the subject as my opinion was that all could add to their income by weaving during winter evenings. The fact is that they had all firmly made up their minds to discard weaving, telling me if they worked all day they were not going to weave at night.' The stubbornness for which the St Kildans were noted whilst on the island was one of the few things they took with them to the mainland. At Lochaline only one family, the Gillieses at Savary, had brought their loom with them.

Nurse Barclay visited all the islanders and reported on them to the Department in Edinburgh. 'I found the Mackinnons very happy and comfortable,' remarked the nurse to George Henderson. 'They had started work and the children had gone to school. At Savary, old Mrs Macdonald and Finlay Gillies were happy, but Lachlan Macdonald was deeply concerned as to how he was to get evening classes to improve himself. Donald Gillies at Achabeg thought his house very good and was liking his work, but was unhappy about his wife. I found her quite hysterical, she is afraid to be left alone in the house. I quite understand this as she was accustomed to neighbours and was rarely found in her own home.' The former nurse of St Kilda was confident that evacuation had been worthwhile. 'Certainly', she concluded in her letter, 'you have spent much time and thought over St Kilda and her problems and while I think they are all very much better off, I realize that it will take time for them to fall into line in new surroundings.'

Christmas Day 1930 was the first the St Kildans celebrated on 25 December. The newspapers were quick to realize the fact, and once again reporters descended upon Lochaline and the surrounding country. The *People's Journal* sent a special correspondent, who called first at the manse where Dugald Munro and his family had taken up residence. 'They seem to have settled down to their new life,' said the missionary. 'At first they were inclined to be restless, due to the vast amount of interest they were creating throughout the country, but that has now passed. I am told they are doing good work and are rapidly making friends with the Morvern folk. Of course, now that the winter has set in there is not much opportunity for the former islanders to continue meeting the country people, as after their work is over for the day the menfolk walk home and spend most of their evenings indoors.'

To those St Kildans who had gone to settle elsewhere than Morvern the new life proved equally hard to accept. John Macdonald had gone to Inverness, where he was employed at the County Road Surveyor's store at Culcabock. Neil Ferguson Senior and his wife had taken a Forestry Commission house at Culross in Fife. He had been offered light work at Tulliallan, the Commission's chief tree nursery. From Oban, the journey to Fife and Inverness had to be made by train, and many stories were told at the time of how the St Kildans coped with this novel form of transport. Sir Compton Mackenzie, who took a close interest in the evacuation, recalled one incident. 'One story I remember,' he said. 'Two old ladies had found for the first time a water closet on the train and thought what a wonderful place for washing up. They washed their china in it. Another old St Kildan who had been told about this thought he was going to do the same thing. Unfortunately, he pulled the communication cord instead of pulling the plug and the train was held up and he was reproved for this behaviour.' It is unlikely that such an incident happened, but such stories were rife at the time.

Neil Ferguson, son of the former postmaster, had been sent to Strome Ferry in Wester Ross. He had chosen to work on the Commission's estate there because he wished to be settled apart from the other islanders and wanted to be away from his overpowering father who had dominated him on St Kilda. For Neil, the youngest married St Kildan, life proved difficult. The work was all right,' he recalls, 'but you had an awful walk, three miles across hills. There was no other road but across the moors to the other side and the same coming back again. You had to go away an hour or more before starting time. Instead of stopping at five o'clock, it would be between six and seven before I got home again. And the wife was in the house all day herself, so that was no use.' Neil, like the other St Kildans in Morvern, was realizing the worth of the companionship they had shared on Hirta, if ever they had doubted its value.

Neil's new home was riddled with rats, and he found it almost impossible to keep them down. Like the other islanders he was faced with the problem of having to buy fuel to heat his house, and in Neil's case he had to travel over two miles with it himself as he could not afford to pay someone to deliver it to him. 'The worst thing we done,' he now says, 'was taking jobs from the Commission. If we had gone on our own and got jobs we'd have been better off. I went to a place away in the wilds, there was only one house in the place. The nearest wee village was about two miles away and there was no roads to it.'

Within a few weeks the St Kildans were writing to the Department of Health to voice their disillusionment. On 11 September 1930, Neil Ferguson Junior wrote from Ardnaff to the Scottish Office in Edinburgh. 'We want you to find us a more suitable place and employment, where I can earn a living as soon as possible,' wrote Neil. 'Under no circumstances will I entertain staying in this lonely place which is nothing like what was promised me before leaving St Kilda.'

Neil had gone as far as to withhold paying part of his rent. 'I wish to inform you,' he added, 'that the croft connected with this house is of no use to me and therefore I will not pay or be responsible for rent on same. As you know we were rushed away from St Kilda leaving boats and other useful things there, and a boat is necessary to take a load of coal, etc., across here. Please let me know what you or party responsible for our evacuation can do in the matter. Meantime, I have started work but trust you will be able to see us better situated very soon.' To aggravate the situation Neil found that work was suspended for a while at Ardnarff estate and he was having to go an additional two miles to Braeintra estate for work. On average, he was having to make do on £3 14s 1d a fortnight. Sutherland of the Forestry Commission felt that Neil had little cause to grumble about his lot, and wrote to MacRobbie at the Department of Health in March 1931. 'It seems to me', wrote Sutherland, 'that the complainer has not much cause to protest. He has not been as satisfactory as others, and has paid no rent since his arrival. I propose that the Divisional Officer should be asked to demand payment now, and also inform Neil Ferguson that unless his rent is paid in full he will not be removed from Strome to Tulliallan.'

John Macdonald, who had moved into the Toll House, Culcabock, near Inverness, was also complaining. 'I thought when you evacuated us from our warm comfortable houses that we had that you were going to situate us in better accommodation,' wrote Macdonald to George Henderson. 'But for us you erected us in the worse place that my eye ever came across. I thought the Department of Health was for Health but it is the other way for us. Now, Mr Henderson, how also do you expect me to make my living out of thirty-seven shillings a week? Life out here is different from St Kilda as you yourself can understand.'

A torrent of correspondence came from John Gillies living at Ardness. 'Please to look in this matter also according to the place I am situated,' wrote the exasperated islander. 'For you knew perfectly well that I had a boy at the age for school and by the means of situated me in such an awkward place. He shall be unable to get to school this year. The house is also too small, no accommodation for sleeping but the one room. The home I had in St Kilda was much bigger.'

Neil Ferguson Senior, earning six shillings and eight pence a day at Tulliallan, took it upon himself to write to the United Free Church of Scotland to see whether they could improve his lot. Upon receipt of the letter, the Reverend John Hall wrote to George Henderson expressing his opinion on Neil's situation. 'If he could be placed at Lochaline', he wrote, 'or elsewhere amongst Gaelic-speaking people he would be much happier. I think it likely he may himself before long request such a change.' The house given to Neil Ferguson left much to be desired. The roof leaked and the doors would not close properly. The gas system to heat and light the rooms was not working properly. The authorities knew from the outset that the Forestry Commission had been hard pressed to provide all the accommodation required to house the St Kildans, and workmen were sent to carry out essential repairs.

The St Kildans appeared ungrateful. It seemed to everyone that all they wished to do was to complain and demand. But their opinions were those of a people who were totally disillusioned. They had expected life on the mainland to be a solution to all their problems – they had been told it would during the long discussions that took place on Hirta before it was decided to evacuate the island. Perhaps the nurse and the missionary, in their desire to convince the islanders of the virtue of evacuation, had been over-generous in their description of what the St Kildans could expect of the mainland. And although there were problems in the early years, some of which were never to be resolved, the St Kildans were not unaware of the debt they owed the British Government. 'We will have to do our best and be content for the time being,' reflected Neil Ferguson in a letter he wrote to the Scottish Office at the end of September 1930. 'We can never forget your kindness to us,' he concluded, 'since all this great change started for our good, I fully believe.'

The government was patient, but not for long. John Gillies continued to write letters. 'Please to understand from this note that I am not going to live in this cottage longer and if you will not look for another home for me more comfortable. This home is worse than the cattle byre I had in St Kilda. I understand from Nurse Barclay that we were to be situated in better homes, but this is worse than a dungeon hole.' Dugald Munro was worried and wrote to George Henderson of the Department of Health for advice. 'The St Kildans must realize', came the prompt reply, 'that while the Government have helped them to leave their island, they cannot regard themselves as a permanently specially favoured community.'

The Department, however, did all they could to provide the islanders with better accommodation. They bought two more houses in Larachbeg, and John Gillies, his mother, and son were offered the tenancy of one, whilst the other was given to Donald Gillies. Donald was not impressed. 'It is a shift out of Morvern altogether I want and I must get it,' he wrote to the Department of Health. 'For your promises to us were a lot before I left St Kilda, but I have not seen any of them fulfill.' But if the government had made promises to the St Kildans, the aspirations of the former islanders were beyond anything that the authorities could be reasonably expected to provide. At a time when several hundred thousand were unemployed on the mainland of Scotland, the government had to be careful not to lavish too great a prize upon the St Kildans. The civil servants were aware that they should not be seen to offer the former islanders more than they had been used to on Hirta.

After all, it was the St Kildans, not the government, who had asked for the evacuation, and there were many watching to see whether the then Labour government would pay too much or too little heed to the needs of a people who themselves had begged for help.

Three months after the evacuation, Donald Gillies was still complaining. 'I shall not take any home here,' he wrote in yet another letter to Henderson. 'For I understand that this place is not suitable for Mother. If you do not so please, send me back to my old dwelling. Please answer soon and let me know.' The Department of Health officials had had enough : they were prepared to be patient but not answerable to every whim of the St Kildans. 'Mr Henderson suggests no action' was scrawled across the top of the letter.

The evacuation had broken up the traditional community of the St Kildan and replaced it with a financially unequal society. On Hirta the islanders had been equally poor, whereas on the mainland they were made financially and hence socially unequal. Some St Kildans became richer than they had ever been in their lives; others became considerably poorer. On Hirta, the old and the young, the widows and the sick were looked after by the able-bodied of the community. Food was always divided out equally, and those who foraged shared their efforts with the less fortunate. The poverty in the last years had been too much for some St Kildans, like the Mackinnons who almost starved, but few on the island were any better off at that time. At Lochaline, the Mackinnon family with four of their number working were able to lead a reasonable life. The older St Kildans who had been able to depend upon the rest found their condition upon the mainland intolerable.

The older St Kildans who could not work were a continual problem for the government. So too were the five widows and widowers. None of the St Kildans was insured; the islanders were therefore not entitled to pensions from the State until they were seventy years of age. Even then, in order to claim ten shillings a week they were subject to the means test and had to prove that they did not earn more than £26 5s 0d a year from other sources. The insurance scheme of the time, moreover, made no allowance for dependants, and the St Kildan widows found life financially difficult on the mainland. The Department of Health took it upon itself to help out. Old Finlay MacQueen, who was seventy-three, was given an additional ten shillings a week for a few months until he settled down. Widow MacQueen was similarly helped, and the Department made an interim maintenance payment of a pound a week to Widow Annie Gillies and her two small girls, Flora and Rachel.

Few of the St Kildans of course had anything in the way of savings. One of the main reasons why they had petitioned the government to evacuate them, in fact, had been because they could not afford to pay for such an exercise themselves. After they came to the mainland, the major financial, as opposed to practical, assistance they were to receive was ultimately the money from the sale of the sheep. It was thought to begin with that the government would keep the money to offset the cost of the evacuation, but public opinion mobilized by the newspapers forced the authorities to think again and agree that the money (nearly £800) be given to the St Kildans. Despite the fact that transportation charges and the cost of auctioning the sheep had cost the Department £506 os 4½d, the government met the bills from their own contingency funds.

The distribution of the sheep money, however, only helped accentuate the differences already existing in the economic condition of the St Kildans. Neil Ferguson Senior, who had owned more sheep on St Kilda than any other islander, laid claim to £184 14s 11d of the money, whereas Widow Norman MacQueen's little flock entitled her to less than £11.

There was only one further source of money available to the islanders – the old Kelsall bequest, known as the St Kilda Fund, which was under the control of the Highland and Agricultural Society of Scotland. Everyone was in agreement that the time had come to close the fund and distribute the proceeds amongst the thirty-six St Kildans. The problem, however, was how to divide out the fund, and to what use the £470 could best be put. The society's members were adamant that they would not hand over cash, for fear of being in breach of the terms of covenant.

Five months after the evacuation, the society were still refusing to allow money from the fund to be used to provide essential foodstuffs for the islanders at Lochaline and elsewhere who were finding it hard to cope on thirty-eight shillings a week. In a letter to George Henderson of the Department of Health, they agreed, in the case of a large family, that part of the money might be expended in the purchase of clothes. 'But', added John Stirton, Secretary of the society, 'my committee at the same time wished it to be borne in mind that, where a public authority was authorized and required to provide clothes, the money now spent from the St Kilda Fund should not be used simply to relieve the public authority of its statutory duty.' They grudgingly committed £20 to help the old and infirm St Kildans. Finally it was resolved that the money would be used to purchase chickens and coops together with various household articles for each new St Kildan home.

The goods, however, were subject to a method of distribution favouring the larger, well-off families. It was thought by the society that the most equitable way would be to employ the age-old system by which grain and foodstuff sent to the island had been shared: namely that every islander – man, woman, and child – be given a part. Nurse Barclay was critical. 'I wonder if it would be just', she wrote to the Department of Health, 'to act on the same basis as the flour and meal distribution. Conditions are now so different, the Mackinnons have a great wage-earning capacity which they did not have formerly, so why should they receive nearly one fourth of the fund? I hear that those at Lochaline have been asked if they wish furniture, cattle, hens, etc., but Widow Mac-Queen and some of the others won't get much of anything if the old rule prevails. Donald Gillies complains that he finds it very hard to live on thirty-eight shillings weekly, the cost of coal and cartage being a big item. Of course, he never had to pay for fuel in his life and it was a case of come easy, go easy.' The Department noted the nurse's comments, but decided they would comply with the method of division suggested by the Highland and Agricultural Society, namely one based upon the number of persons and not the number of households.

It took five months before the government finally decided how the evacuation was to be paid for. On 8 January 1931 a Memorandum was sent from the Department of Agriculture to the Department of Health. 'I have to state that the Secretary of State has instructed', wrote a civil servant, 'that the expenses incurred by your department in connection with the evacuation of the personnel from St Kilda, excluding subsistence and travelling expenses of officials, should be met from the Agriculture (Scotland) Fund in accordance with Section 4 (1)(d) of the Congested District (Scotland) Act, 1897 and that the special provision of £500 made available by the Treasury to cover the expenses of your department should be restored to the Civil Contingencies Fund.' In all, the government of the day spent only £1,000 of British taxpayers' money on the entire exercise.

For many St Kildans, by the spring of 1931 the desire to return to Hirta proved too strong. Less than ten months after they had been evacuated, eleven former Islanders went back to St Kilda for the summer. Some, like Finlay Gillies, the oldest St Kildan, went back to collect a few possessions they had had to leave behind on the island. Finlay, for instance, was eager to claim a rowing boat, and Neil Ferguson Senior was excused from work by the Forestry Commission for two months so that he might collect some personal effects from his old home. Few of those who boarded the first steamer of the year bound for St Kilda, however, felt they needed an excuse to go back.

The *Dunara Castle* and the *Hebrides* averaged six trips to St Kilda each year from 1931 to 1939. The steamship company McCallum Orme was only too willing to encourage the St Kildans to return. As the island boats, for instance, had been left behind on Hirta, the steamship line relied upon the islanders who were there in the summer months to successfully land their passengers. The interest created by the evacuation meant the cruises were always fully booked by some forty passengers a time who wished to make the pilgrimage. For the St Kildans, the cruises offered not only the means by which they could return to Hirta, but also the opportunity of making some additional money at the expense of the passengers, who came out to view St Kilda as they had done in the old days.

Sir Reginald MacLeod of MacLeod was against the St Kildans going back. He was worried about the bird life on the island that might be disturbed, and by the thought of the damage that might be done by tourists in search of souvenirs. He was equally concerned by the obvious danger of his former tenants being stranded on the island. The government officials were totally against even a temporary re-occupation. The Department of Health formally refused to accept medical responsibility for those St Kildans who returned, and the Secretary of State for Scotland did all in his power to discourage resettlement. The GPO refused to re-open the Post Office on Hirta, despite Neil Ferguson Senior's offer to act as unpaid postmaster. They also forbade any mail addressed to St Kilda to be handed over to the steamship company.

The St Kildans were not discouraged. Willie Clelland, who was purser on the *Hebrides*, remembers their excitement as they paid the first visit to their former island home after the evacuation. 'It was their home,' he says, 'and they'd been taken away from it. They didn't like the idea of having lost the island altogether.' It was rumoured in 1931, in fact, that one St Kildan was still continuing to offer rent to MacLeod of MacLeod for his croft on Hirta, believing that, in doing so, he was maintaining his right to return to the island.

When the St Kildans and tourists set foot on Hirta, they discovered the village in a state few had expected. In the previous nine months the cottages had been pillaged by trawlermen. The contents of every home had been looted, and doors had been ripped off their hinges. It was believed at the time that the crew of a Belgian trawler had been responsible for most of the damage. So disgusted was the proprietor, MacLeod of MacLeod, that he promptly appointed Neil Gillies to act as watchman on Hirta during the summer months – a post Neil held until the Second World War broke out.

Although many St Kildans returned for the summer months in years following the evacuation, most of them were those who had taken their leave of Hirta prior to 1930. Malcolm Macdonald, who had left St Kilda in 1924, made several trips and Alexander Gillies Ferguson, the prosperous tweed merchant from Glasgow, regularly returned to St Kilda with his family. In fact, when Ferguson heard that the Post Office on the island was to remain closed, he got a special St Kilda stamping device made. His brother Neil franked the hundreds of postcards he sold to the tourists with the cachet, although the GPO made it clear that such a stamp was invalid. When Alexander or Neil were absent from the island, Neil Gillies was entrusted with the sale and stamping of postcards, which were then put aboard the steamer and posted by the crew when they reached the first post office that was open.

While on Hirta, the St Kildans tried to recreate the simple life they had sought to abandon twelve months earlier. Several hundred sea birds were killed and salted down for eating at a later date on the mainland. Some of the islanders took up weaving. As few of them had taken their looms with them when they evacuated the island, the equipment was still there. Each islander produced six or seven webs of cloth before they took their leave of Hirta on the last steamer of the season.

The following year, the St Kildans set sail once more. The 1932 party included Finlay Gillies, then 68, Alexander Ferguson, his wife and son, and Donald Macdonald who had left the island prior to the evacuation. Neil Ferguson and his son joined them on a later steamer, along with a Mr Cruickshank of Messrs T. & J. Speedy, Estate Agents, who had been instructed by MacLeod of MacLeod to report on the state of the buildings on Hirta.

In 1931, MacLeod of MacLeod decided to sell St Kilda. Despite the fact that his family had owned the archipelago for six centuries, he believed the time had come to give it up. The purchaser was the Earl of Dumfries, a keen ornithologist. 'I always remember in Barra,' recalled Sir Compton Mackenzie, 'Dumfries arriving about midnight one night and knocking at the window and coming in saying, "I've just bought St Kilda!", and telling me about it, very proud of having done this. He was full of plans for the future, there were all sorts of things he was going to do.' The Earl of Dumfries, later to become the 5th Marquis of Bute, saw in St Kilda a chance to own his personal bird observatory to be enjoyed by his family and a few select friends. In 1938 Michael Powell, the film producer, wished to make a full-length feature film on Hirta. He spent some seven years, having read Alasdair Alpin Macgregor's *Last Voyage to St Kilda*, hoping he could make *The Edge of the World* on St Kilda. Ultimately, he had to make the film on the island of Foula. The Earl of Dumfries had decided that the presence of a film crew on Hirta would disturb his birds, his holiday, and his privacy.

The Earl, however, continued to employ Neil Gillies every summer to remain on St Kilda as his representative. Neil was allowed to stay in the factor's house and, together with the other islanders, did much in 1934 to restore the old cottages. On 19 June, Alexander Ferguson wrote to the Earl of Dumfries informing him of the work being done on Hirta. 'Your sitting-room in the manse has been done all white,' wrote Ferguson, 'according to your wish. I supplied Neil Gillies with lime and cement, and my wife superintended the decoration. We cleared all the boulders from the pier entrance, Repaired some habitable cottages, had them Irish lime-washed and the place is once more looking well.' But the St Kildans had an ulterior motive in helping the Earl restore the village. They gave of their labour in the summer months to make habitable not simply the holiday home of the laird, but a possible future home for themselves. 'There is one cottage', wrote Alexander Ferguson, 'I would gladly rent or buy from you. It is Number 11 in the row and used to be occupied by a widow previous to the evacuation.

There is no chance of her coming to stay there, therefore it is available for occupation after being refloored and replastered. I would be prepared to go to all that expense myself if you would kindly consider either let or sale. My brother, whom you met, wants to retain his own ancestral home, so as the manse is being put in order for Your Lordship, I would require some other shelter should I ever visit my native island again.' The Earl refused Ferguson's request to buy or rent a cottage.

In 1936 some St Kildans returned to Hirta to weave a length of tweed for the King. The *Hebrides* left Glasgow on Thursday, 30 May, on its first trip of the year, with a party of St Kildan exiles bent on making their fifth pilgrimage. In all, ten islanders returned that year – the *Hebrides* took aboard several others at Oban and Leverburgh. The party arrived at St Kilda on 3 June and began work immediately. The intention was to prepare a length of tweed from the wool of the wild Soay sheep, which was to be presented to King George V. 'When completed,' said one newspaper report, 'it will be presented to the King by the Earl of Dumfries as a Jubilee gift from the last scattered remnant of His Majesty's old island outpost.' Four out of the five families evacuated in August 1930 were represented on Hirta that summer. The Earl intended at the same time to make a short film about St Kilda and its vanished way of life for posterity, with the help of a personal friend Niall Rankine. A seventeen-foot motorboat was loaded on to the *Hebrides* at Greenock so that Rankine could make the trip to the great stacs and Boreray with the St Kildans and film them.

When the Jubilee Exhibition was held in Glasgow, a group of St Kildans had their own small stand. Surrounded by appropriate paraphernalia including spinning wheels, photographs of Hirta, and stuffed sea birds, they gave demonstrations of spinning and weaving to the hundreds of visitors who came to the Kelvin Hall for the great exhibition. Picture postcards were produced to commemorate the occasion, showing the senior branch of the Ferguson family weaving on a traditional loom. The publicity given to the island at the time gave rise to speculation that St Kilda might again be inhabited.

The rumours that St Kilda was about to be re-inhabited were sparked off when the Wool Owners' Association gave a favourable report on the quality and desirability of the wool from the Soay sheep. The cottages, declared the newspapers, were going to be renovated to house shepherds. 'I am further informed', wrote one correspondent, 'that building operations on quite an extensive scale for shepherds' and other workers' houses are to be started whenever weather conditions permit the landing of a pioneer force.'

'Have you seen the enclosed nonsense about St Kilda appearing in the papers?' wrote Tom Johnston to George Henderson at the Department of Health. Alexander Ferguson had given the *Daily Herald* an interview that gave the strong impression that several St Kildans wanted to go back and live on their native isle, and that the proprietor, the Earl of Dumfries, was prepared to look with favour upon any requests the islanders might make. At a meeting of the Glasgow City Business Club in 1937, the Earl had said, 'As a matter of fact I think it is quite possible that before many years are out there will be people there again. I am not able at the moment to tell you under what circumstances, because I am negotiating with a government department on that question.' The following day, the Glasgow *Evening News* quoted Alexander Ferguson as saying, 'The universal opinion of the islanders is that if Lord Dumfries had bought it a year earlier than he did there would have been a good flourishing population on St Kilda now.' The national press were quick to exploit the rumours; the government was equally swift to collect information to refute any suggestion of repopulation of Hirta.

Dr Shearer, who had been present at the evacuation and had closely followed the St Kildans since they arrived on the mainland, was emphatic that the people who had left in August 1930 had no desire to return. Nurse Barclay agreed, stating that the former inhabitants would not 'put a foot on a steamer' bound for Hirta. To their knowledge there were only two islanders who were complaining about their new life – Donald Gillies, who in one of the numerous letters he had sent to the Scottish Office stated that if he had to starve he might as well starve on St Kilda as on the mainland, and Mrs Ewen Gillies, who had agreed with her cousin Donald because of the pitiful allowance that the Inverness Town Council had agreed to pay her.

For the then Labour Government, St Kilda became yet again an embarrassment which had to be dealt with swiftly. They could not afford political capital to be made of such an emotive situation. Fortunately, the Secretary of State's authority had to be granted before any re-settlement was possible. A condition laid down by the government at the time of the evacuation was that the St Kildans had to formally renounce their claims upon their crofts.

On the other hand, the authorities were aware that as the island belonged to a private individual, he alone 'is at liberty to decide the uses to which it may be put'.

Any further embarrassment was saved by the outbreak of the Second World War. In 1939 the steamers stopped going to St Kilda and so did the former islanders. Hirta was never to be used during the war for military purposes as it had been during the First World War. So for six years the homes of the St Kildans were allowed to crumble before wind and storm. Only Alexander Ferguson was able to continue sailing the Western Isles. A saddened St Kildan, he wrote to the Earl of Dumfries on 20 May 1940 from Leverburgh in Harris, 'I have been touring round these islands for the last three days and have enjoyed every day of it. My health has benefited by the strong air and genial surroundings, but not the same as it would were it St Kilda. I think there is no Paradise on earth like it. Still, we are not allowed to visit it this season for obvious reasons which you know. On Friday last I hired a motor boat to go to Shillay and standing on the top of that island I saw St Kilda under a white cap of summer haze. I felt like Moses when he viewed the promised land from Piscah's heights.' The government had declared St Kilda and the open Atlantic that surrounded it out of bounds to private shipping as long as Britain was at war with Germany.

Some of the able-bodied St Kildans found themselves called up for the first time in their lives. Four St Kildans joined the army and three joined the navy. One was even captured in Germany and held prisoner of war until 1946. Fortunately, patriotism did not demand that any of them be killed. In that respect at least the war proved to be kind.

If disease had been a major cause of the evacuation of Hirta, it was to reap a sad harvest when the islanders settled on the mainland. 'The one thing I was afraid of,' recalls Dr Miller, 'was that they wouldn't have the same resistance to disease as we had.' The St Kildans, unlike those born on the mainland, had no resistance to diseases such as tuberculosis. A community who had been moved closer to civilization for their own good, it was thought, found themselves the helpless victims of the diseases of that civilization. Tuberculosis savagely attacked the family who had stood to gain most from the evacuation. Four of the Mackinnon children died from tuberculosis within six years of the family moving to the mainland.

In the summer of 1935 Norman Mackinnon, the father, contracted lung trouble. The doctor diagnosed tubercular pleurisy. Norman would recover if he took things easy, but he would never again be able to work in the balmy climate of the west coast of Scotland. At that time, Mary Mackinnon was still suffering from TB in the Oban Sanatorium, and Neil, the oldest son, was the only member of the family capable of working. Neil, on his thirty-eight shillings a week, had to support his parents and the three remaining children. The only other money coming into the home was the ten shillings a week that Norman was entitled to under the National Health Insurance Scheme.

The Department of Health applied to the Highlands and Islands Fund to see whether they were prepared to help. The trustees of the fund refused. If there was a financial problem, however, there was also a problem of location. Morvern was obviously unsuitable to a family with a tendency to TB. 'The local doctor is of the opinion that the only chance for the remaining children is to remove the family from the west coast to a less relaxing climate.' So wrote Sir John Jeffrey of the Forestry Commission to the Scottish Office. 'We did what we could', he concluded, 'to settle the St Kildans at the time the island was evacuated, but of course the after care of the islanders, beyond providing employment, does not properly lie within our province.'

Five months later, the civil servants on Tom Johnston's instructions were still searching for a new home for what remained of the Mackinnon family. The Clerk of Inverness County Council had made approaches to Lord Lovat's factor. Lovat owned much of the land in the area and it was hoped that perhaps the noble Lord might have some vacant cottage or croft that could be offered to the Mackinnons. Lord Lovat's factor claimed that nothing was available, despite the fact that Lady Lovat wished to be known for her interest in the treatment of TB. By the autumn of 1936, the civil servants were beginning to feel they had exhausted most of the possibilities. 'The most hopeful area is Inverness County,' wrote an exasperated official of the Department of Health to a colleague in the Scottish Office. 'The Inspector is hopeful that it may be possible to find the family a house, probably at Culcabock, when the houses which the County Council propose to erect there are ready. The case is a very sad one and the delay in moving the family is to be regretted, but the difficulty is to find a suitable house in the right locality.'

It was not until September 1937 that new accommodation was finally found for the family. The Forestry Commission agreed to make available to the Mackinnons a four-roomed house at Findon in the Black Isle, Ross-shire. The six survivors of a family that was once ten strong packed up and moved to their new home. There were now only two breadwinners left – Norman, aged twenty-seven and his only surviving brother Donald, two years his junior. The family that had everything to gain from evacuating St Kilda, and indeed the family who at the time wanted to leave most, had lost virtually all.

The Mackinnon family was not the only one to suffer. Two years after the evacuation, at the age of fifty-nine, John Macdonald died in the Royal Infirmary, Inverness. Tuberculosis claimed a lung from Donald Gillies, who, at the age of thirty-eight had been resettled at Savary in Morvern.

In 1939, St Kilda was not drawn into the theatre of war as had been the case during the First World War. Between 1939 and 1945, in fact, St Kilda was truly abandoned for the first time in recorded history. The islands, however, lay in an important training area for RAF wartime airfields on Scotland's west coast, with tragic consequences, for some young airmen.

A hundred yards from the summit of Conachair lies an airscrew with one blade missing. It belonged to a Beaufighter, LX798, which crashed into the 1397 foot peak in June 1943. The Beaufighter came from 304 Ferry Training Unit which at that time was based at Port Ellen on Islay. At the aerodrome crews were given a two week course preparing them for flying aircraft in India and the Middle East. Just after eight o'clock, on the evening of 3 June 1943 seven Beaufighters took off from Port Ellen on a night navigational exercise. Beaufighter LX798 was crewed by Sergeant-Pilot William Duxbury, aged twenty, and twenty-two year old Wireless Operator/Air Gunner Sergeant Stanley Thornton. Like most wartime airmen they were young; but not without experience. Duxbury had over eighty hours solo flying experience although only five of those were in Beaufighters at night.

At half past midnight Duxbury and Thornton requested a radio fix. They and two other air crews lost their bearings that night. Their message was a routine one: they did not know where they were but gave no indication that they were in trouble. It was to be their last message. When they did not ultimately return to base, a search for the missing Beaufighter was ordered. Nearly three months later, towards the end of August, a report came through that the tail section of an aircraft had been spotted on Hirta. A naval party from HMS

Phrontis landed on St Kilda and found the wreck, or rather what was left of it. The official report concluded that the plane had exploded on impact and that the bulk of the fuselage, probably with the bodies of the two airmen still inside, was catapulted over the 1200 foot high cliffs of Conachair into the sea. The only trace of the crew found was one flying boot and a shoe.

A year later, almost to the day, St Kilda witnessed another more horrendous loss of life when ten airmen were killed. Sunderland flying boat ML858 was based at 302 Ferry Training Unit at Oban. On 22 May 1944 her crew arrived for their final training before being sent to North Africa for convoy protection duties. The Captain of the Sunderland, Warrant Officer Cecil Osborne from New Zealand, was an experienced pilot who had clocked up over eight hundred flying hours. On the night of Wednesday 7 June 1944, the flight plan for Osborne was to fly south from Oban towards the island of Colonsay, then north to Barra Head, then north-west to St Kilda before flying back to base. The weather that night was bad with low cloud and poor visibility, and, as was usual, Sunderland ML858 was ordered to report by radio every hour. A message was received from Osborne at eleven o'clock at night, then the aircraft went off the air.

By dawn it was evident that something had gone wrong and a search began for the missing plane. It was hoped that the Sunderland had come down in the sea and could be recovered and towed back to base. On Saturday 10 June, however, two aircraft sighted the wrecked plane on Hirta and a high speed launch from Stornoway reached St Kilda just before seven o'clock at night. The wreckage, strewn over a large area at the head of Glean Mor, was identified as the missing Sunderland. Her crew of ten, which included six New Zealanders and an Australian, were all dead.

The recovery of the bodies, however, proved to be a problem. No boat was available to go to St Kilda until 13 June, when the armed anti-submarine trawler *Walwyns Castle* was sent to recover the remains of the airmen. On board were Wing Commander Campbell, the Station Commander from Oban, the Reverend Lachlan McLeod, the minister of St Columba's church in Stornoway, who was the acting RAF chaplain, and an RAF bearer party who would also act as Guard of Honour. The trawler set sail in a Force 7 gale and after a difficult journey reached St Kilda. The landing proved difficult and one of the crew had to jump into the heavy sea to bring a line ashore.

The party climbed to the site of the wreck. They found the bodies were badly mutilated and some were incomplete. Sadly, they gathered the human remains, carefully putting them in sacks and carrying them down to the beach from where they were ferried to the trawler in rubber dinghies. Four miles from Hirta, close to Boreray, as the Reverend McLeod read the burial service, the dead were committed to the deep.

The RAF, concerned that the wrecked Sunderland might cause another accident by enticing pilots to drop altitude to investigate, decided to break up and conceal the huge flying boat. On 9 July a squad from 56 Maintenance Unit based at Inverness and two Royal Navy explosives experts were sent to St Kilda to dismantle the wreck. Given the atrocious weather conditions on the island, it took the party two days to find the plane. An attempt to blow up the Sunderland proved futile so they set about hacking the twenty ton plane to pieces with axes.

The party remained on Hirta for nearly a month. They slept in the manse, where the Earl of Dumfries used to stay before the war, and, it is said, worked from seven in the morning until eight-thirty at night. Thirty-seven holes, each eight feet by four feet by four feet deep were dug and the hacked-off sections of the plane man-handled to the holes and buried. Those parts too large to bury were painted reddish brown so that they would not be seen from the air.

On the south-east cliff of Soay, at a height of about 600 feet, is the wreck of another wartime aircraft, of which little is known. Because of the island's inaccessibility, it was not until after the war that attempts were made to research the wreck. Between 1978 and 1979 an RAF Mountain Rescue Team, led by Flight-Lieutenant Hughes made three expeditions to Soay to examine the wreckage and try and identify the crew. The Hughes team concluded that the wreck was definitely that of a Wellington Mark VIII which, at the time of the crash, had been painted black. They failed to find identification tags that could put names to the remains of the six crew members they found, although some items of clothing and footwear together with a Royal Canadian Air Force cap badge were discovered.

The crash of the Wellington on Soay and the identity of her crew remains a mystery. What is known is that the plane crashed before June 1944 because the wreckage was sighted by airmen looking for the Sunderland. Father John Barry, who has painstakingly researched the plane wrecks of St Kilda, has narrowed the Wellington down to one of two possible aircraft; one which went missing on 23 February 1943 and another which was lost on 28 September and is known to have had five Canadians on board.

When peace came in 1945, there were even fewer St Kildans alive on the mainland than there had been before the Second World War. In 1940 Finlay Gillies, the oldest surviving St Kildan died at Pontyfield in Easter Ross. In the same year Neil Ferguson Senior's wife died at Kincardine. 'She died of heart failure,' wrote her son to the Earl of Dumfries, 'and no wonder, her heart was broken since she left the island. Poor soul, she is now at rest.' In 1944 her husband, Neil, died in hospital. When the war ended more than thirteen of the thirty-six islanders who had been evacuated from St Kilda were already dead. Those still alive were never to be constant visitors to St Kilda again, as they had been before the war, although Alexander Ferguson, the Glasgow tweed merchant, revisited his native St Kilda every year from 1947 until his death in 1957, usually in his own yacht *Colonsay*.

In the 1950s, however, the peace and tranquility of St Kilda was shattered. It was decided, for the most modern of reasons, that the abandoned home of the St Kildans, should again be populated.

15
Military occupation

On a bleak morning in April 1957 HM Vessel *Ageila* entered Village Bay. Before her passengers and crew lay the great natural amphitheatre that had witnessed the evacuation of man less than twenty-seven years previously, an event that had had all the marks of classical Greek tragedy. Beyond the storm beach and the meadows stood the empty houses of Main Street, crumbling monuments to man's former presence on Hirta. Despite defeat, man was about to act out another play, to try again to live on St Kilda on a permanent basis. The beginning did not seem an auspicious one: the new settlers were men of the RAF, brought to the cliff-girt isle in a boat crewed by soldiers. Thirty-five airmen landed that April day charged with the task of living on St Kilda, one person less than had been removed to the mainland of Scotland on 29 August 1930. The old St Kildans had asked to be evacuated; the new inhabitants had no choice in the matter. The defence of Britain demanded they live on Hirta whether they wanted to or not.

In 1955 the British Government decided to spend £20 million of taxpayers' money on a guided-missile range. The Minister of Defence, Selwyn Lloyd, told the House of Commons on 27 July that investigations had shown that the best place in the world for such a development was the Outer Hebrides. Within a year of the decision to build the range, officials had selected a suitable site on the north-west corner of South Uist as the launching area for missiles that would be fired out into the Atlantic Ocean.

The proposed range was to be shared by all three services, the Army, the Navy and the RAF and the complex required the Ministry of Defence to purchase land on North Uist, South Uist and Benbecula. The proposal met with much local and national opposition. Critics argued that such a large military establishment would be harmful to the islands' wildlife and lead to a decline in the traditional way of life of the Hebrides. Two world wars, in fact, had already done much to undermine crofting and Gaelic culture and despite island resistance to the scheme, lampooned by Compton Mackenzie in *Rockets Galore*, the range was to provide much welcome employment. Many islanders still receive compensation and the establishment of some five hundred military personnel proved to be a boon to the local economy.

The range needed a corridor of sea a hundred miles long and sixty miles wide, into which could be fired the airborne weapons of the future. The military discovered that not enough sea was British and the navy was sent to formally annex Rockall. Until 1955 Rockall had been the least visited isle on earth, with only five recorded landings on the seventy foot high rock reported in four hundred years. In September 1955, HMS *Vidal* under Commander Richard Connell RN, was despatched to plant the Union Jack upon Rockall because it was feared that the rock would be 'within the orbit of the projected guided-missile range in the Hebrides' and 'it might have been possible for some other power to use it as a post from which to observe our guided missiles'. The Navy landed and cemented a plaque to the rock which declared, to those who might ever be in a position to read it, 'By authority of Her Majesty Queen Elizabeth the Second, by the Grace of God of the United Kingdom of Great Britain and Northern Ireland, and of her other Realms and Territories, Queen, Head of the Commonwealth, Defender of the Faith, Etc, Etc, Etc, and in accordance with Her Majesty's instructions dated 14/9/55, a landing was effected this day upon this island of Rockall from HMS *Vidal*. The Union flag was hoisted and possession of the island was taken in the name of Her Majesty.' A use was also found, once again, for what, until 1930, had been Britain's loneliest inhabited isle. The reason, indeed, why the military had chosen the Outer Hebrides as the site for the new range had been the existence of St Kilda.

In June 1956, the RAF vessel, HMS *Bridport* set sail for St Kilda. Sixty miles west of the proposed range the island group was thought to be an admirable place from which the missiles fired from Uist could be tracked on radar and a constant surveillance kept on ships and aircraft that might stray, by accident or design, into the dropping zone. Under the command of Air Commodore Levis, experts from the army, navy and air force were to recce Hirta. Also on board HMS *Bridport* were former islanders Alexander Gillies Ferguson, then eighty-three years old, and his nephew Neil Ferguson who acted as guides to the expedition. The surveyors took only three days to decide upon the placing of the radar sites and the camp, concluding that some eight acres of Hirta would be needed. Code-named Operation Hard Rock, the occupation of St Kilda would begin in the spring of the following year.

The Earl of Dumfries, who since acquiring St Kilda had become the fifth Marquess of Bute, died in 1956. In his will, he offered the island group to the National Trust for Scotland, that it might hold the fantastic islands in perpetuity for the benefit of the nation. After much deliberation, detailed in the next chapter, the Trust agreed to accept the bequest and, aware that the War Department wished to make use of St Kilda, promptly leased the group to the Nature Conservancy in the Autumn of 1956. At a meeting held in Stirling, it was agreed that St Kilda would formally become a National Nature Reserve the following Spring and that small areas of Hirta would be sub-leased to the Ministry of Defence for a military camp and the proposed radar installations.

In the afternoon of Monday 15 April 1957 the advance party of the Task Force, Operation Hard Rock, set sail from Lochboisdale in South Uist. On board HM Vessel *Ageila*, a Royal Army Service Corps tank landing craft were thirty-five airmen and civilians. The technicians were from 5004 Airfield Construction Squadron, under the command of Wing Commander W. M. Cookson, OBE. Representatives of the Nature Conservancy were accompanying the Task Force to St Kilda. Kenneth Williamson, the Director, and Dr Morton Boyd, the Conservancy's Regional Officer for the Hebrides were to ensure that the military kept to their agreement with both themselves and the Trust.

The *Ageila* beached at St Kilda shortly after dawn. The first day ashore was a busy one as the thirty officers and men manhandled stores and equipment from the landing craft onto dry land across the boulders of the storm beach. By nightfall thirty-seven tons had been dragged ashore. The largest group of people ever to spend the night on Hirta since the evacuation bedded down in the manse and the Factor's house, the only two habitable buildings left on the island. As the men lay in their sleeping bags, crowded into the small rooms of the last 'outsiders' who had lived on St Kilda, there was a sense of trepidation. 'Perhaps we were too conscious,' wrote Kenneth Williamson, 'of those ruined cottages with their broken beds and chairs and derelict pots, pans and bits of crockery – litter everywhere to remind us that man had lived here once and been forced to retreat.'

St Kilda was quick to object to being invaded. The tented camp erected on the second day was blown down after one night. In the space of an hour gusts of nearly a hundred miles an hour put paid to the tents, catapulting tent pegs forty yards away. Equipment was literally blown out to sea to be washed ashore at a later date. During the storm the airmen tried to store everything that was movable in the cleits, just as the St Kildans of old would have done. As the storm abated, the RAF set about re-erecting the camp that would be their home for the rest of the summer, more aware of the fact that St Kilda would not be won easily.

The advance party was followed a fortnight later by more airmen and equipment. The first vehicle ever to be landed on Hirta was a bulldozer. By the middle of June more than three hundred officers and men had arrived by landing-craft. For Operation Hard Rock six LCTs were detailed and they worked a gruelling schedule with primitive navigation aids. It was only when an LCT almost crashed into Dun that the army fitted Decca radar onto the boats. Ashore on Hirta life for the Squadron was rough. Paraffin stoves were all that was available to begin with to keep the tents dry and warm at night.

The old village was nearly bulldozed out of existence. The plan for the road to Mullach Mor originally drawn up by the Combined Services surveyors called for a route that would have destroyed Main Street and used the stones from all but one of the houses and many of the surrounding cleits as foundations. Williamson and Boyd, representing the Nature Conservancy, together with Bob Hillcoat of the Trust and Roy Ritchie of the Ancient Monuments Commission however, managed to persuade Wing-Commander Cookson to take the road through the lower meadows near the shore, thus saving the old village. In return, it was agreed that the army could blast rock from a quarry opened at Creagan Breac and blastings took place two or three times a day for weeks before enough rock was excavated to build the road.

Throughout the summer of 1957, 5004 Airfield Construction Squadron worked round the clock. When asked by the captain of a landing craft how his men spent their spare time, Wing-Commander Cookson is said to have replied, 'When I have finished with them, all they want to do is sleep.' By June a Bailey bridge had been constructed to form a link with the manse, electric light had been installed and the NAAFI opened. The following month excellent showers had been constructed and canteens for the NCOs and the men had been built. So advanced was the work, men were even being allowed to return to the mainland for leave. Operation Hard Rock was proving to be yet another example of what twentieth century man is capable of doing when he puts his will and his technology to use. While a landing-craft was being unloaded in Village Bay, on the night of 25 July, Ken Williamson noted in his diary, 'With amber sodium lamps glowing, and electric lights shining through the fog and vaguely illuminating the forest of mobile cranes and other machinery, this might easily have passed for a corner of one of Britain's great docklands.'

Airmen unable to leave the island were entertained by film shows twice a week. The Church on St Kilda became the island's first cinema. A projector platform replaced the pulpit, and the pews used by the St Kildans while they listened to their minister preaching the word of God, were reversed to face a makeshift screen upon which flickered the man-made fantasies of film studios. The men were also enjoying a regular mail service and three good meals a day. Food for the servicemen was transported in sealed refrigerated containers on trailers. Put aboard LCTs at the Cairnryan base, they were then pulled ashore on Hirta by bulldozer and taken to the cookhouse.

For the airmen that first summer on St Kilda was a novel experience. They had been cast upon an island with none of the diversions British servicemen round the world were used to. There were no women, dance halls, bars or nightclubs. Alone in the Atlantic they faced up to nature. 'It was good to see,' wrote Ken Williamson, 'how quickly many of the townsmen adapted to this remarkable change in their environment: true, there was little else to do but explore the island, developing latent powers of observation and getting to know the ways of the birds and the seals and Soay sheep – and even of the field-mice which invaded their tents at night! I remember one officer who had followed up the Abhainn Mor to its source saying naively to another how the primroses and honeysuckle along the banks reminded him of civilization.' Many airmen took up rock climbing and others became skilled lobster fishermen in their spare time.

During the summer of 1957 there were fortunately only two serious accidents to remind the RAF of their remote and perilous location. The first involved an airman who caught his foot in the wheels of a stone crusher. Within six hours of the accident he had been removed by helicopter. A near fatal accident occurred when a man's thighs were crushed when the draw-bar of a trailer containing fifteen tons of cement collapsed whilst being dragged off a landing craft. The accident happened at night and there was no possibility of a helicopter arriving until dawn. The patient was taken to the make-shift operating theatre at the back of the manse where one leg was removed at the thigh. When a helicopter arrived from RAF Leuchars at first light, he was taken to Benbecula and then by Shakleton aircraft to Renfrew Airport. Within two hours of leaving St Kilda the airman was in Cowglen Military Hospital in Glasgow, where he recovered.

The effort on St Kilda was a prodigious one: within five months the RAF had largely completed the road to Mullach Mor. A miracle of engineering, the first and only road ever constructed on St Kilda rose from sea level to the 1200 foot summit in little over a mile. They had also renovated the Church, the manse and the Factor's house which the Trust had agreed to 'loan' them. In the glebe where once the minister had grazed his cow and grown his crops, solid concrete foundations had been laid for a permanent camp. Concrete huts to house the radar installations had been built. An island that so recently had failed to support one of Britain's most primitive communities now housed one of the most technologically advanced.

In the autumn the airmen, who had given their all that summer were allowed to leave on the last landing-craft of the summer as scheduled. On 19 September 1957, a Fighter Command Care and Maintenance party, commanded by Flight-Lieutenant A. N. Johnstone arrived at St Kilda from North Weald to man the island during the winter. The thirty-strong garrison comprised RAF personnel, a handful of Royal Signalmen and REME technicians. They were to be the first group to spend the entire winter on St Kilda since the evacuation. They were left adequate supplies of food and were linked to the mainland by radio; but otherwise the War Department provided the garrison that first winter with the same infrequent and often unreliable trawler service that had been the lot of the former islanders. In their seven months of isolation there were to be only nine deliveries of mail from the mainland.

Before the evacuation in 1930 the only other regular visitors to St Kilda had been the lobster and crab fishermen of Brittany and trawlermen from the fishing ports of north-west Spain. When the island was abandoned, they continued to land on Hirta for supplies of fresh water and also to raid the bird nests for eggs, shoot the Soay sheep for fresh meat and plunder the rich lobster beds. The Spaniards had a skirmish with the RAF garrison in the winter of 1957 and as a result it was decided to equip the men with a dozen obsolete .303 rifles with which to defend themselves.

Work on St Kilda began again in the spring of 1958, when the men of 5004 Construction Squadron returned. Landing-craft made some twenty-six journeys to Hirta that summer transporting men, supplies and delicate instruments. By August the squadron had completed the work ahead of schedule; but for a time it had looked as though their efforts were in vain.

From the outset the Air Ministry was the sponsoring authority for the South Uist range and had paid the largest part of the construction cost. During 1957 there had been numerous discussions between representatives of the three services and between the Ministry of Defence and the Treasury about the future of the range. When disputes arose about cost and manning, the RAF decided to withdraw from the project. It was planned that the range be operational in 1958 for the first firing of the Army's new Corporal surface-to-surface missiles; but when the RAF refused to finance the project further, it was not until 1958 that funds were made available to the Army to complete the range. The Corporal missiles, therefore, were first tested at the White Sands Missile Range in New Mexico.

The Army, in the guise of The Royal Artillery Guided Weapons Range (Hebrides) formally took over St Kilda on 28 August 1958. The Hard Rock Task Force bade the island farewell to return to RAF Wellesbourne, Mountford. With them went their equipment: the RAF only left behind some essential food supplies, tables and chairs. When the army arrived the sole link they had with the Range at Uist was by way of an old wartime HF radio.

The Range was administered from the Royal Artilley HQ at Woolwich. Technical officers were sent north to St Kilda to survey the island and learn about the radars from the engineers from Decca and Marconi who were installing the system; but as regards other matters, HQ, as Major Riach, the first Officer Commanding St Kilda discovered, knew best. With winter approaching Riach asked for protective clothing for his men. His request was refused and he asked for a meeting to resolve the issue. At a conference held in Whitehall, Headquarters staff claimed that cold-weather waterproof clothing was not required by troops serving in the Pacific. It was only after a lesson in geography pointed out the difference between the Outer Hebrides and the New Hebrides, that the men of St Kilda were supplied with kit that would be most certainly needed in the winter months.

On the basis that Whitehall knows best, the War Office decided that a cutter, with a built-in engine weighing over a ton, should be used by the detachment on St Kilda to ferry men and stores ashore during the winter months when the summer beach would be replaced by boulders and therefore make it impossible for landing craft to be used. It had been suggested by the Trust and others who knew St Kilda well that a dory, which could be easily taken out of the water, was the most suitable craft. During one of the first storms of the winter, the cutter was driven onto the rocks and wrecked.

In 1958, it was decided that the ex-Admiralty trawler, *Mull*, now the property of the Royal Army Service Corps, would be used to supply the detachment once a month. Built in 1941, the *Mull* faithfully did her best to serve the St Kilda detachment from 1958 until 1973. Crewed by civilians, the trawler was never able to tie up, and unloading her in winter was always dangerous. In the first few winters, three cutters and seven dories were damaged beyond repair while attempting to take stores and men to the jetty.

It was originally suggested that the soldiers, like the St Kildans of old, would not use money on the island. The plan, however, was vetoed by the paymaster and the NAAFI who feared the men would run up bills they would not be able to meet when they returned to Benbecula. Finally, it was agreed that everyone would be paid a specific sum of money each week to spend in the canteen. At the end of each week the takings would then be handed over to the paymaster who would use them to give the soldiers their allowance.

The first year for the Army on St Kilda was a dull one. As the Range was not yet complete, their main summer task of scanning the seas with their radars and providing the Range at South Uist with information was not required of the detachment. That first winter there was little maintenance work to do on the installations and their role was reduced to guarding the camp and the radars from being looted by fishermen.

Come the spring of 1959, the Army set about improving communications on the island. On 20 April, a VHF radio station was installed and less than two months later the first telephone call to a number on the mainland was made from St Kilda. In July, the radio system was linked up with the GPO system and henceforth the soldiers could make contact with relations and friends anywhere.

By June the St Kilda detachment was ready to commence the work they had been sent to the lonely isle to do. The Decca radar was fully installed below Mullach Sgar and the Marconi system was in position on Mullach Mor. A radar reflector, twelve feet tall, had also been erected on Levenish, the first time the 185 foot stac had been visited since the evacuation. On 17 and 19 June Maker rockets were fired from the Range to test the system. Rumour had it that one of the guided missiles went seriously off course and ended up near the camp on St Kilda; but the tests were thought a success and the Range regarded as operational.

On 23 June, at twenty-five past four in the afternoon, the first Corporal missile lifted off from the South Uist Range. Eleven more were fired that summer and all were successfully tracked by the men on St Kilda. But despite high technology, the thirty-strong garrison was reminded of their precarious position. On 19 August, the cooks ran out of yeast to make bread and the following day a 3 lb parcel was successfully dropped from an aircraft into the village area. Less than six weeks later, on 2 October, a less successful attempt was made to drop a case of beer for a detachment that had been without a drop for two weeks.

Throughout the autumn of 1959, in readiness for winter, the Army experimented in new methods of supplying St Kilda in need. The *Mull* was fitted with rocket-launching equipment so that in stormy weather the men would not need to take the boat out to get their letters. Mailbags, it was intended, could be fired ashore. But the apparatus was never put to the test. On 11 September the first successful mail-drop from an aircraft took place and from then until June 1961 no less than thirty-five deliveries of mail were made by air to St Kilda. In Gaelic there is an old phrase *Hiort gu Peart* (St Kilda to Perth) that was used to signify a great distance. By using Cessna aeroplanes, Airworks (Perth) Ltd made the journey between the two most distant points in the old Gaelic-speaking nation in ninety minutes. Mail and newspapers continue to be regularly air-dropped and occasionally supplies of foodstuffs and medicines are similarly transported. But in the beginning, trawlers were still used to bring mail, often with near disastrous results. On 22 November 1959, the trawler *St Botolph* entered Village Bay at ten o'clock at night. An army dory went out in the pitch black to collect the mail. The boat was holed and she quickly filled with water and capsized. The crew of seven swam in the icy water for thirty minutes to reach safety and two of the crew who ensured the others survived were rewarded for their bravery. Warrant Officer Bert Jessup RA was awarded the MBE and Private Dennis Hodgson of the Royal Army Service Corps was given the BEM.

The 1960s omened well for the Royal Artillery Range in the Hebrides and the men of St Kilda. British, American and German troops regularly trained during the summer months in the live firing of Corporal and Sergeant surface-to-surface guided missiles. When, however, the Corporal missile, was scrapped in 1966 and the contract for its replacement, the English Electric Blue Water missile, was cancelled, again it seemed the Range might be closed down. To those who served in the most remote station, St Kilda, the last half of the decade was one of boredom.

By this time the normal summer complement of men was between thirty and thirty-five, drawn from numerous military disciplines. The Officer Commanding, usually a bachelor, served nine months on St Kilda. His Battery Sergeant Major was also expected to serve three-quarters of a year on the island; but both men were allowed to take leave during their tour of duty. The Royal Engineers Clerk of Works served six months and the Medical Officer three. During the early years the MO, like the OC was permanently on station. The doctors were usually young National Service recruits and during the long winter months frequently passed the time re-setting the broken legs of gannets and treating seals for pneumonia. In 1966, the post of Medical Officer was replaced with that of a 'Medical Sergeant, a RAMC State Registered Nurse based at the Cambridge Military Hospital.

The rest of the detachment served short tours of duty of four to six weeks; but in a two year stationing at Benbecula would serve on St Kilda several times. A bombardier and three gunners kept the vital generators running twenty-four hours a day and gunners also acted as drivers, storemen and batmen. Another team, made up of a REME senior NCO, two vehicle mechanics, a recovery mechanic, one or two radar technicians and an RAOC storeman, was responsible for repairing and overhauling the vehicles, generators and radars. A small Royal Signals section looked after the cypher equipment, radio and line communications. The Clerk of Works also had under him a carpenter, an electrician and a plumber charged with the task of keeping the camp in one piece. They operated the boilerhouse, the drinking water plant, the sewerage and electrical system. As equipment installed in 1957 became obsolete, their task became an unenviable one. The remainder of the detachment was made up of cooks, whose culinary delights were vital in keeping morale high, pioneers, and RASC military seamen who maintained the boats. Usually, given the size of the little community, men turned their hands to many things.

Although the original camp continued to be used until 1969, many improvements were made. In 1962 work began on a new officers mess and the National Trust for Scotland was given back the Factor's house, which it converted into a home for a joint Trust and Nature Conservancy summer warden. In the same year the Nissen huts were covered with bitumen to reinforce them against the harsh winters. The following year a hundred and twenty civilian contractors spent the summer on St Kilda, carrying out further improvements to the military facilities. The Royal Engineers also deepened the jetty area, almost blowing off the roof of the new Officers Mess in the process with their explosives. As summer drew to a close, the detachment set about preparing for winter. The Nissen huts had to be roped down as did the wooden huts built by the RAF. Stout ropes and heavy iron stakes were needed to prevent them being blown away. Stores for the winter were landed in August, including Christmas dinner. A hundred thousand gallons of diesel fuel also arrived by landing-craft. Each drum containing forty-five gallons had to be unloaded and stacked by hand. Each week of the year the men had to manhandle five tons of oil to fuel the twelve ageing Meadows generators to keep the electricity and central heating going.

In the winter the problem of the detachment's morale was also uppermost in the mind of the Officer Commanding. Captain Stephen Gray, who took charge of the St Kilda garrison in August 1961 and spent over a year on the island claimed, 'By far the most important factor in keeping the detachment happy was the fact that there were on the island only the minimum number to keep the place working and everybody had more than enough work to do.' And there was the geography, climate and history of St Kilda itself. 'There was a slight feeling of adventure about the place the whole time,' commented Gray, 'which, coupled with the need to turn one's hand to unusual tasks, brought out the best in men.'

A licenced pub, the Puff Inn, was opened in the 1960s, complete with inn sign. The pub made a welcome addition to the cinema shows which invariably had old films because the Services Kinema Corporation could never be given any guarantee about when they would get them back. The Puff Inn soon became famous for its low prices and flexible opening hours. Voted 'Pub of the Month' in 1974 by two journalists from the *Daily Mail*, the Puff Inn is still the social centre of Hirta, although non-military visitors to St Kilda are warned by the Army that the pub is 'primarily intended for soldiers and occasionally it does become boisterous and the language can become illuminated.'

Life for the soldiers was not without humour. A signpost at the road junction pointed out to motorists that Nome in Alaska lay in one direction, Moscow the other. A primitive advertising hoarding claimed that 'Fulmar Oil is Best'. A bus stop sign was also erected by the roadside. Practical jokes were invariably played on new arrivals. On one occasion a new Medical Sergeant was persuaded to stand outside the manse for a whole half day, waiting for the bus that would take him to the village on the other side of Hirta.

In winter, the Army is constantly reminded that its hold on Hirta is a tenuous one. Despite modern communications the detachment occasionally has to face up to the same problems as the island's former inhabitants. The soldiers have sometimes been cut off for months on end by storms that have made it impossible for boats or helicopters to chance a trip to St Kilda. Writing in the *Royal Artillery Journal*, Captain Stephen Gray described his experiences. 'The main trial,' he wrote, 'is the incessant high wind and rain. For example, in January 1962 there were seventeen consecutive days when the wind hardly dropped below gale force eight.'

On 26 October 1961, Captain Gray had witnessed a particularly violent storm. 'At 2030 hours,' he wrote, 'there was a violent crash. On going out we found the night full of flying sheets of corrugated iron. It transpired that a gust of about a hundred and thirty miles an hour had torn the roof off the accommodation Nissen hut. The flying sheets had hit a power line, luckily only damaging the earth line and made a hole in the cookhouse. It had also struck the medical centre, cutting through a sheet of corrugated aluminium and a four and a half inch thick wooden beam. Similarly on 21 January 1962, a storm made the anemograph record stops at 130 miles an hour, twenty-seven times in three hours, before it ran out of ink; tore an eleven hundredweight concrete roof slab from the signal centre and lifted the Clerk of Works and me off our feet and carried us twenty yards while we were inspecting the damage. It also blew a bulky cook, chin first, through a thin breeze-block wall, luckily without much damage to him.'

Since the winter of 1959, the men of St Kilda, 'The Furthest Station West', had been made aware of the use made of them by foreign trawlermen. During the winter of 1960, the MO pulled, on average, twenty Spanish teeth a month and in return the detachment was given free fish, wine and brandy, as well as the offer of taking mail to the mainland. But some of the injuries the MO had to deal with were too severe for him to handle on his own.

On 16 March 1961, a Spanish fisherman, Castor Lagos, was landed on the island, having lost a foot in the anchor chain while the trawler *Teresa Lopez* was seeking shelter in Village Bay. The sick bay already had a patient, Sapper William Laity who had a fractured femur, and a helicopter was summoned from Leuchars in Fife the following day to evacuate both sick men. Two months later, another Spaniard with a severe abdominal injury was also evacuated by helicopter.

The military authorities soon began to question whether Spanish fishermen were not abusing the hospitality offered to them by the St Kilda detachment. On enquiry, it was discovered that sometimes the Spaniards were bringing relatives to St Kilda from Spain for free medical treatment. A case of advanced cancer, on one occasion, had to be turned away by the MO, who could do nothing for the sick man whose son had brought him all the way from Spain. After official representations were made to the Spanish Government, the number of Spaniards arriving for treatment waned, although the Army on St Kilda still helped with emergencies.

On 8 April 1963 a Spanish seaman was evacuated by helicopter to Stornoway for an emergency abdominal operation. Just before Christmas, the following year, another sick Spanish sailor was put ashore and taken to the medical centre. Next morning he could not be found and his disappearance is still a mystery. In bad weather, a search for him was organized immediately; but it was not until three weeks later that his body was found on some rocks below Mullach Bi. The Procurator Fiscal was called in from Stornoway to investigate, together with an RAF Mountain Rescue team who recovered the body. The Spaniard was buried at Nunton on Benbecula in the presence of an official from the Spanish Embassy in London. In 1965, another Spanish seaman was brought ashore amidst great secrecy. When he was removed the next day by the Barra lifeboat, the entire detachment was innoculated against typhoid.

In the summer months, injured or sick soldiers and civilian construction workers occasionally had to be quickly taken off St Kilda. On 11 June 1960, for example, the Military Clerk of Works, Sergeant Peter Bennet, suffering from acute appendicitis, was evacuated by Dragonfly helicopter to Benbecula from where he was flown to the Royal Northern Infirmary in Inverness. The helicopter had a bumpy journey and a rotor-blade was damaged by the wind. The rescues, so far, have been fortunate; there has not been an instance yet when bad weather has stopped a rescue from being in time to save a life. The Army are keenly aware that such a tragedy could happen.

Since 1961 teleprinters have been used by the Royal Signal Corps on St Kilda. Messages are transmitted to Benbecula where, if required, the printed out copy can be posted to its destination via the Post Office. Cheaper than a telegram and quicker than a letter, the teleprinter has proved to be the solution to the problem of communication that has plagued the lives of all who have lived on St Kilda. An equally important link with the outside world was established in 1966 when the men of the St Kilda detachment got their first television set. Because the BBC did not regard the island within its range of transmission the soldiers pay no licence fee. In the beginning, the soldiers, in order to watch television, had to drive up to a small room on Ruaival to see their favourite programmes. When the opportunity arose, the Royal Signals set about solving the problem of poor reception. Out of detachment funds, hundreds of yards of expensive coaxial cable were bought. An aerial was erected on the summit of Oiseval and the cable carefully pegged down into the ground, all the way to the camp. It was not until 1976, however, when a new transmitter was opened near Stornoway that reasonable television reception was guaranteed and the soldiers, for the first time, could watch BBC and ITV.

In 1968, it was decided that all British firing of low-level air defence weapon systems, notably Rapier and Blowpipe, would take place at the Uist Range. At a cost of £7 million the Royal Artillery range was to be rebuilt over a period of seven years. The military strength of the establishment was to be increased from 148 to 351 by 1974 and the number of civilian jobs was to more than double. The modernization of installations on St Kilda was to cost some £500,000, and work began the following year.

As a first stage the living quarters on St Kilda were to be improved and enlarged in order that more men might be accommodated on the island at a later date. A new pier that would afford greater shelter was to be constructed together with a new generating station and medical centre. By May 1969 a temporary camp that could house the hundred construction workers from Costain Ltd had been built and the quarry was opened up to blast stone for the new camp and pier. The top of the old jetty which was to be lengthened and strengthened was removed. Landing-craft arrived almost daily, normally at night, bringing yet again to St Kilda bulldozers, stone crushers, cement mixers, bricks and gravel. The detachment, for the first time, began to enjoy the luxury of fresh milk for breakfast.

During the summer of 1970, construction workers outnumbered the army two to one; four army cooks had to serve their 120 'guests' in three shifts because of the shortage of dining space. Within a few years, working mostly in the summer, the new jetty – some twenty feet shorter than planned because of engineering difficulties – had been completed. The modern generating station, that in other circumstances could have provided electricity to a small town, had been built. Nine 12,000 gallon fuel tanks, located by the beach would power the new plant. Soldiers would no longer have to manhandle oil drums.

The Army living quarters were centrally heated and comfortably furnished. The new sick bay was fully equipped to handle minor operations. Attached to modern kitchens that gleam with stainless steel are storerooms to house a dozen deep freezes and sufficient dried and tinned foods to keep the thirty- to thirty-five strong garrison provided with three hot meals a day for anything up to six months. In all the cost of the new complex was nearer a million pounds, a thousand times more than it cost the British Government to evacuate thirty-six St Kildans in 1930. But the expense was justified by the Ministry of Defence on the grounds that in Britain's modern Army home comforts are the prerequisite to adequate recruitment and military efficiency.

The air-dropping of mail and supplies, meanwhile, had not proved to be totally successful. A damper had been put on Christmas in 1969, when out of twelve frozen turkeys dropped for dinner, only two survived. In the spring of 1973 the men on St Kilda decided it would help if the windspeed was checked before a drop was made by landing a toy teddy bear by parachute first, and Warrant Officer E. Bear was enlisted. On 15 May tragedy struck when his parachute failed to open. A formal inquest took place before a death certificate was sadly signed and a coffin made. To this day the battered remains of WO E Bear lie in state in the Puff Inn.

Although the Army have kept records of the weather on St Kilda since they set up camp on Hirta, it was not until April 1976 that the Meteorological Office formally requested a weather report. Since then, on a voluntary basis, the Medical Centre NCO has sent reports to Benbecula regularly. St Kilda is notorious for violent storms, but statistically the island's weather is not unreasonable. In winter the temperature is higher than average for the archipelago's latitude and frost and snow are not that common. Annually, the rainfall is twice that of Edinburgh but lower than that of Greenock or Fort William. The average wind speed on Hirta is about Force 3, the same as the Outer Hebrides in general; but the occasional dramatic gales to which the island is subjected do great damage to the army camp and installations and threaten from time to time the existence of the soldiers themselves. In 1971 the last landing craft of the summer, loaded with six months provisions, failed to reach the island because of bad weather. The *Mull*, moreover, was unable to relieve the garrison for several weeks, and only what was left in the deep freezes and dried goods in the cooks' storeroom kept the men from going hungry. Again, six years later, the weather was so bad that the delivery of bulk supplies for the winter was delayed. The detachment slowly ran out of sugar, potatoes, eggs, milk, bacon, lager and tobacco. An attempt to air-drop sugar ended in disaster and St Kilda was covered with white sweet 'snow'.

In 1978, the Officer Commanding, Captain Forsyth RA, noted in his diary, 'The 28th January was a typical winter's day! Snow, hail, sleet and wind up to 80 knots caused damage to the doors of the power station and tore a door off the officers' mess. A wall in the DDE compound was flattened, the TV aerial blown down three times and two windows were broken by flying pebbles.' In September the same year the tail-end of Hurricane Flossie picked up a 700 lb box of radar components and hurled them sixty yards.

On New Year's Eve, 1980, another hurricane-force storm hit Hirta. When two soldiers attempted to drive the Land Rover up to the radars on Mullach Mor, the vehicle became airborne on the 'S' bend. The vehicle was wrecked and the two men injured. The cover of the NIDIR radar was blown off and the exposed dish ripped off its base. A fifty foot tall mast was also blown down, taking half the building on which it stood with it and throughout the camp windows, doors and roofs were damaged. A concrete wall of a new building which had only been erected the previous summer was blown over. The anemometer cups and the mast supporting them were torn down by winds well in excess of 180 knots, the equivalent of 198 miles an hour and St Kilda entered the *Guinness Book of Records* as the place where the highest wind speeds in Britain have been recorded.

The following winter was almost equally destructive. Just before Christmas the recently erected telemetry mast on Mullach Mor was struck by lightning, damaging many of the expensive electrical components. Two more strikes in January put all the St Kildan radars out of action. January gales in 1982 smashed the reinforced concrete slipway that had only been built the previous autumn. Half ton pieces of concrete were seen being tossed about by the sea in Village Bay like pieces of cork. Another severe winter in 1984 blew a boat out of the sea over a rooftop and it smashed to pieces on the other side. It is with good reason that every winter the soldiers on Hirta retreat to the shelter of their camp. Visits to the radar sites on Mullach Mor are few and the men only venture out when the wind is below 60 knots. Even round the camp area it is normal for them to have to hang on to fixed ropes in order to move about safely.

The summer journey to St Kilda in the old wartime LCTs was an uncomfortable one as the flat-bottomed boats pitched, rolled and corkscrewed their way to Hirta. The old landing-craft, which had been in use for twenty years, were replaced in November 1977 by modern Landing Craft Logistics and when the *Mull* was withdrawn from service in 1973, communication with the island was henceforth by helicopter in the winter months. Because the helicopters cannot carry the same weight as a boat the detachment is kept self-sufficient of foodstuffs, drink and fuel for the six months from October to March. A landing-pad for helicopters was built in Village Bay and now the men of St Kilda, provided the weather allows, are a mere twenty minute flight from the Uist Range.

On 31 December 1985 the Property Services Agency, on behalf of the Minsitry of Defence, lodged a Notice of Proposed Development concerning St Kilda. The MOD wished to demolish the Control Room, radome and two masts on Mullach Mor and replace them with two Watchman Towers, nearly 40 feet high, supporting a radome and build a new equipment room nearby. Also on Mullach Mor, the Ministry wished to erect a new radar system, over 30 feet high which would support a radome and a microwave tower nearly 80 feet high. A new radome, to enclose an existing aerial, was also planned for Mullach Sgar.

The Western Isles Islands Council turned down the application for planning permission on 21 May 1986, on the casting vote of its Convener, on the grounds that there were already too many military installations on Hirta. The Scottish Development Department held a public inquiry. The National Trust for Scotland, owners of the island group, although anxious about the increase in military equipment raised no objection to the MOD proposals in general. The masts, the Trust rightly claimed, would be dwarfed by the scale of Hirta; but they did request that the radomes should be of an acceptable colour and finished in a non-reflecting material.

Conservationists were angry. As the debate continued the *Highland Free Press* argued against the 'militarization' and 'further despoilment' of St Kilda. In fact, only five members of the public and the Scottish Wild Land Group lodged objections to the proposed development and there was a sense in which St Kilda was drawn into the greater and on-going debate in Scotland about the extent to which the country is being used excessively as a military base, particularly of nuclear weaponry.

In December 1986, Malcolm Rifkind, the Secretary of State for

Scotland, over-ruled all objections raised but requested that conditions were met as to the siting of the new buildings and the colours used. Work began in 1987 and again St Kilda was turned into a building site, with the assurance that, on completion of the work, the contractors were obliged, as in the past, to leave the sites tidy to the satisfaction of all concerned.

It is evident, given the fact that £20 million is being invested in modernizing the South Uist Range, that there will be soldiers on St Kilda for many years to come. But in the long run, military occupation will probably prove temporary. The National Trust for Scotland, however, will hold St Kilda in perpetuity for the benefit of the Scottish people. Not surprisingly, perhaps, it has been the fact that the Army has been on St Kilda for over thirty years that has helped the Trust fulfil its aims and justify why it agreed to accept the island group in the first place.

16
St Kilda in Trust

Sir James Stormonth Darling, Secretary of the National Trust for Scotland at the time, has said that the whole affair was 'a damn close run thing'. 'Jamie', to his colleagues and friends, was then, and continued to be until he retired in 1983 the moving force of the organization. A man with a sense of vision, he exercised that attribute to the full when the Trust was offered ownership of St Kilda.

On 14 August 1956, the fifth Marquess of Bute died. In his will he bequeathed St Kilda to the charitable organization provided they accept the offer within six months of his death. A series of meetings of the Executive Committee of the National Trust for Scotland discussed the bequest. Most of the Committee members, of course, had never seen the property they were now being asked to accept on behalf of the nation; but the ownership of an island would not be a novel departure. The Trust had accepted Fair Isle in 1954; but at least people lived on Fair Isle and they had regular communications with the outside world. St Kilda, on the other hand, could prove to be a costly albatross round the neck of an organization that depended upon charity to exist.

Many on the Executive Committee claimed that St Kilda would not suffer if the Trust refused to accept the archipelago. Some argued that the Nature Conservancy would be able to manage St Kilda just as well, despite the fact that the Conservancy had said they could not look after the maintenance of the important archaeological sites on Hirta. Curiously one of those most against Trust ownership was Admiral Sir Angus Cunninghame Graham one of the few to have visited St Kilda. As a young midshipman aboard the armoured cruiser HMS *Achilles*, he had gone to St Kilda in April 1912 and brought relief to the starving community. Those in favour of acceptance argued that the public and those organizations in Scotland concerned with the preservation of wild life expected the Trust to accept the archipelago, visited by few but since the evacuation part of the national consciousness.

The future of St Kilda hung in the balance. In October 1956 a reluctant Executive Committee asked the Secretary to prepare a paper on the property for the next meeting. Jamie Stormonth Darling, instead of producing a document that weighed up the pros and cons of accepting St Kilda, began with the words, 'This is not an impartial document', and then proceeded to list every reason why the Trust had little choice in the matter. After weeks of intensive lobbying both by the Secretary and the Trust's Chairman, The Earl of Wemyss and March, the Executive Committee finally agreed to accept the Bute bequest. On 18 January 1957, the Council of the Trust voted to become the new owners of the islands, just days before the deadline set in the Marquess of Bute's will ran out. Under Schedule 22 of the National Trust for Scotland Confirmation Order Act 1935, the Council also declared the Trust's ownership of St Kilda inalienable and thus provided permanent protection of the island group.

During the debate, the Trust had been concerned about the maintenance of the buildings on Hirta which wind and storm had all but ruined since the evacuation. Those against acceptance had claimed that the public would expect the Trust, at great expense to itself, to restore the old village in its entirety. A compromise was reached when it was agreed that, although the buildings would not be allowed to be destroyed either by the military or nature, no undertaking would be given to restore the entire village. The question of public access to St Kilda was also uppermost in the mind of the Trust. The Nature Conservancy in 1957 took over Rum, but until then the island had been the property of the Bullough family who for decades regarded Rum as a private sporting domain. No member of the general public had landed on the island for years. From the very beginning, therefore, the Trust made plans to organize three or four parties a year to visit St Kilda.

Given the fact that the Trust wished to preserve and restore part of the old village of the St Kildans, it was decided that voluntary work parties would be encouraged. The use of professional tradesmen was ruled out on the grounds of expense and impracticality. In June 1958, George Waterston, who in 1948 had established the famous Bird Observatory on Fair Isle, and his wife Irene led the first of the Trust's work parties to St Kilda. It was not the only expedition planned. Alex Warwick, the Clerk of Works of the Trust, had also hoped to lead a joint schools expedition to St Kilda the year before, only to find himself marooned with his schoolboys on the uninhabited Monach Isles for ten days, an event eagerly taken up by the media.

The Waterstons spent a week on St Kilda. They rebuilt the dry burn bridge and repaired the fall of stones in the drystone wall of the graveyard. The twelve strong party lived in tents loaned by the army, and slept on camp beds bought by the Trust. Each member of the group had to supply a sleeping bag. Cooking was done on two Calor gas grills which the Trust had purchased and the working holiday, to say the least, was rough. The Waterston's group set up camp in the little field beyond the wall of the old minister's glebe, which was used year in year out during the early sixties. Early work parties paid about £16 for the privilege of helping restore a human settlement neglected for nearly thirty years. The joint schools expedition that had been marooned on the Monach Isles the previous summer also finally reached St Kilda. Transported by the Army, the boys camped out in the meadow area below House no 16, to the west of Village Bay.

On 21 May 1959 the first National Trust party of the year, led by Alex Warwick, arrived at St Kilda by fishing boat and continued to tidy up the old village area. His group was replaced on 4 June by a second party of twelve who spent eight days on Hirta. The three parties that year also rebuilt cleits and falls in the unmortared walls of the 1830 black houses that stood gable end onto Main Street.

In June 1960, the *Avocet*, a fifty ton yawl, brought a party of ten volunteers to work on Hirta for two weeks. The skipper of the boat decided to spend some time on St Kilda; but on the first night in Village Bay found it impossible to sleep because the metal anchor chain banged against the bow of his boat. He replaced the chain with a rope the following night in the hope that he might get some rest. The rope snapped and the *Avocet* was blown onto the rocks. Both men and women in the Trust group, working up to their shoulders in stormy water, salvaged what they could of the boat's sails, stores and fittings. The mast of the yawl was later erected on the cliff above the beach, where, as a flagpole it serves as a grim reminder of what St Kildan weather can do. The work party had to be returned to the mainland by Army LCT. In 1961, the first party, who repaired the perimeter wall and cleared the graveyard of nettles, had their stay on Hirta prolonged when the boat that was to take them off the island spent ten stormy days sheltering where it could at various islands in the Outer Hebrides in continuous gales before it could make a dash for St Kilda. In 1966 the first work party of the year had their 160 lb tents blown away in a gale. Again, the Army came to the rescue and moved the women into the officers mess, while the men spent the rest of their visit camped out in the Church.

In the early 1960s, because of the rapid deterioration of the mortar built cottages of Main Street, the number of annual work parties was increased from two to an average of six every summer. Even then, they were always over-subscribed by people prepared to pay for the privilege of working at least twenty-four hours a week on St Kilda. So successful were work parties proving, that they were used, after 1962, on Fair Isle to help lay electricity cables, improve plumbing, lay roads and modernize the islanders' cottages.

By 1967, the work of re-roofing three of the 1860 houses on Hirta was completed. Since then, two have been used as sleeping quarters and one as a common and dining room. But accommodation even behind stone walls was primitive. Washing and lavatory facilities, however, were good, with two WCs, a bath, a shower and two hand basins. But would-be travellers were warned when they applied to go to St Kilda of the disease that in the past had decimated the old St Kildan population. 'Although no cases have yet occurred,' the Trust pointed out, 'there may be some risk of tetanus infection and it is left to members' own discretion whether they have themselves immunized.'

Workers visiting St Kilda were subject to rules. They took orders from their leader and the activities of the military detachment are covered by the Official Secrets Act. Visitors are warned not to ask soldiers questions about their work and they are not allowed to enter any military buildings except the Medical Centre and the Puff Inn.

The Trust, however, did organize more comfortable and less strenuous, though expensive ways for people to visit St Kilda. From 1959, St Kilda was included in the itinerary of the Trust's annual 'Islands Cruise'. On 10 May 1959, ss *Meteor*, a 29,000 ton luxury liner, anchored in Village Bay. The next day 150 passengers were landed on Hirta by half-past-ten in the morning by skilful Norwegian sailors and were taken in relays by Army Land Rover to the top of the island. Not since the old *Hebrides* and *Dunara Castle* had stopped sailing to St Kilda in 1939 had there been such an invasion of tourists. That evening ss *Meteor* made marine history when she became the first ship to sail between the great rocks of Stac Lee and Stac an Armin and Boreray. After a gourmet dinner, Seton Gordon played the bagpipe lament *Leaving St Kilda* for the passengers. 'How exquisite the contrast had become,' wrote Kenneth Williamson and Dr Morton Boyd who had been invited aboard ship, 'half a mile away was the altar of privation, here the dispensation of plenty!'

In 1961, the National Trust chartered British India's ss *Dunera*. Normally used as a 'ship school', the dormitory accommodation was less than luxurious; but few grumbled. Nicknamed 'The Bargain Sail' because passengers paid £15 10s for the first voyage, inclusive of food, 'Big Ship' cruises became a permanent feature of the Trust's policy of providing the public with a chance to see St Kilda. In the *Dunera*, and later ss *Devonia* and ss *Uganda* tens of thousands have viewed St Kilda from the sea.

Given the interest in St Kilda it was obvious that a St Kilda Club be formed. A meeting, indeed, had been held in 1958 in Overseas House in Edinburgh which was attended by those who had visited St Kilda that summer and others of the public interested in the island group. All those who have spent at least twenty-four hours on Hirta are eligible to join. The few St Kildans still alive are Honorary Members and many attend club meetings and dinners. Members receive a free club badge and can buy ties with woven puffin motifs on a maroon background. Before the Club began collecting an annual subscription in November 1964, its running expenses were underwritten by the Trust. When, however, the Club opened its own bank account it gradually became more independent. Since 1964, the St Kilda Club has met on the second Saturday in November every year at Edinburgh's Zoological Park, where members spend the afternoon exchanging experiences, viewing slide shows and ending the day with a dinner. To many, the activities of the St Kilda Club are more social than academically serious and a jolly 'boy scout' atmosphere is present at its meetings; but the club has done much over the years to keep St Kilda in the public eye.

By 1974, the St Kilda Club had 800 members although less than half that number had bothered to pay the annual subscription of forty pence. Three years later, to help stimulate and maintain interest in the archipelago, the Club published the first *St Kilda Mail*, an annual, professionally produced magazine, to keep members informed about what has happened on St Kilda. Funds for restoration work have been raised in novel ways. In 1968, the Trust produced a special issue of stamps. Local carriage labels, they symbolized the payment for the transfer of mail between St Kilda and the mainland only. Visitors sending postcards had to use proper legal stamps as well if their mail was to be handled by the Post Office. The Trust opened St Kilda's first shop in 1976 to look after the needs of visitors. Films, confectionery, specially designed tea-towels and books were for sale. Two years later, it was agreed that the Army take over running the shop selling general goods, together with Trust souvenirs are now stocked.

On 12 August 1971, HM The Queen set foot on Hirta. She was the first British monarch ever to land on St Kilda. Accompanied by the

Duke of Edinburgh, Princess Anne, Princes Charles, Andrew and Edward, the visit was an informal one. It was, however, a surprise visit and the Officer Commanding, Captain Morgan, had to have his Service Dress, which he had left on the mainland, dropped by parachute onto St Kilda.

The frigate, HMS *Ashanti* entered Village Bay at first light, followed by RY *Britannia* at nine-thirty. The two ships first circumnavigated the islands and the Royal Family came ashore on Hirta just before midday. Having toured the Army Camp and the village, they returned to the Royal Yacht for lunch. Given good weather, they spent the afternoon on Dun and only took their leave of St Kilda at nine o'clock at night. So impressed was Princess Anne that she paid a second visit to St Kilda on 26 April 1985.

During the early 1970s, Trust work parties spent much of their time restoring the Church and the schoolroom on St Kilda, as well as making habitable more old cottages. By 1974, overhead electric lighting, powered by the Army generating station, was installed in Houses nos 3 and 4, the schoolroom had been refloored and given new windows and much work had been done to restore the Church to its former simple dignity. The oil crisis and its effects, however, threatened to put paid to further effort.

Inflation had hit hardest the unavoidable costs of sending work parties to St Kilda. The price of oil had risen two hundred per cent, food was up twenty-two per cent. The cost of timber had risen forty per cent. Although subsidized in part by the National Trust, it was agreed that if work was to continue in 1975, party members would have to pay £60 per head instead of £45. The St Kilda Fund, it was claimed woud be empty within a year and only a joint promotion with Burton's Biscuits, which raised £500, meant that the six parties who went to St Kilda in 1975 had the materials to continue work on the Church and prepare another cottage for re-roofing. House no 5 was finally re-roofed in 1976.

By 1976, St Kilda's fame had spread. In that year the Trust began a programme of 'Safari' holidays to St Kilda which were to include tourists from Holland and America. Since then work parties and safari groups have attracted people from Germany, Canada, France, Belgium, Australia and New Zealand, Switzerland and Norway. By 1977 the Trust estimated that more than 1500 people had visited St Kilda on work parties. Many had gone to the island in Bruce Howard's boat, *Charna*. By 1979 he had made some eighty-five round trips, a record that may never be equalled in the modern history of St Kilda.

Many projects take the Trust years to complete, not only because of lack of funds but also because much of each summer is spent on routine maintenance to buidings already restored. When it was decided that the schoolroom should be brought back to its original state a new home had to be found for the little museum of photographs and artifacts the Trust had set up in the room. It was agreed that House no 3 should become the St Kilda Museum.

When the Macdonald family left St Kilda in 1924 for a new life on the mainland House no 3 lay empty up to the evacuation in 1930. It deteriorated, therefore, before many of the other cottages and lay unattended until 1961, when a work party stabilized the walls. In 1980 the gables and chimneys of House no 3 were rebuilt and wall plates and gable joists put in. In early summer the following year, the Army transported the timbers for the new roof from the mainland and the first work party carried them onto the site. The new roof was felted, battened and wired, just as originally done by the St Kildans. New windows and doors were also put in that year and the last party laid a concrete slab floor. In 1982 the old drains were cleared and new ones dug to keep the property as dry as possible. The Trust, in receipt of a generous grant from the Highlands and Islands Development Board for the project, finally opened the new museum in May 1982.

Nine years of work party effort, however, had gone into restoring the Church which was completed in 1980, in time for the fiftieth anniversary of the evacuation. When the RAF arrived in 1957, the Church had few slates left, sarking boards had been exposed, and some had rotted and fallen away. In the early 1960s, the roof of the Church had been temporarily covered with felt so that the Army could use the building as a storeroom as well as a cinema and later as a gymnasium for weightlifting and keep fit classes.

Work parties began renovating the Church in 1971. In just two weeks volunteers had gutted both the Church and the adjoining schoolroom and re-lined and painted the former. The following year the old pulpit and the precentor's desk were restored and the schoolroom re-lined and painted. By 1974 the pulpit balustrade and the newel post had been renovated and new windows fitted into the school. Under floor vents were also cut through stonework two feet thick to help keep the building aired. In 1976, the Church got new windows and three years later recesses were added to them. A new floor was also laid and four of the original pews, together with replicas to replace those lost, were installed. From beginning to end the renovation of the little Church was truly a labour of love. At no time were there more than four skilled men working on the project, usually there were only two. Greenock brassfounders, engravers and engineers gave generously to complete the renovation by providing a replica of the 'Janet Cowan' bell and a belfry which were erected in May 1980. The following year the Robertson family, owners of a shipping company and old friends of the National Trust gave £10,000 for the future upkeep of the Church and the schoolroom so that generations to come may see the buiding that so dominated the lives of the old St Kildans.

On Wednesday 23 May 1979, at eight o'clock in the evening, a Memorial Service was held in the Church. Nearly forty people had come to witness the dedication of a plaque to commemorate the eighteen RAF and RNZAF airmen who died on St Kilda during the Second World War. Five of their relatives were present, including four who had made the long journey from New Zealand. On the plaque space has been left to enter at some future date the names of those who lost their lives when their Wellington crashed into Soay. The Army provided a Guard of Honour and for the first time in its history St Kilda had a war memorial.

For the fiftieth anniversary of the evacuation of St Kilda the Trust invited eight St Kildans evacuated in 1930 to return to see their old homes. Rachel Gillies at first refused the invitation because she hated cameras and questions. She, like all of the islanders who went through the evacuation, has an understandable fear of being exploited and the Trust went to some pains to ensure, as best they could, that the St Kildans would not be again viewed as a 'human zoo'.

The eight St Kildans returned to St Kilda, as they had left in 1930, by way of a Royal Navy ship. HMS *Shetland* made the 110 mile journey from Argyll and a further twelve St Kildans, who had left before 1930 with their wives and relations were taken to Hirta by LCL *Arakan*. The official party for the Service of Rededication of the Church on St Kilda left Mallaig on 23 August 1980. An island on which few ministers before 1930 had been prepared to tend to the spiritual needs of the old St Kildans was to have a surfeit of them for the anniversary. The Reverend Charles B. Edie left Mallaig in the company of the Reverend John Barry and the Reverend Donald Gillies, a St Kildan who is a minister of the United Presbyterian Church of Canada. A helicopter was also bringing to St Kilda the Army Chaplain from the Uist Range and the Reverend Donald A. MacRae, the Church of Scotland minister on Benbecula. Two officials from the Post Office were also brought to St Kilda. A government agency that had begrudged what it cost to provide the old St Kildans with a decent mail service, were now glad to stamp 40,000 special covers in a replica of the St Kilda Post Office which the Army had built of timber and corrugated iron for the occasion.

The Army spent much of the day of 27 August ferrying people ashore and providing refreshments. Fires had been lit in some of the restored cottages, no doubt, it was thought, to make the St Kildans feel at home. For many of the former islanders, questioned by the Press, it was a time to reflect on the past, on why fifty years before it had all gone wrong. Andrew Macdonald, whose family had left St Kilda before 1930, claimed 'money was the end of it. People had been used to barter and sharing what they had,' he told a *Sunday Times* reporter. 'But strangers came,' he continued, 'and offered them money and gifts. You know what money does to people. They get greedy.' Macdonald's grandfather had been a businessman, and in his wallet that day Andrew Macdonald had a visiting card. 'William Macdonald, Tweed Manufacturer,' read the card, '3 Main Street St Kilda. Orders will receive prompt and personal attention.' Morag Macdonald, who was eight years old when she left Hirta with her parents, remarked, 'An odd thing was we never sang songs on St Kilda.' Ministers of an unbending faith and over-zealous missionaries had seen to that and many of the younger islanders were glad to shed themselves of the grim sabbatarianism of their youth when they settled on the mainland. Yet within hours of their landing, the St Kildans were summoned by a replica bell of the 'Janet Cowan' to attend service in the restored Church.

All the St Kildans sat together. One family occupied the same pew they had sat in on that last call to prayer in 1930. The service began at five o'clock in the afternoon and only a reading and part of a prayer were in Gaelic. The President of the St Kilda Club, Alex Warwick, acted as precentor and led the singing. The St Kildans with the rest of the congregation sang *We love the place, O God* and listened to the Reverend Donald Gillies preach the sermon in a booming Canadian accent. His grandfather, he said, had spent all his life on Hirta and had a voice that could carry two miles.

During the service, news came through of a gale. By seven o'clock most of the congregation was leaving Village Bay. Some of the St Kildans spent the night on Hirta in the cottages restored by the Trust and the next day HMS *Shetland* circumnavigated the islands to give them a chance to view the archipelago that had been not only their home; but that of their ancestors. The correspondent of the *Sunday Times* noted that only the islanders remained on deck – and they were singing.

From press reports, that day in August 1980 was a non-event. It had somehow gone wrong. For whom one might question had it been staged – the Trust and its working parties, the Press, or the few St Kildans left? In the crowded Church on 27 August, they had had to share their Church with Trust officials, the Press and a camera crew from the BBC, who were later criticized for not having included more of the church service in their programme *Return to St Kilda*. Such is the way, passionately concerned with concepts of conservation and preservation, we city dwellers often do things. The old St Kildans had experienced the same before. How strange, perhaps, that the Trust had chosen to spend so much effort, care and money on two buildings – the Church and the schoolroom – that in times past had done so much damage. Before 1930, the morale of the islanders had been fatally sapped by those from the mainland who had used them to preach and to teach a life that was better.

It was not until 1987 that a Bible in Gaelic was placed on the the pulpit, alongside the Testaments in English. A printed token to a lost way of life and our inability, given an ever increasing distance in time and culture to fully know the real meaning of what it was like to live on St Kilda. We continue to show our concern and try and refute the attitudes and decisions of those who went before. Perhaps, on reflection, a more fitting tribute in August 1980, would have been to allow the few remaining St Kildans, at our expense and in peace, to do on Hirta what they themselves would have wished to do. The writer, Catherine Lucy Czerkawska, wrote of the event in *The Scotsman*, 'One can't help feeling that all the interest has come about 100 years too late for the St Kildans. Having complacently watched something die, it is as if we then embalm the corpse and hallow it. In a sense the heart has gone out of the place as surely as those last fires smouldered away to ash . . . Now there are calendars, pictures, tea-towels with puffins on them. We make our films, write our articles, record our interviews. We boast that we have spent so many days on the island. But we are merely playing the twentieth century game of toying with the wilderness . . . Better perhaps to leave St Kilda to the wren, the mouse and the sheep. Or to the Army who have a job to do.' Perhaps she is right.

17
Of mice, men and other life

While man lived on Hirta *mus muralis* thrived. Within a year of the evacuation in 1930 the unique St Kildan house mouse was extinct. The fate of man and house mouse, it seems, had been inextricably bound. The latter could not exist without the former – the warm glimmer of man's turf fire, his household rubbish and his scraps of unwanted foodstuff. After the evacuation, the stronger St Kildan field mouse, also a unique sub-species, moved into the crumbling houses of Main Street and put paid to the remaining house mice. Such is nature's way. In olden times it was thought that the soul of man, at death, left the body in the form of mice. Strange, perhaps, that when the native community left in 1930, so too, perhaps, did its soul in the form of *mus muralis*.

The dominant St Kildan field mouse weighs twice as much as his mainland cousin, has larger ears and back feet and a tail as long as his body. Having killed off his cousin, his habits changed. Formerly a nocturnal animal, he now feels free to show himself during the day.

When the Task Force of Operation Hard Rock arrived in 1957, the field mouse, who had not seen man since 1930, except occasionally, adjusted. 'The young of 1957,' wrote Williamson and Boyd in *St Kilda Summer*, 'were born into a very different environment from their parents': gone were the dark nights with only the sigh of wind in the grass and the call of the snipe overhead – instead there were floodlights everywhere, and the perpetual roar of generators and the sound of human voices. There was a whole complex of fright and attraction, temptation and disillusionment – beguiling aromas to be followed to their source, warm places in which lie a bewildering array of new and exciting materials from polythene piping and rubber door stops to lard, putty, chocolate and potato skins in which to sink optimistic teeth.' Given man's new presence, the mice learnt quickly what was good and not good for them. Since 1957, the population of St Kildan field mice has prospered.

Declared a National Nature Reserve on 4 April 1957, St Kilda was one of the first reserves to be established in Scotland. Given its remit, it seemed there would be problems between the military and the Conservancy from the outset. Anxious in case rats might be brought to St Kilda for the first time in its recorded history, the Conservancy insisted that the landing craft servicing Hirta be carefully examined by pest-control experts and certified 'rat-free' before embarking on trips to St Kilda. To the layman the Conservancy's condition seemed petty; but the introduction of rats would have been disastrous. Their presence could not only have annihilated the St Kildan field mouse; but could also have put paid to the smaller petrels, the Manx shearwaters and the vast colony of puffins. The Conservancy's association with the Army since 1958 has been amicable. The latter has not only provided transport, but also assisted by deep freezing vital specimens.

Before the Nature Conservancy had an interest in St Kilda, the archipelago was probably the most closely studied, and certainly best documented area of wildlife in Western Europe. The heyday of the tourists, who were also naturalists had been from the last quarter of the 19th century up until the outbreak of the First World War. Many had been remarkable people, like the Kearton brothers and Norman Heathcote and his sister. In a long dress and straw hat she climbed Stac Lee. Most had been serious observers and their comments and bird counts have proved invaluable ever since. Well over a hundred books provide us with extensive information about St Kildan bird and animal life. Indeed, as R. Niall Campbell, the Conservancy's Regional Officer for the North West of Scotland, wrote, 'The natural history of the archipelago was pretty well buttoned-up by the time the Conservancy arrived on the scene.'

There was much for the Nature Conservancy to do. In 1958 they produced a Management Plan which stated their primary aims. First they declared their intention to safeguard the St Kilda group from development which would be harmful to the preservation of the wildlife. They also wished that St Kilda would remain unspoiled and a vital area for research. The Conservancy also declared the intention of researching into the ecology of St Kilda, particularly the animal population, and that the geology, climate and archaeology of the group should be subjects of study. The fact that man has ceased to plunder the soil, beasts and birds of St Kilda has enabled the Conservancy to carry out several important ecological studies. Most notable has been their research into the life-cycle of the Soay sheep.

James Fisher, the noted naturalist, once described the mouflon sheep of Soay as 'primitive fossils'. First brought to the British Isles around 5000 BC, the unique breed had lived on Soay, untended and undomesticated since time immemorial. Until the evacuation in 1930, the sheep had been confined to the island of their name. The Soay grazing, in fact, belonged to families who went to Australia in the 1850s and the owner of St Kilda, MacLeod of MacLeod had purchased the flock before the emigrants left for a new life. St Kildans before 1930 had gone to Soay. Having climbed the thousand feet cliffs to the lush plateau on which the sheep grazed, the islanders then hunted down the best beasts and shot them for fresh meat.

The Earl of Dumfries had a balanced flock transported from Soay to Hirta. His 107 sheep, brought off Soay by the St Kildans who went to the islands in the summer months, had increased to about 500 head by 1939, and to about 700 by 1948. Before, however, the Conservancy took over St Kilda the sheep population appears to have fluctuated considerably, and the agency was concerned to find out why.

In 1959, the Soay Sheep Research Team was constituted. The interested parties were many. Scientists representing the Hill Farming Research Organization, the Royal Veterinary College, London, the Animal Breeding Research Organization, the Ministry of Agriculture, the Rowett Research Institute, Aberdeen and the Conservancy itself all went to make up the Team's sixteen members. Their brief was summarized by Dr J. Morton Boyd. 'The team,' he said, 'hope to describe the sequence of events which control the size and structure of the population. The number of places in the world where it is now possible to perform such a study on a large mammal in natural conditions is becoming rapidly fewer. St Kilda is one of the last remaining sites in Europe.'

The research team first compared physically the Soay breed with other existing sheep. They then set about discovering why there were such fluctuations in numbers over the years, what made for increased reproduction and what caused mortality. In order to examine at close quarters the genetic make-up of the Soay sheep, specimens of the flock were taken from St Kilda to both London and Edinburgh Zoos. The St Kilda Club annually has contributed to the upkeep of a ram, who in turn has repaid his benefactors by his virility.

The importance of the cleits to the life-cycle of the Soay sheep soon became apparent to the scientists. They noted that the animals retire to them when sick or about to die and the ewes were observed using cleits to lamb, and sheep of all ages and sexes used them in times of bad weather. Given their discoveries, the question might be posed whether the St Kildans of old, perhaps, built so many of the structures in order to conserve their own flocks of domesticated animals.

After years of study a pattern emerged. It seems that the Soay sheep increase in number to a peak population, which is then followed by what is called a crash. In 1960, of 1344 sheep counted the previous autumn, no less than 820 had perished during the winter. Malnutrition, due to over-grazing, and the presence of parasites seems to have brought about death, especially among the rams, although year-old sheep of both sexes died.

In the years following the 1960 crash, the numbers of sheep increased again despite a poor lambing in 1962. By 1963 the Conservancy counted 1589 Soay sheep on Hirta and forecast, correctly, that there would be another crash in the foreseeable future. The pressure on the island's grazing, which itself is subject to change, appears to be increasing and may be responsible for the ups and downs of the sheep population. The scientists believe that the flock, so recently in ecological terms, removed to a new habitat, may not stabilize until the turn of the century. The primitive sheep of St Kilda are telling zoologists and conservationists alike much about the management of big game and other animal life, information pertinent throughout the world. As Williamson and Boyd remarked in *St Kilda Summer*, 'provided man does nothing that will destroy their habitat, there may well be sheep grazing these rich maritime pastures for milleniums to come'.

Other notable St Kildan survivors have been the plants that grow on the archipelago. The peaty soil of Hirta supports more than a hundred and thirty flowering plants and almost two hundred varieties of lichen, as well as mushrooms, which many a Trust work party has devoured with relish. The botany of St Kilda is important to scientists. St Kilda escaped the rigours of the Great Ice Age and on the islands are found pre-glacial plants which are helping to explain the origin and distribution of vegetation in the British Isles today. In 1971 an intensive study of the lichen discovered 194 species, some of them extremely rare. The most significant change in the island's vegetation since man left in 1930 has been the increase in heather moorland in Village Bay which scientists are also monitoring.

The bird life of the St Kilda group is, perhaps, the jewel in the crown of the Nature Conservancy. St Kilda boasts eighteen breeding species of seabirds and at least 260,000 occupied nest sites have been noted. Boreray, with a quarter of the North Atlantic population of gannets is the largest gannetry in the world. By 1973, 59,000 pairs were breeding on Boreray and the stacs. Fulmars nest everywhere on the cliffs of Hirta, the oldest and largest colony of the birds found in Britain. Ornithologists estimate there are 40,000 pairs of fulmars on the island group. Given the other sea birds, notably guillemots, kittiwakes and puffins, the archipelago is the largest breeding area in north-west Europe, with over a million breeding seabirds.

The fulmar colony has increased since the evacuation. In the 1930s, James Fisher estimated there were about 30,000 pairs. Since man has stopped slaughtering the fulmars in their thousands for food, feathers and oil, the population has been allowed to grow naturally. The number of gannets has also grown. In 1931 it was estimated that there were only 16,500 pairs. By 1957 over 40,000 pairs were breeding on Boreray, Stac Lee and Stac an Armin.

Gulls have been the birds most closely affected by the evacuation. The St Kildans killed them because they interfered with more valuable birds; but since 1957 scientists have noted increases in the populations of the lesser and greater blackback, and the herring gulls. The colony of Leach's petrels that nest on Dun, Carn Mor and the Cambir is one of the five main colonies in the Eastern Atlantic. The St Kilda wren is unique. It has a larger beak than wrens found on the British mainland and a different song. Some 250 pairs are estimated to live on St Kilda.

The seabird found in greatest number on St Kilda is the puffin. At one time they bred in huge numbers, estimated at between two and three million and the Conservancy has done much research into why the colony declined, especially in view of the fact that they were no longer cropped in their thousands by the St Kildans. From 1973 to 1980 NCC staff made a special study of the colony on Dun, which showed that the puffin population seems to have stabilized and gave possible reasons for the puffins' decline in the late 1940s and 1950s. Compared to puffins found elsewhere in Britain, those on St Kilda appear to have great difficulty finding food. During the middle part of this century the sea around St Kilda became slightly warmer, affecting the fish upon which the puffins feed. Now that the warming-up of the sea seems to have stopped so has the decline in the number of puffins. The Conservancy scientists concluded 'this is surely not a mere coincidence'.

Since taking over St Kilda, the Conservancy has been wary of those who have wanted to climb the highest sea cliffs in Europe, for fear that the bird life might be disturbed. In 1987, however, Chris Bonnington and a team of professional climbers scaled Conachair for the first time since the evacuation. It was not the first time that experienced climbers had been interested. In 1969 Chris Brasher hoped to follow up the successful live broadcast of the climbing of the Old Man of Hoy for BBC television. He stayed on Hirta for a week but concluded that the project was not feasible. Five years later Joe Brown and Hamish McInnes also went to St Kilda hoping they might scale the cliffs of Boreray. Given the vast population of gannets, with wing-spans of six feet and over, they decided that the climb would be too dangerous. One of the few climbs of Boreray was made in July 1980. A party from the University of Durham, who wanted to study the ecology and wild life of the island, scrambled ashore, with the help of the Army. The group of seven men and a woman stayed on Boreray until 25 July and were thus able to claim the longest inhabitation of the island since the evacuation.

The St Kilda group also attacts archaeologists. In 1967, J. F. Davidson, from Dundee University, who went to Hirta to help with the first Ordinance Survey archaeological study, drew attention to a group of boat-shaped settings of stone and suggested they were probably cairns and graves. In 1973, after samples had been radio-carbon dated, Davidson suggested that a small human settlement, which may have introduced sheep and goats to St Kilda, may have existed on Hirta about the year 2000 BC. Davidson's finds, he claimed, could have been used for human burial but there is no factual evidence as yet and archaeologists have not found evidence of the domestic structures used by those early settlers.

Remains also survive on Hirta of a souterrain, an underground passage and chamber, of the period 400 BC to 500 AD. The Earth House, as it is called, would probably have been connected to houses on the surface and artifacts have been found including Hebridean Iron Age pottery. An underground chamber has also been found on Oiseval which may prove to be more modern. Two Christian crosses found on St Kilda, engaved into stone, also suggest a pre-Viking settlement. The Vikings, we know, knew of St Kilda and they may, indeed have settled on the island. Two tenth century Viking brooches, a Viking sword and other artifacts have been found, which may have come from a burial mound.

The three churches, thatched drystone buildings, mentioned by Martin Martin in the seventeenth century, have gone; but if found, together with the monkish cells, will be of considerable importance. In Glean Mor archaeologists are also interested in the Amazon's House and the complexes of small chambers that are similar to Iron Age settlements which have been discovered in the north and west of Scotland. Calum Mor's house, north of Village Bay, is in the same tradition, but may prove to be an eighteenth century structure. The old bothy on Boreray, used by the St Kildans for shelter when they were on the island, may date back to the Iron Age, and it is hoped there are substantial remains underground.

In May 1984 Durham University made an initial assessment of the archaeological possibilities on Hirta and a year later was formally invited to undertake excavation work in association with the National Trust. Early findings proved promising. A mound by the east gable of House no 8 was excavated in 1986 and discovered to be the site of a midden. Vast quantities of interesting household rubbish were uncovered. Both the house and the midden overlay the remains of an improved blackhouse, built in the 1830s, but unfortunately the archaeologists found little else. They returned in 1987 to continue their work.

There is little more to be learnt from the few surviving St Kildans; we will have to use disciplines other than oral history to discover the past. Archaeologists have much important work to do and it is likely that future Trust work parties will be involved in helping scientists carefully dig and sift through the peaty soil of Hirta. There are centuries, indeed, milleniums of St Kildan history we know little about. Who were the first St Kildans and where did they come from? Why do some of the archaeological remains on St Kilda look like those found elsewhere in Scotland, while others do not?

The scientists of the Nature Conservancy also have much work to do in the future. They plan to make a detailed study of the changes in vegetation in the Village Bay area which may affect the habitats of the wildlife of St Kilda, notably the Soay sheep. More study needs to be made of the St Kilda wren and the field mouse and the Conservancy would like the shearwaters and petrels to be studied, especially the Leach's petrels because there are so few colonies of them in Britain.

There are many questions to which scientists, hopefully, will find answers in the future. Where, for instance, do the St Kildan puffins spend the autumn, winter and spring months? How far do gannets fly to find food? Why do the Soay sheep not totally overgraze Hirta and thus destroy themselves? The research work of the Nature Conservancy is less obvious to the visitor than the efforts of the Army and the Trust work parties; but will probably continue long after the soldiers and the volunteers give up their present occupation of St Kilda.

18
A far better place

St Kilda has not been allowed to die. Her native population may have been evacuated in August 1930; but man has continued to rise to the challenge of living on Hirta. Our modern occupation of the islands has taken effort and cost lives and money. The British taxpayer has already paid for the Army to inhabit St Kilda longer this century than the native St Kildans did. The Army presence, in turn, has enabled the National Trust for Scotland to exploit the most remote property in its care. More people probably visit St Kilda now than ever did before the evacuation. In 1986 more than a thousand people landed on the island by way of sixty-seven boats and fourteen helicopters.

The Trust work parties continue to be popular; but it is likely that renovation work will soon reach an optimum. Each year an increasing amount of time is devoted to maintaining and repairing the five cottages and the Church and schoolroom already restored. During 1984 work began on renovating the old feather store which was slated and floored by 1986; but it may have to be the last major example of restoration work.

St Kilda can now boast a prodigious list of honours, bestowed on the little archipelago since 1957. We may have neglected the St Kildans; but we have gone out of our way to preserve the island itself. St Kilda is not only an inalienable property of the National Trust for Scotland and a National Nature Reserve but has also been designated a National Scenic Area and an Ancient Monument by the Secretary of State for Scotland. The island is also a notified Site of Special Scientific Interest and receives statutory protection under Section 28 of the Wildlife and Countryside Act 1981. The islands are also listed as a key site in the Nature Conservation Review published by the Nature Conservancy Council and Natural Environment Research Council in 1977. St Kilda is also a Biosphere Reserve established within UNESCO's Programme on Man and the Biosphere and the same international organization gave St Kilda its greatest accolade to date in 1986 when the group was added to UNESCO's World Heritage List, a collection of 'wonders of the world'. St Kilda now rubs shoulders with the Pyramids of Egypt, the Taj Mahal in India, the Great Barrier Reef and the Grand Canyon.

On 11 August 1987, more than forty people attended a short service in the Church to commemorate the listing of St Kilda as a World Heritage Site. The congregation sang Psalm 121, *I To The Hills Will Lift Mine Eyes*, and Bernd von Droste of UNESCO unveiled a plaque. 'St Kilda,' he said, 'is a testimony to the powerful work of nature and to the tenacity but ultimate fragility of human settlement.' The formal British Government submission to UNESCO had stated, 'The fact that the island community held out until its eventual evacuation in 1930 is a remarkable enough story. But what is most tragic is that a community which had survived the remoteness and physical hardships for over 2000 years should finally succumb to the influences of modern civilization.' Fine words from the Scottish Office, which in 1930 grudgingly paid the bill of £1000 to clear St Kilda.

St Kilda continues to cast a genuine spell and inspire those who visit the islands. There have been poems written and published in the *St Kilda Mail*, and Scottish country dances devised. Filmed at Applecross in 1982, *Ill Fares the Land* became the second feature film to tell the story of St Kilda. Written and directed by Bill Bryden, the film unfortunately, like Michael Powell's *The Edge of the World*, could not be filmed on Hirta and suffered as a consequence. A composer, Jerold James Gordon, has written a *St Kilda Requiem*. His second symphony, the Requiem is in one movement for a large orchestra, chorus and soloists and is largely based upon the few fragments of St Kildan music, real and invented, that have been handed down to us. St Kilda has entered the consciousness of many, not the privileged few, thanks to the Army and the Trust.

Some of the soldiers who have served on St Kilda are less enchanted. They cannot understand why such a lot of fuss is made about what to them is 'just another island'. They too have written songs. One sung to the tune *Galway Bay* contains the verse:

> No there's not a lot to see upon St Kilda
> Two dozen empty bothies and a wall
> It's a dreary little dot of desolation
> One hundred miles due west of buggar all.

But many soldiers, notably the officers and NCOs, have fallen under the spell. Pat Blenkinsopp, who was OC St Kilda in 1981, wrote, 'Whilst there one is constantly reminded about the history of the islanders and of the savage conditions which they had to endure. The army detachment, on the other hand, will complain when the potatoes run out and they have to eat rice as an alternative.' Some of the soldiers have become students of St Kildan fauna and history and some, indeed, have found it difficult to take their leave of the island. Sergeant Mickey Bowe, REME, a radar technician holds the record for having served on St Kilda longer than anyone. In March 1979, he left the island after a posting that had lasted four and a half years. A bachelor, Bowe had only reluctantly taken any leave during that period, usually, it was said, when the Trust work parties disturbed the peace of Hirta.

Under the sub-tenancy lease with the Ministry of Defence, a vital clause demands that when the Army leaves Hirta, all their buidings, radar masts and scanners may have to be removed at the Trust's discretion. Already, obsolete installations have been taken away and those buildings initially commandeered by the military have been handed back, like the Church, the schoolroom and the Factor's house. Only the old manse, now the sergeants mess, is in Army hands.

The Army not only makes life easier for the Trust but indeed possible. Work parties and Nature Conservancy personnel are able to use the deep freezes, the Gemini boat crew, unlimited electricity and hot water, and the Puff Inn. Most important, the Army maintains twenty-four hour communication with the mainland, and their presence on St Kilda throughout the winter stops the Trust restoration work from being vandalized by trawlermen. Many regard the military presence as a blot on the landscape; but without the Army and their facilities, as Alex Warwick has stated, 'National Trust for Scotland working parties would have had to have been organized on a quite different basis if at all.' A Nature Conservancy warden on the island concurred: 'Whilst it is impossible,' he wrote, 'to put thirty men on a small island and render them invisible, as I am sure some conservation interests want, for me their presence and help outweighed any minor effect on the environment.' For the Trust and the Conservancy it will be a sad day when the Army takes its leave.

And what of those original St Kildans, that ever-dwindling group, our fragile link with the past? Most still remember their former home with affection; but few talk about the old way of life freely. The trauma of the evacuation and those early years on the mainland has left an indelible mark. They do not understand why people should still be interested in them and would much prefer to be left alone with their memories. 'I am not a bit ashamed to be a St Kildan,' Lachlan

Macdonald told me in 1971. 'I can be quite proud of myself sometimes. I mean, I didn't do any harm or anything. I had a good life with the islanders and I don't feel ashamed.' In 1971, Lachlan returned to St Kilda and found his old house a roofless shell. The sight of his birthplace reduced him to tears. But he has returned to St Kilda several times since then and frequently attends the St Kilda Club functions where he is made warmly welcome. On 4 June 1987, at the age of eighty-one, Lachlan paid what may be his last visit to St Kilda and for four days was entertained by the officers and men of the St Kilda Detachment. Over a dram in the Puff Inn, one of the last remaining old St Kildans told the young military occupiers of his island what life was like in his day. Lachlan's reason for visiting St Kilda one more time was a simple one. 'I want,' he said, 'to stand in the graveyard where my ancestors are buried and to pray in the church.'

The Gillies sisters have also gone back to Hirta on several occasions. Catherine Gillies was eleven years old and Rachel seven in 1930. On one visit, in July 1979, even the atrocious weather could not prevent them from walking down Main Street to look at the remains of House no 13, where they were both born. They ended the day by taking a bath, the first, they said, they had ever had on St Kilda.

The St Kilda of the past and that of the present is uniquely united in one family, the Macdonalds. Malcolm Macdonald was among the young men who left St Kilda shortly after the First World War. The sixteen year old did many jobs: he worked for the Earl of Dumfries for a while on one of his estates and in 1937 was a pantry boy on the *Hebrides*. In later years he became a gentleman's valet at the Grosvenor House Hotel in London and lived with his family in a council house in Wandsworth. When he took his leave of Hirta in 1924 he never imagined that the time would come when his kinsmen would abandon the isle forever. In 1930, he was a saddened man. Gone was the possibility that Macdonald might be able to retire to St Kilda. He, like the others, had to be satisfied with making occasional visits to the island of his birth. 'Even when I visited the island four years ago,' he told me in 1971, 'I felt I didn't want to leave it again. I was feeling so contented in myself. I don't know if I was living in the past or what, but I just felt contented. I didn't feel I wanted to come back to London. I suppose I was born and brought up in the island, so I'm not used to the turmoil of life in a big city.'

Malcolm Macdonald died in London in 1979. His wife contacted the Army and the Trust to ask whether her husband's ashes could return to St Kilda. Her request was granted and the Reverend Ian Forbes, the

Minister of the Church of Scotland kirk at Griminish on Benbecula held a short memorial service for Malcolm in the old church on St Kilda. His ashes were buried in the little oval graveyard. A headstone was brought over from the Hebrides. On it were engraved the words, 'Malcolm Macdonald. Born on Hirta 1908.' It does not say what happened to him in life or where he died: both to Malcolm had been irrelevant.

In 1980, on the first anniversary of Malcolm Macdonald's death, three of his children, Elizabeth, Marion and Neil, together with his niece Maria, went to St Kilda as members of a Trust work party. On Hirta, they helped restore House no 3, Malcolm's old home which was to become the St Kilda Museum. Stationed on St Kilda that year was Andrew Gibbon from Doncaster, a Plant Operator with the 11th Field Squadron, Royal Engineers. Andrew and Elizabeth Macdonald fell in love and were married on 21 August 1982. The following year they emigrated to Australia and now live in Taringa, Queensland. It is a quirk of history that they should choose to settle in the same country to which thirty-six St Kildans had gone in 1852 considerably weakening the strength of the community left behind on Hirta, as indeed had the departure of the Macdonald family in 1924. Elizabeth's father, Malcolm, had had longer than most St Kildans to try and readjust to a new life on the mainland; but he was never to find the qualities that to him were so much part of his young life on St Kilda. 'You had peace of mind,' he told me, 'quietness and a way of life I don't find on the mainland. To me it was peace living in St Kilda, and to me it was happiness, dear happiness. It was a far better place.'

Aristotle said that the plot of true tragedy, 'ought to be so constructed that , even without the aid of the eye, he who hears the tale told will thrill with horror and melt with pity at what takes place.' There are few tales in Scottish history more fitting that definition than that of St Kilda, a story that is finished, and yet not quite over.

Bibliography

Bibliography

Books

ATKINSON, G. C., *A Few Weeks' Ramble Among The Hebrides in the Summer of 1831* (Bute Collection)

ATKINSON, R., *Island Going*, 1949

BENNETT, Edward, *The Post Office and Its Story*, 1912

BROUGHAM, Lord, 'Tour in Western Isles, including St Kilda in 1799', *The Life and Times of Henry, Lord Brougham*, 1871, vol. ii, p. 99.

BUCHAN, Rev. Alexander, *A Description of St Kilda*, 1732 (reprinted in *Miscellanea Scotica*, 1818, vol. ii)

BUCHANAN, M., *St Kilda, a photographic album*, Edinburgh, 1983

CARRUTHERS, R., *The Highland Note-book; or sketches and anecdotes*, 1843

CLARKE, E. D., *The Life and Remains of Edward Daniel Clarke*. Ed. Rev. William Offer, two volumes, London, 1825; second edition contains 'Visit to St Kilda in 1727'

CONNELL, R., *St Kilda and the St Kildans*, 1887

CUMMING, Gordon C. F., *In the Hebrides*, 1883

DUNN, D., *St Kilda's Parliament*, London, 1981

FERGUSON, M., *Ramblers in Skye, with a sketch of a trip to St Kilda*, 1885

FORSYTH, R., *The Beauties of Scotland*, vol. 5, 1808

GORDON, S., *Afoot in the Hebrides*, 1950

GRANT, I. F., *History of a Clan*, 1954

HEATHCOTE, N., *St Kilda*, 1900

INNES, Hammond, *Atlantic Fury*, 1962 (fiction)

JEWELL, MILNER and MORTON BOYD, *Island Survivors: The Ecology of the Soay Sheep of St Kilda*, 1973

KEARTON, R., *With Nature and a Camera*, 1899, pp. 1–134

KENNEDY, J., *The 'Apostle' of the North*: The Life and Labours of the Rev. Dr John MacDonald, 1866

LAWSON, R., *A Flight to St Kilda in July 1902*

LESLIE, Bishop, *The History of Scotland*, written 1596

LOGIE, D. W., *An Account of a trip from Stirling to St Kilda 12–17 August 1889*, 1889

MACAULAY, Rev. K., *The History of St Kilda*, 1764

MACCULLOCH, J., *A Description of the Western Islands of Scotland*, 1819

MACDONALD, Rev. J., *Journal and Report of a Visit to the Island of St Kilda*, 1823

MACGREGOR, A. A., *A Last Voyage to St Kilda*, 1931
The Farthest Hebrides, 1969

MACKAY, J. A., *St Kilda, its Posts and Communications*, 1963

MACKENZIE, Rev. J. B., *Episode in the Life of the Rev. Neil Mackenzie at St Kilda from 1829 to 1843*, 1911

MACKENZIE, O., *A Hundred Years in the Highlands*, chapter 6, 1924

MACKENZIE, W. C., *The Lady of Hirta, A Tale of the Isles*, 1905

MACLEAN, C., *Island on the Edge of the World; The Story of St Kilda*, Edinburgh, 1977

MACLEAN, L., *Sketches of the Island of St Kilda*, 1838

MACPHERSON, H. A., *A History of Fowling*, 1897

MARTIN, M., *A Late Voyage to St Kilda, the remotest of all the Hebrides*, 1698 (reprinted 1934)

MUIR, T. S., *St Kilda, a fragment of travel*, by 'Unda', 1858
Ecclesiological Notes on some of the Islands of Scotland, 1885

NICOL, T., *By Mountain, Moor and Loch to the Dream Isles of the West*, 1931

PIGGOTT, T. Digby, *London Birds and London Insects* (Chapter V), London, 1892

POWELL, Michael, *200,000 Feet on Foula*, 1938

QUINE, D. A., *St Kilda revisited*, 1982

RUTHERFORD, I., *At the Tiller*, 1964

SANDS, J., *Out of the World, or Life in St Kilda*, 1878

SETON, G., *St Kilda Past and Present*, 1877

SMITH, R. A., *Visit to St Kilda in the 'Nyanza'*, 1879

SPACKMAN, R. A., *Soldiers on St Kilda*, Uist Community Press, 1982

STEEL, Tom, *The Life and Death of St Kilda*, 1965

SVENSSON, R., *Lonely Isles*, 1954

THOMSON, Francis, *St Kilda and other Hebridean Outliers*, 1970

TROLLOPE, A., *How the 'Mastiffs' went to Iceland*, chapter 3, 1877

WILLIAMSON, K. and MORTON BOYD, J., *St Kilda Summer*, 1960

WILSON, J., *A Voyage round the Coasts of Scotland and the Isles*, 1842, vol. ii, pp. 1–113

Periodicals, Manuscripts and Newspapers

(ANONYMOUS), 'Life in St Kilda', *Chambers's Journal*, vol. liv, pp. 284, 312, 331

ATKINSON, G. C., 'An Account of an Expedition to St Kilda in 1831', *Transactions of the Natural History Society of Northumberland*, 1832

BAGENAL, T. B., 'The Birds on St Kilda 1952', *Scottish Naturalist*, 65, 1953

BAILLIE, Lady (of Polkemmet), 'A Short Visit to St Kilda', *Church of Scotland Missionary Record*, January 1875

BOYD, J. M., 'St Kilda in 1952', *Scottish Field 50, No. 598*, 1952
'The Gannetry of St Kilda', *Journal of Animal Ecology*, 30, 1961

BRAZENOR, H., 'Proposed Dealer's Raid on the Birds of St Kilda and the Outer Hebrides', *Annals of the Scottish Natural History Society*, 1908

BURRILL, Major John E. O., 'Gunners on St Kilda', *Journal of the Royal Artillery*, 1958, 85: pp. 97–101

CAMERON, Mary, *Childhood Days on St Kilda*, 1973
'Our Childhood on St Kilda', *Scots Magazine*, March 1969
'Some Memories of a St Kildan Childhood', *Oban Times*

CHAMBERS, W., 'The Story of Lady Grange', *Chambers's Journal*, No. 551, 1874

COCHRANE, D. and FRASER, A., 'Men May Go', *Farmers Weekly*, December 1957

COLLACOTT, R. A., 'Neonatal Tetanus in St Kilda', *Scottish Medical Journal*, 26, 1981

DENNY, A., 'Outpost of the British Isles', *Travel*, October 1907, pp. 158–63

DIXON, C., 'The Ornithology of St Kilda', *Transactions of the Royal Society of Edinburgh*, 5th Series, III, 1885

DOTT, H. E. M., and others, 'Aberdeen University Expedition to St Kilda, 1968, Report on seabird studies', (unpublished), Aberdeen University, 1969

DREWE, Charles, 'Specks off the Mainland', *Stamp Collecting*, 1958

DRYDEN, James, 'St Kilda's Floating Mail', *Gibbons Stamp Monthly*, December 1930

ELLIOT, J. S., 'St Kilda and the St Kildans', *Journal of the Birmingham Natural History and Philosophical Society*, I, 1895

FLEGG, J., 'Lost at Sea? The decline of the puffin', *Country Life*, 14 February 1974

GIBSON, G., 'The Tragedy of St Kilda', *The Caledonian Medical Journal*, April 1926

GILMOUR, H., 'Mail Boat from St Kilda', *Post Office Magazine*, December 1958

GRANGE, Lady Rachel, *Epistle from Lady Grange to Edward D—, Esq.*, London 1798

GREEN, F. H. W., 'The Weather of St Kilda, Winter 1957-8', *Weather*, 14, 1959

HARRIS, M. P., 'Monitoring of puffin numbers. Final Report', *Nature Conservancy Council Chief Scientific Team Report No. 299*, 1980

HEATHCOTE, E., 'A Visit to St Kilda', *Wide World Magazine*, August 1900

'A Summer Sojourn in St Kilda', *Good Words*, 1901, vol. xlii, p. 60

HUXLEY, J., 'Birds and Men on St Kilda', *Geographical Magazine*, 1939, vol. 10, pp. 69-82

KEARTON, R., 'Strange Life of Lone', *Wide World Magazine*, February 1897

LUNGATOO, F. M., 'St Kilda Mail Via Shetland', *St Martin's le Grand*, 1906

MACCALLUM, H., 'St Kilda', *Caledonian Medical Journal*, vol. vii, 1907

MACDIARMID, J., 'St Kilda and Its Inhabitants', *Transactions of the Highland and Agricultural Society of Scotland*, 1878, vol. x, p. 232

MACDONALD, C. R., 'St Kilda: its Inhabitants and the Diseases peculiar to them', *British Medical Journal*, II, 1886

MACDONALD, J., 'Journal of a visit to St Kilda, etc.', In an appendix to SSPCK *Sermon Preached by Rev. W. A. Thomson, on June 6, 1882*

MACGREGOR, D. R., 'St Kilda', *Scottish Studies*, vol. 4, Part 1, 1960

MACINTOSH, C. F., *Parish of Harris*, St Kilda contained in Antiquarian Notes, Inverness, 1897

MACKENZIE, Sir George, 'An Account of the Misfortunes of Mrs Erskine of Grange, Commonly known as Lady Grange', *Edinburgh Magazine*, I, 1817

MACKENZIE, H. R., 'St Kilda', *Celtic Magazine*, XI, 1885

MACLACHLAN, A., 'Diary', from August 1906 to May 1909 (Bute Collection)

Macfarlane's Geographical Collections, vol. iii, pp. 28, 94, 291

MACLEOD, Lieut.-Col., 'Notice on the Present State of St Kilda', *The Scots Magazine and Edinburgh Literary Miscellany*, December 1814

MACLEOD, B., 'Aunt Emily Goes to St Kilda', *Countryman*, Summer, 1953

MATHIESON, J., 'St Kilda', *Scottish Geographical Magazine*, vol. xliv, No. 2, pp. 65–90, 1928

'The Evacuation of St Kilda', *Scottish Geographical Magazine*, vol. xlvi, 1930

'Lone St Kilda, an Historical Note', *SMT Magazine*, August 1930

'Survey of St Kilda – an Expert's Self-imposed Task', 1927 (Bute Collection)

MILLS, S., 'Graveyard of the puffin', *New Scientist*, 2 July 1981

MITCHELL, A., 'Consanguineous Marriages in St Kilda', *Edinburgh Medical Journal*, April 1865

MORAY, Sir Robert, 'A Description of the Island of Hirta', *Transactions of The Royal Philosophical Society*, 1678

MORGAN, J. E., 'The Falcon among the Fulmars', *Macmillan's Magazine*, June 1861

'The Diseases of St Kilda', *British and Foreign Medico-Chirurgical Review*, 1862, vol. xxix, p. 179

MORGAN, JOHN E., 'Six Hours at St Kilda', *Macmillan's Magazine*, 1861

MURRAY, G., *St Kilda Diary*, from June 11, 1886, to June 11, 1887 (Bute Collection)

MURRAY, S., 'A count of Gannets on Boreray, St Kilda', *Scottish Birds*, II, 1981

Peoples Journal, The, 'St Kildans' First Christmas on Mainland', December 13, 1930

PRICE, E., 'Voyage to St Kilda', *The Scotsman*, July 21, 1906

POMFRET, Surgeon Lieut.-Comm. A. A., RN, 'The Evacuation of St Kilda', *Journal of the RN Medical Service*, 1931, vol. xvii

ROSS, A., 'A Visit to the Island of St Kilda', *Transactions of the Inverness Scientific Society and Field Club*, 1884, vol. iii, pp. 72–91

ROSS, J., *Notes on the island of St Kilda*, made while schoolmaster in St Kilda, 1887–8 (Bute Collection)

St Kilda Mail, (annual publication of the St Kilda Club), 1977–86

Scottish Society of Antiquaries, Proceedings of:

Vol. vii, 1867, 'On primitive dwellings and the Hypogea of the Outer Hebrides', by Capt. F. W. L. Thomas

Vol. x, 1872–14, pp. 702–11, 'Letter from St Kilda', by Miss A. Kennedy, with notes by Capt. F. W. L. Thomas

Vol. x, 1875; Vol. xi, 1876, 'Lady Grange on the Island of St Kilda', by D. Laing

Vol. xii, 1876–8, 'Notes on the Antiquities of the Island of St Kilda', by J. Sands

Vol. xxxv, 1901, 'List of Accounts of Visits to St Kilda (1549–1900)', by A. Mitchell

Vol. xxxix, Fourth series, vol. iii, 1904–5, 'Antiquities and old customs in St Kilda', by Rev. J. B. Mackenzie

SMALL, A. (Ed.), 'A St Kilda Handbook', Edinburgh 1980

SMITH, J. A., 'An Isolated and Intermittent Post Office', *St Martin's le Grand*, 1911

TAYLOR, A. B., 'The Name "St Kilda"', *Scottish Studies*, vol. 13, 1969

THOMSON, D. C., 'St Kilda as it was a Century Ago', *The Scotsman*, November 30, 1957

TURNER, G. A., *Glasgow Medical Journal*, March 1895

WIGLESWORTH, J., 'St Kilda and Its Birds', *Transactions of the Liverpool Biological Society*, 1903

WILLIAMSON, K., 'Ancient St Kilda', *Scottish Field*, March 1958

WINTER, G., 'The death and rebirth of St Kilda', *Country Life, 168*, 1980

Official Documents

AGRICULTURE, Department of, FILES:

Provision of nurse (1890)

Provision of supplies – naval visits (1893–14)

Report of visit by HMS Starling (1894)

Remission of Rates (1897)

Provision of pier and harbour (1878–97)

Report on visit by HMS Bellona (1901)

Press cutting – condition of islanders (1903)

Communications with mainland during winter months. Conveyance of mail (1904–8)

Report by Captain Christie, RAMC (1906)

Provision of supplies. Visit and report by HMS Achilles (1912)

Provision of telegraphic facilities (1912)

Communications with mainland during winter months. Conveyance of provisions and mail (1912–13)

Provision of wireless facilities: application by Daily Mirror to set up a station (1912)

Influenza epidemic. Relief measures. Medical report on health of islanders (1913)

Illness of individual. Appeals for medical assistance. Reports by nurses (1914)

Parliamentary Question put by Mr Hogge. Provision of medical facilities (1914)

Influenza epidemic (1914)

Parliamentary Question put by Mr Hogge. Proposal that Treasury take over wireless installation (1914)

Transport and disposal of cattle from island (1916–17)

Proposed government take-over of wireless installation (1919)

Arrangements for mail service (1920)

Epidemic of mumps (1920)

Police report on conditions on island (1920)

Repair of pier (1921)

Proposed visit by medical officer (1922)

Reports on conditions of inhabitants. Proposed removal (1923–30)

Mail service (1924–30)

Fuel supplies (1924–29)

Wireless station. Proposed re-establishment (1929)

Parliamentary Questions by Mr Ramsay. Removal of inhabitants (1930)

Parliamentary Questions by Mr Ramsay. Resettlement of islanders on mainland (1930)

Miscellaneous correspondence arising out of evacuation (1930–1)

Resettlement of islanders on mainland. Highland and Agricultural Society Fund (1930–1)

Conditions on island. Enquiries, etc. (1930)

Parliamentary Question by Maj. Gen. Davidson. Sale of islanders' stock (1930)

Removal of inhabitants (1930–1)

Parliamentary Question by Mr Lewis. Establishment of bird sanctuary (1931)

Raiding (1931)

Press cuttings (1931–7)

Explosion on island (1935)

Enquiries, etc. (1935–7)

Parliamentary Questions by Messrs McGovern and McMillan. Applications by islanders to return (1937)

After-care of islanders (1935–7)

Re-occupation (1937)

CENSUS, Government, *1851, 1861, 1871, 1881, 1891, 1901, 1911, 1921*

CROFTERS COMMISSION, *Report of, 1886*

HEALTH, Department of, for Scotland, *Report of visits to and arrangements for the evacuation of the Island of St Kilda*, 1930–4 (six files)

HERON, R., *General view of the Natural Circumstances of those islands adjacent to the North-West Coast of Scotland*, drawn up for the consideration of the Board of Agriculture and Internal Improvement, 1794

Inverness Education Authority, *Log Book of St Kilda School* (Held by the Authority in Inverness)

MACNEIL, M., 'On His Visit to St Kilda', Annual report of the Board of Supervision, 1884

Parochial Registers: *St Kilda. Births, 1830–51, Marriages, 1830–49, Deaths, 1830–46* (initially kept by Rev. Neil Mackenzie. Now in Register House, Edinburgh)

POST OFFICE, GENERAL, Documents in care of, *regarding postal service to the islands of St Kilda*

SSPCK *Minutes of Committee*, c 1710 (In the Scottish Record Office, Register House, Edinburgh)
The State of the Society in Scotland for propagating Christian Knowledge, 1729

Index

Index

The Celts

Frank Delaney

The Celts have been described as 'one of the great barbarian peoples of the world', much given to ferocious, excitable and warlike behaviour. But despite their numerical smallness they made a major and lasting contribution to Western civilisation.

Beginning in the plains of Hungary and progressing through Austria, Switzerland, southern Germany and France into Scotland, Wales and Ireland, Frank Delaney traces the origin, growth, flowering and eventual decline of a people whose very name conjures romance and adventure.

The Celts brushes aside the clichés in a refreshing and entertaining way, revealing much about the people who sacked Rome, penetrated the sacred heart of Greece by pillaging Delphi – and attracted the name 'the fathers of Europe'.

ISBN 0 586 20349 4

Legends of the Celts

Frank Delaney

'Over the sea, there lay a realm of glory, a skyline so bewitchingly clear that men set sail, futilely, to find this eternal place . . .'

The Celtic people fed on a rich mixture of legends and myths which, in many versions and derivations, were told around the firesides of Europe and passed on from generation to generation. They are tales of brave warriors, feuding families and conniving kings that have become embedded, in different forms, within many of the world's mythologies.

Now, Frank Delaney has produced a popular version of these fantastic stories. Delaney has been fascinated by the Celtic legends since childhood and in this volume he draws together their main strands, bringing them to life in vivid, often thrilling detail. He not only recaptures an ancient world for the modern reader, but, through a revealing Introduction, sheds new light on many of the motifs which Celtic mythology shares with other ancient civilisations.

'Frank Delaney writes the way he speaks . . . full of enthusiasm. He vividly conveys his interest in Celtic legends and literature.'
Sunday Times

ISBN 0 586 21151 9

Nick Danziger

Danziger's Britain

A Journey to the Edge

'A chilling indictment of what we've let happen in the past two decades . . . At every turn you feel the stress, the rage, the pain and the despair. Through these bitter scenes, Danziger's writing remains fluent, lucid and humane . . . Danziger deserves all praise, and the widest possible readership . . . This book is so important that every one of us should read it and weep.'   PETE DAVIES, *Independent*

Danziger's Britain is a hair-raising account of the author's journey among the 'other British' – the huge ranks of the excluded and marginalised people of Great Britain. It is as gripping and extraordinary as any of his famous travels in Asia, and illustrated by his own haunting and remarkable photographs.

'His account of how, where and why the poor of Britain live grips and appals the mind. Danziger travelled the length and breadth of breadline Britain, focusing on old industrial and maritime cities but also taking in the Scottish Highlands and rural Suffolk, Cornwall and the old Welsh coalfields. As he goes . . . he invites people to talk – thieves in Brixton, Somalis in Liverpool, junkies in Glasgow, mental health workers in Barrow-in-Furness, teenagers in Bradford and Salford, kneecapped Belfast joyriders, a hardworking councillor in the ravaged west end of Newcastle . . . The sheer extent of civil catastrophe and human waste revealed here threatens to beggar belief.'   SEAN O'BRIEN, *Sunday Times*

ISBN 0 00 638249 5

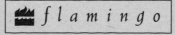

In Search of Churchill

Martin Gilbert

'A fascinating account of tireless and resourceful detective work . . . Gilbert's zeal in pursuit of every scrap of evidence on Churchill's life is an example to all biographers. The work he has done puts all historians of the twentieth century, and all students of Churchill, incalculably in his debt.' JOHN GRIGG, *Sunday Telegraph*

Martin Gilbert's biography of Churchill is probably the longest biography ever written, and in the opinion of many one of the greatest. *In Search of Churchill* is the story of Gilbert's thirty-year quest for his subject. He reveals the staggering extent of his historical labour and shares with the reader some of the great moments in his pursuit. It is also the story of those who have helped Gilbert along his way, as they had earlier helped Churchill on his. Secretaries, assistants, diarists, correspondents, soldiers, politicians, civil servants; the eminent and the humble: all of them had tales to tell, many of them published here for the first time. The portrait that emerges of Churchill is almost tangibly intimate. Here, perhaps more than in any other book about him, is the character of the man, untrammelled by formalities, as seen by those who were with him at his most unguarded moments.

'This book, part intellectual autobiography, part coda to his monumental Churchill biography, is required reading for Churchill enthusiasts. It takes on all the pace of an adventure novel.'
ANDREW ROBERTS, *Literary Review*

'Any world statesman close to the end would be grateful for a Martin Gilbert. What better way to meet your maker than in the happy knowledge that a leading scholar is devoting his career to tracking down, codifying and publishing every detail of your own? Gilbert is a careful scholar with a proper respect for evidence, fact, accuracy . . . His primary concern is setting the record straight - and in this entertaining and enjoyable book he explains how he sets about it.' BEN PIMLOTT, *Guardian*

ISBN: 0 00 637432 8